PRAISE FOR *100 WAYS TO IMPROVE CUSTOMER EXPERIENCE*

'The vital importance of customer-centricity is an enduring business truth. Newman and McDonald's book creates a contemporary perspective on how businesses can embrace this goal in new ways. Typically, their ideas are hugely practical and straightforward for organizations to implement.' **David Wild, CEO, Domino's**

'A pithy, practical, enjoyable and thought-provoking book that brings new insights into consumer behaviour and how to improve the experience you deliver. This book will appeal to anyone who works in a consumer business, irrespective of the sector. A book that you can read from cover to cover and then dip in and out of when you are looking for inspiration to change the way you might be framing a consumer challenge. I really love the practical and relatable examples.' **Debbie Hewitt MBE, Chairman, White Stuff**

'Written by one of the world's leading multichannel customer experience experts with the support of one of the world's leading marketing academics, this practical guide to improving customer experience is essential reading for anyone who wants to thrive in an increasingly disrupted, hyper-local, mobile world. I have worked with both of them separately, but this author combination provides a powerful fusion.' **Andy Rubin, Chairman, Pentland Brands**

'100 ways to turn disruption into opportunities. This book should become your best friend in a fast-changing retail environment. Newman's common sense is brilliant!' **Paul Delaoutre, President, Al-Futtaim Retail**

'If you are a CEO, buy this book for your team and devote an off-site day (or two) to undertaking an honest appraisal of how you score against Martin Newman's 100 recommendations for transforming your service culture. If you are not a CEO, buy this book and give it to your CEO.' **Richard Pennycook, Non-Executive Director and Chairman, retail sector**

100 Practical Ways to Improve Customer Experience

Achieve end-to-end customer engagement in a multichannel world

Martin Newman
with Malcolm McDonald

KoganPage

Publisher's note

Every possible effort has been made to ensure that the information contained in this book is accurate at the time of going to press, and the publisher and authors cannot accept responsibility for any errors or omissions, however caused. No responsibility for loss or damage occasioned to any person acting, or refraining from action, as a result of the material in this publication can be accepted by the editor, the publisher or the authors.

First published in Great Britain and the United States in 2018 by Kogan Page Limited

2nd Floor, 45 Gee Street	c/o Martin P Hill Consulting	4737/23 Ansari Road
London	122 W 27th St, 10th Floor	Daryaganj
EC1V 3RS	New York, NY 10001	New Delhi 110002
United Kingdom	USA	India

www.koganpage.com

© Martin Newman and Malcolm McDonald, 2018

The right of Martin Newman and Malcolm McDonald to be identified as the authors of this work has been asserted by them in accordance with the Copyright, Designs and Patents Act 1988.

ISBN   978 0 7494 8267 1
E-ISBN   978 0 7494 8268 8

British Library Cataloguing-in-Publication Data

A CIP record for this book is available from the British Library.

Library of Congress Cataloging-in-Publication Data

CIP data is available.

Library of Congress Control Number: 2018027582

Typeset by Integra Software Services, Pondicherry
Print production managed by Jellyfish
Printed and bound by CPI Group (UK) Ltd, Croydon, CR0 4YY

CONTENTS

Please visit:

www.koganpage.com/100-practical-ways-CX

or:

www.100practicalways.com/customerexperience

to download a printable **best-practice checklist for apps** (as detailed in Chapter 6).

ABOUT THE AUTHOR

Widely considered a global thought leader, Martin Newman is known globally as one of the foremost authorities on customer experience.

Martin's achievements cover over 30 years in retail, including heading up the multichannel operations of some of the world's leading brands, including Burberry, Intersport, Pentland Brands (Speedo, Berghaus), Harrods and Ted Baker.

Martin has been listed in various industry leader lists, including being listed on Retail Week's Top 50 eTail Power List for five years in a row; he has been named in Retail Insider's Top 100 Retail Movers and Shakers list and on the British Vogue Online Fashion 100.

He judges numerous awards, including the World Retail Awards, the Customer Experience Awards, the Retail Insider Awards, the PayPal eTail Awards and the Online Retail Awards of Australia.

Martin presents keynotes and moderates panels at more than 20 events annually, some of which have included:

- Customer Futures (Hong Kong)
- Global e-Commerce Leaders Forum (New York)
- Retail Week Hackathon Head Judge (London)
- Shop.org (Chicago, Las Vegas)
- Retail Week Live (London)
- Seamless Retail (Dubai, Singapore, Australia)
- World Retail Conference (Dubai, Rome, Paris, Madrid)
- Retail Plus (Amsterdam)
- Savant e-Commerce (Berlin and London)
- iMedia (Australia)
- Sports Interactive (Amsterdam)
- Sun Capital (Mountain View, CA)
- UPS (Rome)
- Etail (London)
- Etail Connect (Chester)

Martin is a regular contributor to various industry titles including *Retail Week* (UK) and *Power Retail* (Australia) and has been cited dozens of times in other publications. Martin can also be seen predicting the performance of Black Friday on the BBC and on 11/11 singles day on Alizila, as well providing thought leadership for a host of global organizations.

He has shared a stage with the founder of the world wide web, Sir Tim Berners-Lee, at the World Retail Congress, to talk about what is next for the web and what it means for retailers.

Martin regularly advises the boards of his clients on their key strategic questions and challenges, including how to put the customer first; omnichannel strategy; the role of the store; how they should prioritize their investments and road map for growth; how to internationalize and into which markets; how to turn their data into insight; and how to structure the organization to be customer-centric.

Martin is also a board member of renowned retail companies, including the multichannel fashion retailer White Stuff. He sits on the KPMG IPSOS Retail Think Tank and is on the advisory board of Yext, the digital asset management platform.

ACKNOWLEDGEMENTS

There are a number of people whom I want to call out for their support during the process of writing the book. My wife Laura, and my daughters Antonia and Saskia, are always supportive of my exploits and have had to endure a fair chunk of time without me during this process. Not only due to writing the book but my extensive travels have meant that I've spent much time on a plane of late. Great for writing the book, not great for reminding Laura and the girls of why I'm such a wonderful husband and father!

I would never have written this book had I not met the amazing Malcolm McDonald and convinced him to contribute to the book. He also put me in front of his publishers Kogan Page. There is no doubt that a referral from Malcolm carries some weight. I also have to thank him for the excellent comments at the end of each chapter. I wanted to provide the reader with both practical and academic perspectives of what it means to put the customer first. In that respect, I think we have achieved a really good balance.

I will always be indebted to my executive assistant, Tiffiny, without whose support I would never have completed the book in the time allotted for doing so, nor anywhere close to it. She has provided so much help with sources, interview sign-offs, editing, coordinating with Malcolm and with Kogan Page, and also with formatting the manuscript. Thank you Tiff. Tiffiny's assistant, Martha, has also provided sources and research for the book and for that I thank her.

I have interviewed a number of my friends, peers and industry thought leaders, all of whom have helped me to substantiate some of the key messages I want to impart. I'm humbled that they all gave of their time and knowledge to support me. Thank you very much to the following people:

- Morgan Tan, President, Shiseido (Hong Kong)
- Aaron Faraguna, Retail Director, David Jones (Australia)
- Andy Harding, CEO, Alamy (former Chief Customer Officer, House of Fraser)
- Robin Phillips, former Director of Omnichannel, Boots
- Nadine Neatrour, Ecommerce Director, Revolution Beauty
- Ruth Chapman, Co-Founder, Matches Fashion

- Tim Kobe, Founder, Eight Inc
- Livia Firth, Founder and Creative Director, Eco-Age
- Dave Elston, former Digital Director Europe, Clarks
- Philip Mountford, CEO of Hunkemöller
- Julian Burnett, former CIO, Executive Director, Supply Chain, House of Fraser
- Mike Logue, CEO, Dreams
- Craig Smith, Digital Commerce Director, Ted Baker
- Jonathan Wall, Chief Digital Officer, Missguided
- Sean McKee, Director of e-Commerce and Customer Experience, Schuh
- Dr Leila Fourie, Chief Executive Officer, Australian Payments Network

I want to thank *Retail Week*, for whom I'm a columnist, for allowing me to use content from my many columns over the years, and to Retail Insider for enabling me to leverage examples from their digital innovations report.

I want to thank the publisher Kogan Page and the delightful Charlotte for her support and feedback. I hope I've done a good job of repaying your confidence in me with the book that I've produced.

Last but not least, I want to thank my colleagues from Practicology, both for their support during this process as well as for the ongoing thought leadership that they create, some of which is contained within key elements of the book.

Introduction

If you're reading this book then you know **why** it's so important to put customers first. I cover all of the elements I believe consumer-facing brands need to face in order to get closer to their customers and to deliver a more relevant proposition. This answers **what** you need to do to put customers first. At the end of the book, I will leave you with a clear set of next steps for **how** to begin the transformation of your business to a customer-first organization.

Whatever consumer-facing sector you're in, this book will not only arm you with more than 100 practical tips to improve customer experience and, therefore, your commercial performance, it also provides a clear view of what is coming in the future and what it means for your business. I detail the serious threats that all consumer-facing brands will come up against, and the solutions I recommend to counteract these.

As a proof point for predicting the future, to follow is the last paragraph of my column that appeared in *Retail Week* (Newman, 2013): 'While it would be folly to try and predict Amazon's strategy, a move into multichannel retailing is highly probable, with a move to bricks and mortar to enable its customers to "choose how they shop".' Suffice to say, I was right. Amazon are now multichannel, with book stores, AmazonFresh, their acquisition of Whole Foods, and Amazon Go.

Amazon and others have demonstrated that putting the customer first delivers **significant shareholder value**. I asked Mike Logue, Chief Executive Officer (CEO) of Dreams, the UK's leading bed and mattress retailer, what does being a customer-centric business mean to you and how have you helped to transition Dreams towards delivering that proposition? He said that simplicity is at the heart of it: 'Dreams as a customer-centric business is an organization where the colleagues, all of the employees, have an understanding that the customer is paying their monthly wage. The company doesn't pay the wages. The customer has the ability to make it successful or impact upon their future growth, and how that affects everyone in the business.'

Furthermore, I asked Mike, 'How do you back that up?' He said that you must ensure that every colleague has visibility of what the customer is saying about the business. Dreams has created 'pillow talk', where 3,500 customers share on a weekly basis with Dreams their experience around home delivery and how that was, their instore experience, the quality of the product and their experience online. Therefore, colleagues don't just hear from management about the customer, they hear directly from the customer. So, colleagues understand whether they are going forwards or backwards as a business. Obviously for some, this visibility will provide a direct opportunity for how they can help to address any issues customers are experiencing. Mike told me that 'It's not about what I think or any of the senior team thinks, it's all about what the customer experience is. If we disappoint customers, it's a disaster for the organization.'

Assuredly, the first thing they review at every meeting is the customer data and feedback. Therefore, everyone who comes into contact with Mike realizes that he puts the customer first in every meeting! They see the leadership team working in the stores, the factory and out on deliveries. Colleagues don't see customer-centricity as a management mantra sitting on the wall. It is being executed every day.

Moreover, with £100 million like-for-like uplift in sales and £50 million growth in profits in four years, I think it is fair to say that Dreams' focus on the customer has really paid off. They have gone from essentially being bust to now being the most profitable and recommended bed company in the world.

Nevertheless, in case you need a further proof point for the commercial benefits of improving customer experience, KPMG Nunwood produced a report in 2017 called 'The Connected Experience Imperative' (KPMG, 2017). It uses research from the Customer Experience Excellence Centre (CEEC), which conducted eight years of ongoing research with 1,550 detailed brand reviews across 17 markets. During this research and the production of the report, they compared two groups of companies: one the FTSE100, and the other, the top 100 customer experience leaders within the CEEC report. The findings are very telling. Here is what they found the revenue growth comparison to be in three key verticals:

- Financial services – top 100 customer experience leaders' revenue growth was 2x larger than that of the FTSE100.
- Non-grocery retail – top 100 customer experience leaders' revenue growth was 3.5x larger than that of the FTSE100.
- Travel and hotels – top 100 customer experience leaders' revenue growth was 1.5x larger than that of the FTSE100.

If the shoe fits...

Another retailer that benefits commercially from its very strong customer focus is Schuh, a leading European footwear retailer.

They have always had a focus on the customer and good service: 1) they have tended to interpret where they can get volume consumption; 2) where can they play to their strengths, eg same-day delivery. They are system-oriented and have tight control over their inventory and therefore are well positioned to deliver a great experience.

Sean McKee, Director of e-Commerce and Customer Experience, described an e-commerce arms race to do the sexy and exciting things. From his perspective, it is about how to judge what is not worth doing and how to prioritize things that will add real value to the customer and to the business. 'However, you don't want to be so risk averse – a little bit of failure is a good thing.'

Schuh has been an early adopter of technology that delivers great customer service. They implemented live video chat. They also provide text-based customer service; 60 per cent of customer service is now through mobile-led text interaction.

Furthermore, Schuh has also transitioned to a more customer-centric business by recognizing the type of experience customers demand – an example of this being that all inventory is available in near real time across all channels, therefore they can satisfy customer demand. They use all stores as fulfilment hubs and are fulfilled four times per day. They have 90-minute home delivery from most stores. They have mobile point of sale (POS), which reduces customer wait time, has shaved 100 seconds off transaction time and is great for e-receipts. They have even repurposed cash-desk areas as children's areas. All of the above delivers a return for shareholders.

The key to success

Timpson is the UK's leading shoe-repair and key-cutting business with over 1,800 shops and more than 5,000 staff. The founder John Timpson empowers his staff with the freedom to look after customers as they see fit. In fact, he says that they have an upside-down management structure with the CEO at the bottom. They empower colleagues to spend up to £500 to solve customer issues before they need authorization from a manager. Timpson has a turnover of more than £260 million and profits of over £20 million (Timpson. co.uk). Empowering staff to look after customers clearly pays off.

Don't think this book is only about retail, it is most definitely not – it is about customers

Whatever consumer-facing sector you operate in, whether it is financial services, travel, leisure, automotive, casual dining/food and beverage, your customers spend more time in retail than in your vertical. Therefore, there are lots of lessons to be learnt from the retail sector in terms of understanding customer behaviour.

You must be clear about the threats you face

This book will detail what the threats are to retailers, banks, insurance companies, automotive dealers, restaurants, travel companies and more, and provide detailed recommendations for how to defend your position by getting closer to your customers. In a world where all consumer-facing verticals are being disrupted, it is quite simply no longer acceptable, nor is it sustainable, to pay lip service to putting the customer first.

Many businesses talk about it, and sometimes it is even explicitly stated in the company's mission statement or vision. However, in reality, it is rarely executed well, if at all. Consumer-facing businesses largely take their customers for granted. Think about it for a minute. How many times a day do you touch a consumer-facing brand? When was the last time you had a truly fantastic customer experience? You can normally count these on one finger, if at all. That's why when you do have a great experience it stands out and you remember it. It is a rare experience to come across a business that truly understands what putting the customer first really means. As a result, it resonates even more when this does occur and can become a key differentiator for your business.

As more and more disruptors come into all verticals – be that Uber, Airbnb, Tesla, Alibaba or Amazon – at the very least, businesses must get the basics right. That must start with putting the customer first. Failure to do so will only see them lose market share and quite possibly go out of business as they are overtaken by customer-centric organizations that have built a culture, systems, people and processes all around putting the customer first.

Figure 0.1 shows that there is a lot to do behind the scenes to transform to a customer-centric business, much of which you can do in the short term. Later on in the book, I provide an extensive checklist of all the quick wins and low-hanging fruit you can use in order to drive an immediate uptick in sales performance.

Figure 0.1   Customer-centric transformation

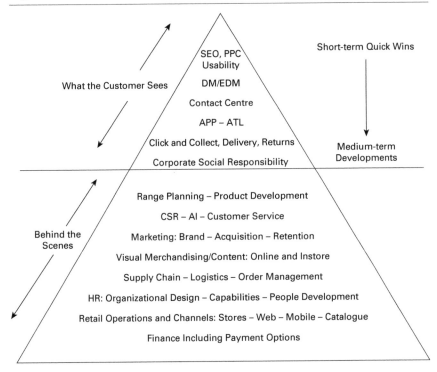

Some examples of the quicker wins include search engine optimization (SEO) and pay per click (PPC) acquisition marketing, which enable the right customers to find you more easily and improve the usability of the website, thus making it easier for customers to make a purchase. Other quick wins include improving your direct and electronic direct mail to customers (DM/EDM) and your above-the-line (ATL) advertising.

There are lots of other elements that take longer to effect change and improvements from the product or service you offer, such as defining your approach to corporate social responsibility (CSR) and integrating that into your business, as well as leveraging artificial intelligence (AI) to drive efficiencies.

Unquestionably there are lots of things a business can do in the short term to improve the experience for the customer. For example, my experience of buying a new car.

I fancied a Jaguar. I searched online and found Lookers. They were the furthest away from me but they came top on the search rankings and they also had a paid search ad. From the moment I called them, I knew I was in the hands of a very professional organization. The receptionist asked me a whole suite of questions in order to ensure she passed me through to the most appropriate salesperson. In this case it was Jason. He managed my expectations really well. After ascertaining my budget and the spec of car I was after, he told me he'd get back to me the next day. He did. I received a text with a link to a personalized video of Jason showing me the car he had quoted me on. Wow! I'd never had that experience before and it really was great. It brought it to life, it made the experience really personal and engaging.

When I turned up at the dealer's showroom for my test drive, I was greeted by a drink (non-alcoholic) and a snack while I waited for Jason and the demonstrator I was to test drive to be ready. I test-drove the car. I was hooked. I bought the car. I was made to feel important and valued as a customer.

Subsequently, since purchase, they have e-mailed me with a survey to gauge my experience and gain my feedback on anything they could improve as well as simply to thank me for my purchase. This is not representative of a business only focused on customer acquisition. More importantly, they are absolutely doing all they can to ensure I always think of them first in the future when I'm looking for a new car. Not only that, but I'm far more likely to tell my friends, family and work colleagues about how great an experience I had with them. Referrals and word of mouth are the life blood for any business. That is what I consider to be a business with a true customer retention focus and one that takes a view of customer lifetime value. Of my experiences with car dealers, 99 per cent have felt as though they couldn't care less if I never came back, as long as I purchased the car they wanted to sell me on that given day.

All of the above are quick wins. None of it is rocket science.

I keep hearing the term 'digital transformation'. Maybe that's the answer? No, it's a misnomer. Digital is technology. It's the conduit and enabler to delivering the appropriate customer experience. It's not the starting point. It should really be called **customer-centric transformation**, as that would then set the agenda for leveraging technology to put the customer first.

This book will enable you to gain a far deeper understanding of what makes customers tick in this multichannel world, and will provide practical examples and frameworks for how businesses can create lasting value and defend their market positions by becoming truly customer-centric – all delivered by the UK's leading marketing strategist, Professor Malcolm McDonald, and global retail and customer experience thought leader (that's me), Martin Newman.

To follow is a breakdown of the key points I cover in each chapter:

Chapter 1: Put the customer first – if you don't, someone else will:

- How the balance of power has shifted from brand/retailer to the customer.
- The type of experience and service the customer expects to receive.
- It is okay to mimic successful businesses.

Chapter 2: Marketplaces and disruptors are eating your lunch (taking your market share):

- The specific threat posed to retailers by marketplaces.
- Marketplace strategy is to go multichannel.
- Defending your position: strategic options to maintain market share (includes exclusive or unique products, building relationships with customers, creating engaging store experiences).
- Marketplaces also present an opportunity as a new channel to market. Should you take part or not?

Chapter 3: Removing friction from the customer's journey – getting the basics right in travel, retail, food and beverage, leisure and financial services:

- Key points of friction within each vertical and each channel.
- I provide a view of how the disruptors are creating highly effective customer value propositions and provide case studies of how disruptors are winning market share.
- Highlight some clear untapped opportunities to drive sales.
- The focus is on hotels, restaurants, automotive, health and leisure, media, utilities and the travel and holiday sectors.

Chapter 4: How to be disruptive in your own business:

- From Uber to Airbnb, all verticals are being disrupted by new entrants that offer customers new and more relevant value propositions.

- How to become a disruptor in your own business – creating and leveraging innovation labs to help your business evolve.
- The requirement to adopt agile business development to stay one step ahead of your competitors.

Chapter 5: The role of the store and its new footprint:

- How to leverage digital instore to drive customer acquisition, conversion and retention.
- Why product and brand immersion are key components for customer engagement and what this means for the new store footprint.
- As digital grows, how many stores do you need?
- Case studies of brands that have reimagined their stores to deliver unique customer experiences.

Chapter 6: We live in a hyper-local world where mobile is key:

- Developing a mobile-first strategy.
- Customer expectations of mobile.
- Mobile versus app – or do you need both?
- Mobile usability.
- The role of mobile in the store.

Chapter 7: Organizational design to put the customer first:

- How organizational structures are evolving to put the customer first.
- Capability gaps that need filling to be more customer-centric.
- How operating models are adapting to a customer-first approach

Chapter 8: Cultural change – must be top down and bottom up:

- The CEO must be the one person obsessed more than anyone else about putting the customer first.
- How to drive customer-centric cultural change.
- How to empower staff to put the customer first.
- Case studies of brands that do this well.
- The importance of transparency in all customer interactions.

Chapter 9: Less about corporate, more about social responsibility:

- What you stand for counts. Here we demonstrate brands whose social responsibility has had serious cut-through with customers (examples include Toms, Warby Parker, Magrabi).

– Why millennials care, and how to position yourself with authenticity and credibility.

Chapter 10: Retail as a service:

– Consumer-facing businesses need to become service providers.

– How can retailers add value to customers by providing services such as auto-replenishment of bulky or regularly purchased items?

– How can other verticals become more service-oriented?

Chapter 11: Winning the hearts and minds of customers in international markets:

– Customers in international markets have different elements that matter more to them; for example in Germany, paying by direct debit or bank transfer is key (free returns are also very important in Germany as it has a strong catalogue heritage and propensity to return products).

– How to win the trust of customers in new geographical markets.

– Options for structure and operating models.

– China and the opportunity there.

Chapter 12: Customer-centric marketing communications:

– How the mix of marketing communications has changed and what that means for skill sets and activity.

– Growth hacking explained, and the opportunity it offers.

– The opportunities presented by proximity marketing.

– The evolving customer journey, and what that means for acquisition activity.

– The owned, bought and earned touchpoints on the customer journey.

Chapter 13: A new framework for the marketing mix – the Customer Mix or 6Ws:

– Why the 4Ps marketing mix is no longer relevent.

– The new 6Ws framework – the Customer Mix.

– What the key levers are to deliver a customer-first strategy.

Chapter 14: Strategic social media and its importance to the whole organization:

– Social media should not be run by the youngest person in the business just because they are on Instagram and Pinterest!

– Understanding the strategic opportunities and imperatives of social media.

– What areas does social media impact, eg service, product development, customer sentiment etc.

Chapter 15: The impact of AI, augmented virtual reality, machine learning and voice on customer experience:

– Chat bots are all the rage. Who is using them and are they delivering better service?

– What other areas of customer engagement are likely to be impacted by machine learning and AI?

Chapter 16: The rise of the 'ations' in driving differentiation:

– Premiumization.

– Customization.

– Personalization/me-ization.

Chapter 17: Understanding customer behaviour – turning data into actionable insight and the key drivers for customer relationship management:

– What can be achieved with a single view of the customer.

– What is the hierarchy of customer relationship management (CRM), from sending gender-relevant e-mails to full personalization?

– Case studies of brands that communicate highly effectively with customers.

– How do you surface a deeper understanding of customer behaviour?

– What should you be looking for in the first place?

– How can this insight help you to deliver an even better customer experience?

Chapter 18: So where do you start to transform your business?:

– A practical plan of action for undertaking your journey to being a customer-centric business.

– As with each chapter, we will now hear comments by Professor Malcolm McDonald, who will share his thoughts on the topics from an academic and marketing viewpoint. We hope this gives you further food for thought.

Over to Professor Malcolm McDonald

Customer-centricity can also have its downside for suppliers unless great care is taken. There are a vast number of scholarly studies that prove that long-run financial success is caused by the following:

- Deep understanding of how the market works and who makes the decision on what to buy.

- Needs-based segmentation – that is, buyer needs-based segmentation, as opposed to sole focus on common business-school topics such as socio-economics, demographics, geodemographics and the like. (After all, Ozzy Osbourne and Prince Charles are both socio-economic group A but they don't behave the same!) The truth is there is no such thing as a customer/consumer. They are all different and we have to look for groups with the same or similar needs. These are 'segments'.

- The development of value propositions for each segment. Some segments will inevitably be more important to a supplier than others. The main point here is that the customer service that each requires will be different in all cases. So, branding and positioning will depend on how well an organization carries this out.

Steven Sheil from L'Oréal said: 'L'Oréal is consumer-centric but in a special way. It is about understanding when our consumers want to be communicated to and in what way. Consumers look for different types of information in different places and want to have different interactions with their brands' (Sheil, 2017).

The best we have been able to get to in the so-called 'science of marketing' is to put our millions of customers into groups who share approximately the same or similar needs and behaviours. These are called 'segments'. There is a process for this that is central to customer-centricity and we will expand on this later in the book.

I would like to complement Martin's thoughts on customer experience with some further worrying trends. For example, the airline model of squeezing extra customer pennies is being replicated in hotels. IHG, Hilton, Marriott, Choice, Wyndham and Hyatt now have about 60 per cent of all hotel rooms in America and are now starting to copy the additional fees similar to baggage and ancillary charges made by the big four airlines. All this, of course, is to grow profits, whilst forgetting the whole concept of customer satisfaction.

References

KPMG (2017) [accessed 18 December 2017] The Connected Experience Imperative: 2017 UK Customer Experience Excellence Analysis [Online] http://www.nunwood.com/media/2216/the-connected-experience-imperative-uk-2017-cee-analysis-single-page-spread.pdf

Newman, M (2013) [accessed 23 October 2017] Comment: Amazon's Dogged Determination Will Continue To Threaten Other Retailers [Online] https://www.retail-week.com/online-retail/comment-amazons-dogged-determination-will-continue-to-threaten-other-retailers-/5053953.article?authent=1

Sheil, S (2017) [accessed 23 October 2017] L'Oréal On Why Communicating the Science Behind the Beauty Takes True Collaboration, *Marketing Week* [Online] https://www.marketingweek.com/2017/08/03/loreal-science-behind-beauty/

Put the customer first

01

If you don't, someone else will

The web changed everything, for ever

- It drives proliferation of choice.
- It drives transparency on pricing.
- It forced new, more convenient logistics propositions.
- It put the power in the hands of the consumer, NOT the retailer or the brand.

In this chapter, I detail the different types of experience and service that customers demand across various consumer sectors and what happens when their requirements are not met. I provide my top five practical tips for putting the customer first, which apply across all consumer verticals and can help you to make an immediate difference to your business.

Picture the scene of the future. Your stores are shut. Your website can no longer take payment from customers. You have laid off all of your people. The admin staff, human resources, buyers and merchandisers, visual merchandisers, digital and brand marketing, finance, retail operations, store staff, supply chain and logistics, customer service, property and, of course, the board. All gone. Every last one of them, yourself included. You have gone out of business. You are feeling fairly sorry for yourself. You just didn't see it coming. Yet only five years ago you were doing well. Sales were up like-for-like, the web was growing nicely and everything seemed fine. So, what happened? Well, you took your customers for granted, that's what happened.

Today is not the 1990s when customers had limited choice of where to buy their goods, their flights, their holidays and so on. The web was in its infancy and therefore customers only had retail stores to buy from, most of which were on their local high street, and a handful of catalogues. Therefore, you could rely upon their custom. The web has changed everything. It has created proliferation of choice for consumers, and it has put the power in their hands: where, when, how and whom they buy from... *they are in control, not you.*

The traditional 20th-century retail organization is at odds with 21st-century customers' needs and wants. We moved away from the old key driver of 'location, location, location' to 'convenience, convenience, convenience' – and now provide the only model the customer is really interested in, which is 'anything, anytime, anywhere'.

It does sound ridiculous to talk about the fact that the reason you went out of business is that you did not put the customer first. But that is the reality and a harsh one at that. You didn't put your customer first, while lots of your existing competitors, and some who didn't exist a year ago, did. They ate your lunch, right in front of your eyes. With their market-leading logistics and fulfilment propositions, their price transparency and increasingly relevant range architecture, marketplaces including Amazon also consumed a fair bit of your customer base.

As I talk about at length in Chapter 2, marketplaces have very compelling value chains. Table 1.1 provides a high-level view of what their value chain looks like compared to most retailers.

If you think this book is fiction, then think again. Just ask the former CEOs of the original Clintons Cards, American Apparel, Jaeger, HMV, Blockbuster, Kodak, Brantano, Woolworths (UK), Borders, Comet, Maplin, Toys 'R' Us

Table 1.1 The marketplace value chain

Source	Range architecture: breadth of range	Price architecture: spread from low to high	Supply chain	Logistics/ delivery	Customer service
Marketplaces such as Amazon and Alibaba	✓	✓	✓	✓	✓
Retailers	Can't compete	Can't Compete	Most can't compete	Can't compete with speed nor with the Prime delivery proposition	Can compete, but most don't currently

(UK), Aussie Farmers Direct and more. Some did not see the change coming, some were unable to react quickly enough. Along came the internet and the opportunity for new brands to come in and remove friction from the customer's experience and make it easier for them to purchase products in their respective categories. Arguably, many retailers were too slow to adapt both to the multichannel world but also to new or existing competitors who had also upped their game on their product proposition and had created more compelling customer value propositions.

It is easy to get caught up in the here and now. In retail, probably more so than any other consumer-facing sector, you live and die by current performance. Arguably not enough emphasis is put on the medium to long term. I appreciate it is often a catch-22. While cash flow, levels of debt and bank covenants are all short-term in focus, and understandably so, if you are not also playing the long game you may find that 18 months to three years down the line your business model is no longer relevant. Your customers will have long since migrated onto other businesses that have more relevant, more convenient, customer-first propositions. Therefore, consumer-facing brands must find other measures of value over and above short-term return to shareholders. Otherwise, they will not make the investments required to ensure their long-term relevance to customers.

Top practical customer experience tips

Centred around *putting the customer first* in any consumer market:

1 Always start with the customer. Otherwise, how can you possibly know what you need to do to be successful?

2 If you can't beat them, join them: it's okay to mimic successful businesses.

3 Think of yourself as a customer service business that just happens to sell stuff.

4 Think customer empowerment: what can you do at every step of the way to truly empower your customers?

5 Always empower your staff to deliver the right experience for customers.

Expanded on below.

Always start with the customer. Otherwise, how can you possibly know what you need to do to be successful?

Never, ever, ever start with the technology. Technology is an enabler; people and processes are required to deliver the appropriate customer experience.

The excuse for many businesses not putting the customer first is their legacy technology. Again, this is focusing on the wrong thing entirely. While I fully appreciate the challenge that legacy systems can cause in relation to the speed at which a business can transform itself, you must start by understanding what the experience is that your core customer segments require. What is the strategy? Only then can you decide what technology you require to deliver the right experience. When you are making decisions about technology, you also need to be clear about your long-term strategy. Otherwise, you will end up having to re-engineer your systems, or rip out the web platform, CRM application, enterprise resource planning (ERP), or other technology you acquired in the not-too-distant future. The advantage that pureplay web-based businesses potentially have is that they don't have legacy technology. Therefore, they are able to create system architecture that is fit for purpose for the short, medium and long term.

I firmly believe that legacy systems are overused as an excuse for not being able to deliver the appropriate customer experience. A great example is when I purchase Lab Series skin cream as my male grooming brand of choice. I used to buy these products from John Lewis. I stopped buying from them in 2014 for two reasons: 1) I couldn't tick a box to request that they send me the same products every six weeks – I had to keep reordering; 2) they were sending me e-mails to 'spruce up my women's work wardrobe'. Contrary to popular belief, I don't wear women's clothes!

In this instance, flagging my gender in the database would have been an easy fix. I believe they have since rectified both of the above. Unfortunately, too late for me, as I now buy directly from the brand.

If you truly understand your customers, you will know that consumers are increasingly looking for experiences, and are no longer driven by 'buying stuff' in the way they were in the past. This has led to the mash-up of social environments with a traditional retail proposition. In the Emporium Shopping Centre in Melbourne, Australia, the retailer Autonomy has integrated espresso/coffee bars within their retail store. A barber in the shopping centre offers a free beer with a haircut. These are both aimed at adding value to the customer experience, socializing it and, in Autonomy's case, also encouraging dwell time.

At White Stuff, where I have the privilege of being a non-executive director, we have been practising social retail for years. In the same vein, we have a tea room for customers in the store. It encourages dwell time and allows the customers to immerse themselves in a White Stuff brand experience. They can read a magazine, discuss new designs in the range with store colleagues or socialize with friends or other customers.

Good customer experience is about getting the basics right

Practicology analysed the multichannel experience of 30 leading non-food UK retailers in 2017. Somewhat surprisingly, we found that many retailers were not even doing the basics very well, below are some of the findings (Omnichannel CX Report, 2017):

- 50 per cent reply to an e-mail query within 24 hours.
- 37 per cent have live chat on their site.
- 43 per cent offer a store stock checker on their website.
- 37 per cent offer e-receipts when you purchase instore.

It is astonishing that in this day and age, when customers expect both instant gratification and feedback, over half of the leading retailers we surveyed did not respond to e-mail queries within 24 hours. The same service levels would be expected of consumers who engage with banks, restaurants, car dealers and other business-to-consumer (B2C) verticals.

Only just over one-third had live chat functionality on their website. For the 63 per cent who did not, this is a lost sales opportunity. We are living in a digital world and, while more and more sales are being driven online, some customers simply seek the reassurance of entering into a dialogue with someone before making a purchase. In fashion, people want to know, 'Will my bum look big in this?' 'Does this dress go with that blouse, or this suit with that colour of shirt?' They would ask the same questions instore. It will be interesting to see if AI bots, which are increasingly delivering the live chat services, can answer the array of nuanced, and sometimes quite personal, questions that customers ask.

Of the retailers in our research 57 per cent did not offer a store stock checker on their website. It would be good to know what the impact of that is on lost demand. How many customers would have gone to their store to make a purchase but didn't bother as they couldn't be sure that what they wanted to buy was in stock in the store? This is not only a retail requirement. If you were looking for a restaurant, particularly a popular one, you would want to reserve a table rather than risk turning up on the night without a reservation. If you were going to a bank you would want some clarity online of what financial products were available. If you were looking to buy a new car, you would want to book a test drive at the dealership; you would certainly want to know whether or not the car you wanted to buy was in stock.

Only 43 per cent of retailers in our survey offer e-receipts. What a wasted opportunity for the other 57 per cent of retailers to capture customer data, move towards a single view of the customer, drive conversion by enabling customers to check out quicker, and have the opportunity to cross-sell to them. Practicology found:

- 63 per cent offer free Wi-Fi instore.
- 67 per cent promote their online channels instore.
- 37 per cent have dedicated click-and-collect desks.
- 10 per cent provide the location of click-and-collect desks on their store details page.

One-third did not think it was important to promote the website instore. It is dangerous to assume that all customers know that you have a transactional website. Remove any potential doubts they might have. What you really want to do is promote a proposition to 'shop your way'. That is the ultimate customer empowerment proposition (CEP). Buy online, instore, on your mobile, click and collect, ship from store. Ultimately you want the customer to choose where they buy from and where they have their order delivered to or fulfilled from. This is a truly segmented service proposition, as 'shop your way' helps to meet the needs of different customer groups.

I specifically refer to these gaps outlined above as *micro moments of disruption*. Not disruption in the positive sense that a new technology or service has improved my daily life – it is the opposite. It is when I have an experience that makes me question whether I want to engage again with the business I was transacting with.

I know some of you reading this will be of the mindset that we should not always pander to customers and that we need to provide services that suit us as retailers, and that deliver an appropriate margin. First of all, you cannot afford not to offer the right 'shop my way' customer experience, because there are plenty of your competitors who will offer this to customers. This is about meeting customer expectations and having the adaptability and responsiveness to remain ahead.

Second, most customers are multichannel. Sometimes they prefer the ease of buying online without visiting a store. However, when on average more than 50 per cent of a retailer's customers 'research online and purchase offline' (ROPO) they will drive a significant percentage of instore sales. Therefore, there needs to be a line in the profit and loss (P&L) to reflect this – as this then starts to demonstrate the true value of the web. It is not just about incremental sales. Of course, not forgetting that from a pure P&L perspective a multichannel customer is significantly more valuable than a single-channel customer. 'Shop your way' increases the propensity for customers to become multichannel customers. It also makes them 'more sticky' and loyal, due to the convenience of 'shop your way'.

Only two-thirds of the retailers who were surveyed offered free Wi-Fi instore. While many customers visit the showroom instore and look at pricing elsewhere before deciding to buy, whether you offer free Wi-Fi or not you are not going to change this behaviour. Therefore, why not do what David Jones does in Australia and make a virtue of free Wi-Fi?

In our report, only 37 per cent had dedicated click-and-collect desks. What about all those customers who chose click and collect in the 63 per cent of retailers who didn't have a dedicated click-and-collect desk? What are they supposed to do? Wander aimlessly around the store asking members of staff where to find their order? Retailers who don't take this seriously cannot complain when click-and-collect orders are not utilized to full potential. Not only that, but they will lose out on the benefits that click and collect offers, whereby it presents store staff with the opportunity to cross-sell to customers.

If you can't beat them, join them: it's okay to mimic successful businesses

You don't have to create something new for the sake of it. Some of the most successful businesses in the world are modelled on similar businesses in other markets.

With Amazon offering Prime, where customers can not only pay a one-off fee to have as many deliveries as they want throughout the year, but where they can also now select a one-hour delivery slot within main cities and conurbations, retailers need to work very hard to compete on logistics options. Best-practice fulfilment options include:

- Order by 10 pm the night before (some offer orders up to midnight) for guaranteed delivery before 10 am the next day.
- A guaranteed one-hour time slot for delivery.
- Specified date delivery.

According to UPS's 'pulse of the online shopper' research, 52 per cent of shoppers find the number of shipping options offered important when searching for and selecting products to buy online (UPS, 2017).

If you can't beat them, can you join them? Can you offer a similar delivery proposition to Amazon that increases propensity to buy and encourages customers to think of you first as they have already subscribed to an annual delivery proposition?

Think of yourself as a customer service business that just happens to sell stuff

Think of yourself like a customer service business, rather than a retail bank selling financial services, or a travel company selling holidays or a retailer selling fashion. If you were the former, then rather than behaving like a traditional high-street bank, you would behave more like Metro Bank, arguably the leading challenger bank in the UK. Some of the biggest issues with traditional banks are the opening hours; historically the hours would be 9 am to 5 pm, Monday to Friday, or sometimes Saturday mornings. Many consumers want the added flexibility of coming in at the weekends or before or after work hours, as that is what suits them better.

Net-a-Porter are working hard to position themselves as service providers and go beyond traditional delivery methods. As part of 'You Try, We Wait', Net-a-Porter's personal shopping assistants will deliver orders to their extremely important customers (EIP – extremely important people) at their home on the same day as they place their request. They will then wait until the customer has tried on the pieces they ordered, and take back anything that the customer does not want to keep – the big change being that customers no longer have to book an extra pickup for items they want to send back. This puts the customer in control. It is more convenient and will undoubtedly lead to an uplift in items per order purchased and overall sales from EIPs. There are additional services that they offer, including 'Net-a-Porter at Home' and 'Mr Porter at Home', whereby personal shoppers present customers with a curated edit of new-season items in addition to items they already have on their wish lists. It not only enhances the relationship with the customer, it makes their busy life easier as it is such a convenient proposition. It also recognizes the multichannel opportunity that customers present.

Retailers and other consumer-facing brands in other verticals have to think and behave like service providers. They need to engineer opportunities to engage with customers outside of the traditional experience, but not with gimmicks, where they can genuinely add value and make the customer's life easier (in Chapter 10, I talk extensively about why retail needs to become 'retail as a service' or RAAS).

Direct Line claims to be the only insurer who gets you a taxi after a car accident. It may seem like a small gesture, but one that would be very welcome when you have just been involved in an accident. After all, the last thing you would want to do would be to get behind the wheel of a car yourself or potentially be stranded waiting for someone to come and collect you from an obscure place. Getting home would be top of mind and therefore a taxi would help you to get home and begin the recovery process.

Key performance indicators

If you were truly customer-centric, you would not only focus on commercial key performance indicators (KPIs), of which there are many, including:

- conversion rates (by channel);
- sales;
- average order values;
- units per transaction;
- traffic (unique and repeat visits);
- recency–frequency–value;
- footfall;
- yields achieved (airline, train seats, entertainment venue tickets etc).

You would also measure the following customer-facing KPIs:

- Net Promoter Score (NPS);
- levels of customer retention and customer churn;
- customer ratings and review of products or services;
- sentiment analysis on social media channels;
- customer satisfaction levels;
- referral rates.

To truly think of yourself as a customer service business means that at every step of the way you will put the customer first. You will engineer a business that has a customer-first value chain.

After all, operational and commercial KPIs are backward looking; customer-led KPIs are mainly forward looking. See Table 1.2 for the customer-facing value chain.

Think customer empowerment: what can you do at every step of the way to truly empower your customers?

Retail

I know many retailers who charge customers to return their online orders, the mantra being that free returns erode margins. Well it also erodes conversion rates! At the very least you should be testing the impact on conversion by trialling free returns. Too many retailers make decisions without testing the impact on customers. You need to trial different options to find out what works best for different segments of customers and therefore for the business.

A survey of respondents across the United States, the United Kingdom, Spain, France, Germany and the Netherlands suggested that 76 per cent of shoppers view a retailer's returns options before placing an order; 51 per cent fail to proceed with a purchase because the returns process offered was not easy or convenient for them (IMRG MetaPack UK Delivery Index Report, 2015). This will also include customers who choose not to buy due to there being a cost associated with returning items. According to UPS's 'Pulse of the Online Shopper' survey in 2017, 75 per cent of customers consider free return shipping important when selecting whom to buy from online.

Table 1.2 The customer-facing value chain

Product or service development	Your people	Marketing	Supply chain	Logistics	Customer service	KPIs and measurement
You would always start by involving customers in product and service development and innovation	You would always empower your colleagues to 'do the right thing', to delight customers and not to only do it by the book	You would not only focus on customer acquisition; customer relationship management (CRM) would be more important	You would ensure that you always had products customers wanted in stock	You would ensure that you had delivery options that put the customer in control of when they received their order; you would offer free returns and make it easy for customers to return their goods	You would offer service levels that were instantaneous; no need for customers to wait 24 hours for a response – you would offer service when customers wanted it	You would develop KPIs and performance measurements that were driven by customer satisfaction

Returns are not the only issue: delivery of orders placed online is still an issue for customers. If the retailer offers a generic message such as 'delivery in 1–3 working days', how is the customer supposed to know when they will get their goods? Does Saturday count as a working day? It is at this point that customers start asking themselves questions such as: 'What happens if I'm not in when my order arrives? Will they card me? Will they leave it with a neighbour? What happens if I don't want my neighbour to know what I've just ordered? Will I have to take time off work to be there?' It leads to a sense of complete lack of empowerment and loss of control of the situation. This is one of the main reasons that an ever-increasing number of customers have chosen click and collect as their choice for order fulfilment. It is because it puts them in control of the following:

- When they pick up their goods.
- If they don't like the product they have bought they can return it there and then.
- They can be reimbursed there and then as well.
- They can also choose other products that might be complementary to what they have chosen online.

Travel

In the travel sector, there are blockers that stop customers from longer-term engagement. I fly a lot to Australia. I used to fly on Emirates. While they are a fantastic airline in terms of both the in-airport and online experience, I found that when I was trying to use my air miles to book a reward flight, if I didn't have enough miles I couldn't top up the rest with cash, as is the case with most other leading airlines. I therefore switched my custom to the One World Alliance network and AVIOS in 2015 – BA, Qantas, Cathay Pacific et al. Emirates has since rectified this issue, but unfortunately too late for me.

If you thought about how customer empowerment might apply to taxis, then it would relate to being able to book a cab, get it within a couple of minutes, and rather than wondering when your taxi would turn up, or whether it would turn up at all, you could see the exact location of the taxi. Boom! Along came Uber, Gett and other virtual taxi apps that addressed this issue by putting the control and power into the hands of the customer. It also helps that you know up front exactly how much the journey will cost. Getting into a taxi in an area you are unfamiliar with can sometimes feel as though you are opening yourself up to being taken around the houses and paying far more than you need to.

Financial services

If a financial services provider wanted to empower its core customer segments , then it would start by being open when customers want to visit or contact them. They would provide added benefits by enabling customers to service all of their financial requirements in one place and where the customer was given recognition for obtaining all these products from the one provider. This might include:

- your mortgage;
- loans or leasing agreements for all of your family's cars;
- car insurance;
- household insurance;
- travel insurance;
- currency;
- pension.

This would be someone who could offer you a more personalized experience. An experience based on products and services you actually want, that are tailored to your lifestyle. Why don't financial service providers offer segmented products based on life stage? The creation of an ecosystem of products for the family, eg a loan for offspring when they go to university, a loan for their first car. A special account for your new baby so that you can save an amount of money that will pay for his or her university education, etc. Given that traditional financial service providers struggle to deliver a more tailored proposition, it is no surprise, therefore, that traditional banking faces an uncertain future.

Are online banking apps the equivalent of Web 2.0 but, in this case, Banking 2.0?

According to CACI, in 2015 current-account customers visited their banks 427 million times. Although this appears to be a significant volume, consumers checked their banking details online 1.6 billion times. Online banking users have more than doubled since 2007 (*Financial Times*, 2016). Why would you queue in a bank when mobile offers you the ability to sort things in seconds, coupled with more personalized products and services? This means that few customers will require the traditional offline banking experience. Online banks also appear to be delivering a more personalized and relevant customer experience. Leaders include Atom and Monzo.

Monzo Bank, a mobile-only bank that launched in 2015, is disrupting the banking sector. They leverage customer data to track their spending habits and in turn provide customers with advice on how to save money. A good example of how they are leveraging customers' data to help provide customers with advice and better services is that 30,000 customers use their cards to pay for public transport in London (Tube and buses). The bank has data on those people: where they live, where they travel, how much they spend etc. As such, they are able to recommend to customers that they would be better off getting a year-long travel card and saving a couple of hundred pounds. Analysing data to help customers improve their finances is a core part of Monzo's value proposition. They are able to provide customers with financial advice that is actually based on their spending patterns. This enables customers to save money, budget more responsibly and to find the best deals. Monzo's algorithms can identify when a customer has changed how they pay for their gas and electricity, in some cases moving from paying a monthly money-saving tariff to a more expensive standard variable rate. In this scenario, they might suggest that the customer could save money by finding a new supplier (Raconteur, 2017).

Always empower your staff to deliver the right experience for customers

It is important to remember that often when poor service is delivered it is due to the rules set down by the organization. While rules are a necessary requirement, as long as your people are empowered to make exceptions when they feel it appropriate, and to delight the customer, they will deliver the right experience.

Are your colleagues truly empowered to 'do the right thing' for your customers or are they directed to follow the rules? Is your organization one that penalizes staff when they do not follow the rules? Or one that empowers staff with the flexibility to work outside the rules in order to delight customers?

Does it really cost anything to say to a customer 'yes you can' as opposed to 'no you cannot'? You can be discreet about it. You can even tell customers that you wouldn't normally do what they have asked you to do and that it is not company policy. If you provide the right levels of customer service, it will pay back many times over.

Over to Professor Malcolm McDonald

How can we put our customers first? We have said that 'location, location, location' has given way to 'convenience, convenience, convenience', and although this is largely true, there are of course exceptions to this mantra. I live in an Anglo-Saxon village and there is a pub/restaurant that is full seven days a week, 52 weeks a year, yet the food is truly below average. People go there because the staff are nice, the ambience is great and, above all, it is conveniently placed in the high street. They attend for both location and convenience. Meanwhile, London is full of places like this where it is impossible to get served, but importantly, they are available when we want them.

I used to run 125 pubs in London. The most successful had a combination of a good landlord and a deep understanding of how to match the service to the most important demographic segments in their location. So, let's be careful about discussing convenience as the only key variable.

Expanding on the need to combine online and offline channels. Martin mentioned Blockbuster at the beginning of this chapter – in 2008 they had 650 stores, a turnover of around £300 million and were making a healthy profit (Hobbs, 2017). Although the company started an online rental business, they didn't really take it seriously that the future would be in digital downloads and online ordering, because the company executives all had retail backgrounds and the priority seemed to be to save the high-street shops at all costs. They even introduced food lines such as popcorn and ice cream. This online division appeared to have been treated as something inferior to traditional retailing with the possibility of cannibalizing high-street sales. Even sadder is the fact that Blockbuster had millions of members' details about purchasing behaviours – and their customers were very fond of the company. However, the message here is that you have to evolve your customer priorities or progress will catch you out sooner or later. It is only by understanding the future picture of individual activity across online and offline that you can really understand customer behaviours and preferences.

I should like to make one further point here; of the five practical tips for customer experience within Chapter 1, I personally believe the most important is 'think of yourself like a customer service business', in which the customer experience at all touchpoints is seamless and outstanding. You will read more about this in this book.

From a slightly more academic perspective, I return to the research mentioned by me at the end of the Introduction. The first factor linking long-term financial success is a deep understanding of how the market works.

What 'a deep understanding of how the market works' involves are tasks such as mapping quantitatively the flow of goods and services from suppliers through to end user. This entails an awareness of how channels and new influences are affecting the working of the market. This also involves observing what these trends are and predicting the future.

It is extremely dangerous just to be vaguely aware of changes taking place in the market. This is why the very best and most enduring companies build this into their formal planning processes.

References

Financial Times (2016) [accessed 18 December 2017] Growth
    Of Mobile Phone Apps Threatens UK Bank Branches, 9 March [Online]
    https://www.ft.com/content/a7d81bb0-e609-11e5-bc31-138df2ae9ee6
Hobbs, T (2017) [accessed 5 December 2017) From Iconic To Punchline:
    Blockbuster's CMO Reflects On Failure [Online] https://www.marketingweek.
    com/2017/07/03/blockbusters-cmo-failure
IMRG MetaPack UK Delivery Index Report (2015) IMRG, London
Omnichannel CX Report (2017) Practicology, London
Raconteur (2017) [accessed 23 October 2017] Getting Personal With Customers
    Is The Future Of Financial Services [Online] https://www.raconteur.net/finance/
    getting-personal-with-customers-is-the-future-of-financial-services
UPS (2017) [accessed 12 December 2017] Pulse of the Online Shopper, *Pulse*
    [Online] https://solutions.ups.com/ups-pulse-of-the-online-shopper-LP.html?WT.
    mc_id=VAN701693

Marketplaces and disruptors are eating your lunch

02

(Taking your market share)

WHAT YOU WILL LEARN IN THIS CHAPTER

- You will read about the specific threat posed to retailers by marketplaces as well as the opportunity they present to extend your reach to both new customers and new markets.

- On the former, you will learn about lots of strategic opportunities and practical tips on how to defend and maintain market share (includes exclusive or unique products, building relationships with customers, creating engaging store experiences).

- Even if you are not a retailer, this chapter will resonate well with you as disruptors are all around and currently planning how to provide a better, more relevant experience for your customers.

- There has never been a more important time to have a strategy and plan in place for marketplaces.

If you're not careful, marketplaces might eat your lunch, your dinner and, if possible, your breakfast too. Or at the very least, provide a channel for your competitors to eat your lunch. There can be no doubt that marketplaces are a threat to retailers; however, they also present an opportunity to extend your reach and engage with consumers who may well not otherwise have bought from you or have even heard of your brand before. They bring a volume of traffic and customer base that you could never hope to reach on your own.

Let's start with the threat element

Retailers tend to obsess about their traditional competitive set, when marketplaces in fact pose a bigger threat. Department stores in the US such as Macy's, Saks and Niemen Marcus, or in the UK, such as John Lewis, Debenhams or House of Fraser, are more likely to lose market share to a marketplace than to another department store. House of Fraser's well-documented challenges are many but there can be no doubt that they lost market share to Zalando, Amazon and others, contributing to their decline in commercial performance.

With this in mind, it is surprising that very few boards have a plan for combating marketplaces. It's a challenge often passed to the e-commerce team, when the response in fact requires a strategy and direction from the board.

As the saying goes, keep your friends close but your enemies closer. To defend your position against marketplaces, you need to understand their modus operandi.

Both Amazon and Alibaba provide a route to market for other brands, while also developing their own multichannel retail propositions. Amazon prides itself on being customer obsessive. That can certainly be evidenced by the Amazon Prime delivery proposition that enables consumers to pay a one-off annual fee and have as many deliveries as they want throughout the course of the year as part of this 'delivery subscription' model. In addition to this, they have Amazon Prime day, which to some extent is their own version of Black Friday. It is a deal-and-discount-led day whereby they offer incentives to purchase or trial Amazon products as well as encouraging brands who use their marketplace to offer deals to customers. As of July 2017, Amazon had 85 million Prime customers in the United States, up 35 per cent year on year (Consumer Intelligence Research Partners, 2018).

In 2017, they also added a proposition called 'Amazon Prime Fashion' whereby consumers can order up to 15 items of clothing and have free returns for the products that don't fit or that they don't want to keep. It's a smart play. It will drive up average order values and the numbers of units per transaction that customers buy. It also makes their Prime delivery proposition even stickier and will increase the propensity for users to leverage it as well as act as a fairly effective customer acquisition tool. Amazon also have a good track record on delivery service levels and generally deliver on their promises.

In 2018 Amazon led across the value chain:

- It is hard to compete with their logistics network, proposition and pace at which they can fulfil orders, in addition to their Prime delivery proposition. Once you have paid for that annual delivery service, why go elsewhere?

- They have a broader range of products than anyone else.
- They have a better supply chain.
- They have a better price proposition than anyone else.
- They use customer, product and pricing data more effectively than probably any other retailer, to the point where their ultimate objective is to send you something before you even know that you want it!
- They have better overall customer service than most.

In addition, 2017 research in the United States found that Amazon was the most respected brand by US consumers (Harris Poll, 2017).

It is important also to understand the Amazon culture. Jeff Bezos is well quoted as saying that every day at Amazon is day one. Day two is excruciating, painful decline. Essentially, he has created a business that thinks and behaves like a start-up, there is so much innovation emanating from Amazon on an almost daily basis. Good is never good enough. They are continually looking to improve every aspect of their business. The innovation that this generates makes it extremely challenging for even the largest, most established retailers to compete with. To put this in context, according to Slice Intelligence, in 2016 Amazon took 53 per cent of all sales growth in e-commerce in the United States and 43 per cent of total US online revenue (Rupp, Coleman-Lochner and Turner, 2017) (see Figure 2.1).

Figure 2.1   Online retail sales growth in 2016

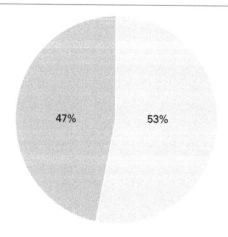

47%   53%

Amazon.com   Rest of market

SOURCE Emarketer.com (2017)

This, along with the continuing shift in a sizable percentage of consumer spend going online, has led to the prediction by Credit Suisse (2017) that approximately 25 per cent more stores will have been closed in the United States in 2017 than during the global financial crisis of 2008.

While Amazon's move into multichannel retail has only begun to evolve in the past two years, they continue to extend into new product categories. Furniture is being muted as their next offline, bricks-and-mortar proposition to complement their move into grocery and book stores. Yes, your eyes don't deceive you. Book stores. Who would have believed that when just a couple of years ago it looked as though physical book stores would surely become consigned to the annals of history? They are also reportedly planning to leverage augmented reality and virtual reality tools and technology to enable customers to get a virtual reality-driven idea of how furniture products might appear in their own home and environment.

In addition, they are also rumoured to be exploring an electronics concept store similar to Apple's retail stores, to promote sales of Amazon devices and services such as Amazon Echo. They have launched Amazon Go, a grocery/convenience proposition where busy consumers don't even have to get their wallets or purses out to pay.

In April 2017, Amazon revealed details of their grocery click-and-collect locations in Seattle, to be branded AmazonFresh Pickup. This offers a wide range of grocery and household items available for online ordering and pickup, free to its Amazon Prime members. Having acquired Whole Foods in 2017, you can expect this to expedite their move into multichannel grocery.

Amazon have not stopped at retail (Amazon.com, 2017). Amazon Prime TV is taking on Netflix and other pay-to-view providers. Like everything else they do, they will do it better than most, if not anyone else. Amazon's market capitalization is significant. Their stock market value is considerably higher than that of Walmart, Sears, Macy's, JC Penney, Best Buy Nordstrom and Kohl's put together. Essentially, and in my humble opinion, Amazon are beginning to own the customer. They are creating an ecosystem of value and such a compelling customer experience proposition that it is an increasingly hard decision for customers to go elsewhere. I don't believe they see themselves as retailers, more an ecosystem of convenience. A true one-stop shop.

As Amazon build out their infrastructure, they also have incredible opportunities to scale one of the most profitable parts of their business, Amazon Web Services (AWS), and to leverage their logistics to become a key third-party logistics provider for other retailers. Not long after launching in Australia in 2018, they were selling their own logistics network to other retailers under the 'fulfilled by Amazon' proposition.

So where does this leave Alibaba, owners of Tmall, TM Global, Taobao, Ali Pay and Ali express?

Below is a column I wrote for *Retail Week* after my trip to Singles' Day in Shanghai. Published with kind permission of *Retail Week*, the full article, published on 4 December 2017, titled 'How Alibaba is Really Reinventing Retail' can be accessed here: https://www.retail-week.com/opinion/opinion-how-alibaba-is-really-reinventing-retail/7027765.article.

I recently had the privilege to attend Singles' Day, or 11/11 as it is known locally (now rebranded as the 'global shopping festival'). With over 140,000 brands, of which 100,000 are international brands, and with US $25.4 billion of sales from over 200 countries (in one day), I think that is an appropriate title.

Alibaba has a strong community aspect to its business. A good example of this is Ling Shou Tong, which is an Alibaba business that provides small independent retailers with a POS system, analytics, digital ordering, supply chain, merchandising and mobile payment solutions; as well as a team of advisers who are able to help them maximize various aspects of their operation such as promotions and instore merchandising.

Alibaba will look to extend its HEMA grocery concept. Unencumbered by legacy, HEMA has created a highly experiential retail space with a fusion of live produce, multiple instore dining options and solutions such as home delivery trolleys. Shopping carts even have kids' toy cars built into the frame. There is a gym, nail bar and other community-based services, all of which increase footfall, dwell time and potential spend per customer.

Alibaba is reinventing retail. Executives call it 'the new retail'. I call it 'customer first'. The business is taking its immense technical capabilities and marrying this up with consumer needs and use cases, to deliver convenience and experiential retail on a level previously unseen before.

This is leading digital innovation globally. 'See now, buy now' allows customers to order items worn or displayed during its gala countdown show in the lead up to 11/11. It is leveraging AI to drive more efficient and effective customer service. Its mobile virtual fitting rooms enable customers to 'virtually try on outfits', and Alipay is revolutionizing payment solutions.

How not to respond to the threat of Amazon and other marketplaces

Short-term gain for long-term pain is the order of day for too many retailers. We have seen this with John Lewis, House of Fraser and TK Maxx, amongst others, charging customers to click and collect orders below a threshold. It is a reaction to maintaining margin and mitigating the 'cost to serve'. One reason for the margin issue is that many retailers incur additional costs as they fulfil click-and-collect orders from their distribution centres, and not stores. In some cases, this means they can only offer a next-day click-and-collect service; it raises the question of whether the operating model is appropriate to meet customers' needs. While John Lewis downplayed their £2 charge – only 18 per cent of collected orders fell below its £30 threshold – that is missing the point. Free and convenient fulfilment has become a core part of consumers' multichannel shopping journeys. So, retailers will struggle to wean customers off free delivery or collect offers. *Retail Week*'s research in 2016 found that three-quarters of consumers did not believe they should pay for click and collect.

In December 2015, it was revealed that John Lewis would plough £500 million into driving online sales, including IT staff, systems and warehousing (Gallagher, 2015). Hopefully this included examining its business model to deliver customer experience improvements.

My fear for retailers is that trouble is being stored up by targeting shorter-term financial goals over ensuring a relevant customer experience. This becomes more important when you consider Amazon's continued march into new categories, along with its market-leading fulfilment and one-click-to-order customer experience – all of which make it increasingly likely that even retailers' most loyal customers will have their heads turned. It is inevitable that they will increasingly buy from whoever provides the strongest value proposition – combining range, value and convenience/service. I'm sure these are the key drivers behind Sainsbury's acquisition of Argos. Not only does it enable the grocer to broaden its range, but it has acquired a distribution capability that arguably competes with Amazon's.

You cannot out-Amazon Amazon, nor should you try to. However, retailers need to redefine their own operating models in order to maintain their relevance to their customers. In Chapter 3, I talk about the disruption that is taking place across all consumer-facing sectors, from automotive to financial services, and from retail to travel. I will also share what businesses can do to become disruptive.

The meek shall inherit the earth

There is a feeling amongst some in the retail space that there will be a backlash against the likes of Amazon at some point, as they will have become so big and so dominant that consumers will choose to go elsewhere to buy their goods. While I accept this is a possibility, as they continue to broaden their range of products and services I can only see Amazon's proposition becoming even more relevant, more convenient, over time.

FMCG and CPG brands find new routes to market

In 2017, the CEO of one of the world's largest fast-moving consumer goods (FMCG) companies stood up at a conference and said, 'Why do we need retailers any more?' It was slightly tongue in cheek and probably aimed as a direct challenge to the retailers in the room. However, there is some truth in what he was saying. Many brands are growing their sales by going direct to consumer. While some are doing this via their own newly created direct-to-consumer sites, much of the growth is coming from sales through Amazon and other marketplaces. Brand owners are alert to the requirement to enable consumers to purchase their products any time, any place, and that means being in the channels that consumers are frequenting. There is a genuine belief within many FMCG and consumer packaged goods (CPG) brands that many of their existing retail customers whom they sell through at present will not be there in the future. One of their tasks is to determine what the channels to market will be in the future and to prepare their businesses for the change that is coming.

Top practical customer experience tips

1 Exclusive products can help you to defend your position.

2 Listen to the voice of the customer.

3 Don't cut off your nose to spite your face… marketplaces are an effective route to market.

4 Deliver a seamless multichannel experience.

5 Consider offering an Amazon Prime-type delivery proposition.

6 Keep your friends close and your enemies closer.

Expanded on below.

Exclusive products can help you to defend your position

Retailers can choose to play on marketplaces but develop exclusive ranges in order to differentiate the marketplace offer from their own direct-to-consumer (D2C) proposition. I have spoken to various retailers in markets where Amazon have just entered, including Australia. Some categories such as furniture retailers with their own brand feel they will not be too badly affected due to having their own brand. However, Amazon will simply reach out to other similar brands in the category to build a furniture proposition.

Listen to the voice of the customer

Listening to the voice of the customer and capturing their sentiment is key to knowing what you must do. It is vital that retailers understand that simply transacting with customers, and having the right products at the right time, is no longer a defendable position. You must earn customer lifetime value. Customers need multiple reasons to come back to you time and again. As highlighted in Chapter 1, getting the basics right is a given. But you need to go further. Sending generic e-mails doesn't cut it. Customers want to be treated as individuals and to receive a personalized level of service and experience. I expand upon this in Chapter 17.

Don't cut off your nose to spite your face: marketplaces are an effective route to market

Marketplaces offer a route to market and also enable your customers to buy from you through their channel of choice. If you are not there, another competitive brand will be. Don't forget, more customers in the United States and the United Kingdom start their product search on Amazon than they do on Google.

Deliver a seamless multichannel experience

Consumers want to 'shop their way'. They demand *what* they want, *when* they want and *wherever and however* they want it fulfilled. You absolutely have to be able to offer that. If you are a pureplay internet-only business, or have a limited number of physical stores, you can still offer a multichannel proposition by enabling customers to pick up or return their goods at your local store using collect plus or similar propositions.

Consider offering an Amazon Prime-type delivery proposition

The same applies to the fulfilment proposition. What if you were to offer an Amazon Prime-type experience? Sell a delivery proposition that gets in cash up front and drives the propensity of customers to buy more frequently from you, as they have already paid for the delivery. Why couldn't this work for jewellery products? For sportswear? For fashion? For homewares? At the very least, test and learn. Try it. If it doesn't work, fail fast. At least you gave it a go.

Table 2.1 provides a list of some of the key marketplaces you might want to consider leveraging as an additional channel to market. After all, marketplaces deliver additional traffic and potential customers. They are also a good way to dip your toes when internationalizing your business, before committing to new markets.

Table 2.1 Leading marketplaces

Marketplace – primary	Country
Amazon	United States, United Kingdom and Ireland, France, Canada, Germany, Italy, Spain, Netherlands, Australia, Brazil, Japan, China, India and Mexico
Tmall	China, United Kingdom, Canada, Italy, Germany, Denmark, Netherlands, Belgium, United States, Norway, France, Spain
Ali Express	China to sell worldwide
Zalando	Germany, United Kingdom
Zalora	Indonesia, Singapore, Malaysia, Philippines, Hong Kong, Taiwan, Brunei
Lasada	Indonesia, Malaysia, Philippines, Singapore, Thailand and Vietnam. Lazada also has offices in Hong Kong, Korea, United Kingdom and Russia
Noon	Middle East
Namshi	United Arab Emirates, Saudi Arabia, Kuwait, Bahrain, Oman and Qatar

(continued)

Table 2.1 (*Continued*)

Marketplace – primary	Country
Flipkart	India
eBay	United States, Canada, Argentina, Brazil, Mexico APAC: Australia, Japan, China, Korea, Hong Kong, Malaysia, India, Singapore and Taiwan Europe, Middle East and Africa: Belgium, Ireland, Russia, Czech Republic, Spain, Denmark, Israel, Sweden, France, Italy, Switzerland, Germany, Luxembourg, Turkey, Netherlands, Norway, Poland and United Kingdom
Flubit	United Kingdom and Ireland
Price Minister	France, Switzerland, Belgium and Canada
Alegro	Austria and Germany
Etsy	United Kingdom, France, Spain, Italy, Germany, Netherlands, Australia, Luxembourg, Austria, Canada, United States, New Zealand, Poland, Finland, Sweden, Belgium, Singapore, Ireland and Greece
Pixmania	United Kingdom, Ireland, France, Portugal, Spain, Germany, Italy, Belgium, Finland, Netherlands, Luxembourg, Austria, Sweden and Norway
Jet.com	United States
Mercado Libre	Latin America – Argentina, Brazil, Chile, Columbia, Costa Rica, Ecuador, Mexico, Peru, Uruguay and Venezuela
Fruugo	Denmark, United Kingdom, France, Spain, Italy, Germany, Netherlands, Russia, Luxembourg, Australia, Austria, Sweden, Canada, United States, Poland, South Africa, Finland, Portugal, Belgium, New Zealand, Ireland, Switzerland and Norway
Cdiscount	France
Fnac	France, Spain, Italy, Brazil, Belgium, Portugal and Switzerland
Otto	Germany, Austria, Belgium, Netherlands, Russia
Real	Germany
Newegg	United States, Canada, United Kingdom, Netherlands, Ireland, Australia, Poland, India, Singapore and New Zealand
Sears	United Kingdom, Brazil, Spain, Italy, Germany, Netherlands, United States, Mexico, Japan, Finland, Australia, India, China, France, Greece and Hungary
JD worldwide	China

(*continued*)

Table 2.1   *(Continued)*

Marketplace – primary	Country
Rakuten	Japan
Trade me	New Zealand
Linio	Argentina, Chile, Colombia, Ecuador, Panama, Peru and Venezuela
ASOS	United Kingdom, United States, Australia,
Game	United Kingdom
Tesco	United Kingdom

Keep your friends close and your enemies closer

Keep a close eye on competitors and the rapidly changing landscape in your sector. Things are moving at such a pace that if you're not also focused on your competitors you will have become obsolete before you know it.

Over to Professor Malcolm McDonald

Retail outlets will not disappear, in spite of the Amazons of the world. This is because there will always be segments of customers who actually enjoy the process of travelling to a shopping centre to experience the true retail adventure. These people will always be there. But, if we listen to Martin's advice, their experience should be greatly improved. Then there will be more of them!

Nonetheless, there is no doubt that in order to survive, retailers have to significantly up their game. 'Survival', however, is not enough. If they are to thrive and prosper and continue to create shareholder value added, the shopping experience has to be extraordinarily good for each of the different consumer segments they choose to serve.

Take Marks & Spencer, for example, who had their biggest market decline in 2016, driven by clothing (Wood and Farrell, 2016). I believe their relative decline is more to do with positioning in the market. The brand was founded on a vision of aspirational value and quality that resonated brilliantly with the 20th century. The point I am trying to make is that even though Marks & Spencer have a useful and efficient model of online and offline, they, and indeed any organization, have to get their market positioning right, in addition to their online/offline mix.

Marks & Spencer's middle-market position has become an increasingly unpleasant place to inhabit. In 2017, they are working hard to combat the decline in clothes sales by addressing complaints regarding ill-fitting clothing and overly modern styles. They are also seeing stronger sales driven by food (Armstrong, 2017), all of which hopefully will improve their market position. I refer back to my comments at the end of the Introduction, when I spelt out that positioning and branding depend entirely on a deep understanding of the needs of specific segments rather than trying to be all things to all people.

References

Amazon.com (2017) [accessed 29 November 2017] Amazon.com: AmazonFresh Pickup [Online] https://www.amazon.com/afx/nc/aboutpickup

Armstrong, A (2017) [accessed 29 November 2017] Marks & Spencer Slows Rate of Decline in Clothes Sales [Online] /http://www.telegraph.co.uk/business/2017/07/11/marks-spencer-slows-rate-decline-clothes-sales/

Consumer Intelligence Research Partners (2018) [accessed 23 March 2018] Amazon Prime Reaches 85 Million US Members [Online] https://www.cirpllc.com/blog/2018/1/14/amazon-prime-reaches-85-million-us-members

Credit Suisse (2017) [accessed 29 November 2017] Retailing Quarterly [Online] https://research-doc.credit-suisse.com/docView?language=ENG&format=PDF&sourceid=csplusresearchcp&document_id=1073325671&serialid=EyVXtoz87yovWNNAvcZfsquqOSSytpm8w1T1EClqtRo%3D

Emarketer.com (2017) [accessed 29 November 2017] Share of US Retail Ecommerce Sales Growth, Amazon vs. Rest of the Market, 2016 [Online] https://www.emarketer.com/Chart/Share-of-US-Retail-Ecommerce-Sales-Growth-Amazon-vs-Rest-of-Market-2016-of-total-retail-ecommerce-sales-growth/204745

Gallagher, P (2015) [accessed 30 November 2017] John Lewis Investing £500m Into eCommerce [Online] https://www.retailgazette.co.uk/blog/2015/12/john-lewis-investing-500-pounds-into-ecommerce/

Harris Poll (2017) Harris Poll names top nonprofit brands for 2017, *Nonprofit Business Advisor*, **2017** (334), p 7

Rupp, M, Coleman-Lochner, M and Turner, M (2017) [accessed 28 November 2017] America's Retailers Are Closing Stores Faster Than Ever [Online] https://www.bloomberg.com/news/articles/2017-04-07/stores-are-closing-at-a-record-pace-as-amazon-chews-up-retailers

Wood, Z and Farrell, S (2016) [accessed 28 November 2017] Marks & Spencer Suffers Biggest Clothing Sales Fall in 10 Years [Online] https://www.theguardian.com/business/2016/jul/07/marks-spencer-suffers-big-fall-in-clothing-sales

Removing friction from the customer's journey

03

Getting the basics right in travel, retail, food and beverage, leisure and financial services

WHAT YOU WILL LEARN IN THIS CHAPTER

- I discuss what the key points of friction are within each consumer-facing vertical.

- I provide a view of how the disruptors are creating highly effective customer value propositions and provide case studies of how disruptors are winning market share.

- I also highlight some clear untapped opportunities to drive sales, focusing on hotels, restaurants, automotive, health and leisure, utilities and the travel sector.

All consumer verticals are going through varying degrees of disintermediation, which is the reduction of intermediaries between production and consumers. In other words, the consumer is able to bypass one layer and go directly to the manufacturer, as is increasingly the case in automotive. Consumers are now able to purchase a car directly from a car manufacturer as opposed to having to go to a car dealership. You could also apply this in the reverse where customers can go to an aggregator that offers choice rather than the one option. An example of this would be Airbnb in travel or GoCompare.com in financial services.

The pace of change and disruption is astonishing

Things are evolving at such a pace that the threat of disruption is real across all categories and verticals. Just ask London, New York or Las Vegas taxi drivers and cab company owners, how many of them could ever have imagined an Uber-like model coming into their sector and taking away so much market share? Or how all the greetings card retailers felt about the prospect of customers buying their cards online. Did they see Moonpig or Funky Pigeon coming? Or were they just not able to react quickly enough? Did the traditional tour operators see Lastminute.com or Expedia coming? Equally, the online booking sites such as Booking.com may not have seen Airbnb on the horizon. So even the disruptors are being disrupted! Back in the 1990s, did British Airways see easyJet and Ryanair in their rear-view mirror?

Disruption is nothing new. It has been going on for millennia. The difference now is that digital technology provides the platform for the rapid deployment of new business models. That is why businesses in all consumer-facing verticals must change their approach to business development. After all, how can you prove a business case when what you are looking to do has never been done before?

Let's start with the travel and holiday sector

Travel websites were the early innovators in the online space. Fairly rapidly, travel bookings moved from the high street to online. Consumer adoption of travel sites was rapid (May, 2014). Online pureplays (online-only retailers) offered a quicker and more cost-effective way to book a flight or buy a holiday than traditional bricks-and-mortar travel agents. However, despite their success, there are still some glitches and barriers to customers buying their holidays online. As a father of two daughters, our key requirement when they were growing up was to have adjoining rooms with a connecting door so that my wife and I could be secure in the knowledge our kids were safe and we were there to comfort them when required. I am still, in 2018, not aware of a single travel website that can assure you that adjoining rooms will be available; or, if this is the case, one that has advertised this. This in turn led to us continuing to book holidays through a travel agent, offline, until our kids were old enough that adjoining rooms were definitely not appreciated!

Players such as Airbnb have further disrupted this space. If you are going on holiday or a short business trip, then Airbnb offers a great alternative to either the pureplay travel-booking engines such as Booking.com or Expedia, and at the same time offers a very strong customer value proposition:

- **Range/choice:** a broader choice than any other online site and something to suit all tastes and requirements with very effective categories such as 'just booked', 'food and drink experiences', 'featured destinations' and so on.

- **Price:** to suit anyone's budget.

- **Availability:** you will only see what is available for when you want to travel.

- **Peer credibility:** the first things you see are experiences and accommodation viewed by your friends.

Automotive sector

A good example of a brand that has developed not only a hugely innovative new product but also the channels in which their cars can be purchased is Tesla. They were the first car brand to disintermediate and go direct to consumer. You can only buy directly from them (Forbes.com, 2016).

One thing I would say that could definitely be improved in the car sector is the location of the dealer. Most car dealerships are in remote locations, primarily because they require a large amount of land, and this is more cost-effective on the outskirts of a town than in its centre. However, this is not always the most convenient for potential customers. It certainly doesn't capture any 'passing trade'. You need to have the intent to visit a car dealer. Tesla's move to open retail outlets in traditional shopping environments is very smart play. It extends the reach of the brand and potentially pulls in new customers who may have been 'passing trade' and spontaneously decided to go into the Tesla showroom. It also **democratizes the car-buying experience**; it takes the brand to the customer rather than the other way around. It makes it accessible to anyone who wants to experience it. Skoda are just one of a number of other brands looking at following the Tesla model.

Rockar empowers car brands, including Jaguar Landrover, to open their own direct-to-consumer showrooms as well as opening their own digital car outlets – some standalone, some in other retail environments including the fashion retailer Next.

Toyota is among a number of car manufacturers that are working with visualization platform ZeroLight, which enables potential car buyers to put on a headset in, say, an office, shopping centre or small city centre dealership and be transported into the car. The car can be examined closely and the configurations determined by the user. ZeroLight has been integrated into Amazon Alexa whereby car buyers can explore, interact and make changes to the model being viewed by giving simple voice commands.

Health and leisure sector

PureGym have shaken up the gym market in the UK by creating a very strong proposition in the health and leisure sector:

- **Location:** good locations usually served with parking, or good public transport access; often in and around workplace environments.
- **Price:** low cost.
- **Flexibility:** people hate to commit to annual contracts. No need to do so with PureGym. They have no contracts; you can buy a pass for a day or membership for a month and beyond.

Again, this is about customer empowerment. Flexibility puts the customer in control, not the other way around.

Food and beverage sector

The pub and casual dining market feels like it could be the next to be disrupted. How much money does the average pub lose because there are too few staff behind the bar? How many more drinks could they have sold? When was the last time they did an A/B split test to see what was the impact on sales and profitability of having more staff behind the bar? Wetherspoons in the UK have implemented an in-venue feature where, using their app, you can pay and request them to bring your drink to you. Now that's a nice experience.

I should be able to click and collect my drinks order the same way I can now click and collect my Starbucks. I don't want to wait in a queue. I just want to get drinking!

When you are buying a coffee, often on the way to work, you're in a hurry. Starbucks continues to develop its extremely popular mobile Order & Pay app with My Starbucks Barista being added to enable customers to order and pay for their food and drink just by speaking in a conversational exchange.

The success of the ordering-ahead capability, which in 2017 accounted for 7 per cent of all transactions in the United States, has led Starbucks to open a mobile order-and-pay store at its Seattle headquarters (Retail Insider, 2017).

Aside from the app, I often wonder why the process of serving coffee cannot be made more linear and process-oriented. Every time I go into any of the leading chains, and I frequent all of them, I have an inconsistent experience. It could be more consistent, streamlined and efficient.

I'm buzzing about restaurants

In a restaurant, why don't they introduce a silent buzzer system so that you can alert the waiting staff when you are ready to place your order, order another drink or pay your bill? It is embarrassing for both the customer and the waiting staff when the customer has to flap their arms around or call the waiter over for service. Working in partnership with Mastercard, Wagamama has introduced an app that allows pre-registered customers to pay and go.

Newspaper and media sector

Sadly, newspapers have been disrupted for the best part of 20 years. Really, since the internet took off in the mid-1990s, gradually most traditional press media has been losing market share. This happened steadily to begin with and then rapidly over the past decade as our media consumption has moved to free media online (ONS, 2017). There are some titles, including *The Times* in the UK, that have been able to maintain a reasonable percentage of their market share by migrating customers to their paid content online. Others have suffered a significant decline in circulation and sales. There is no easy answer. Although some titles have switched to a model whereby the paper is free and they generate their revenues through advertising alone, other media owners, including Condé Nast, have tried valiantly to create retail propositions online, such as with their style.com proposition.

Utilities and telco sectors – the next to be disrupted?

Utilities and telco are consumer-facing verticals that feel as though they are ripe for disruption. Consumers seem to have limited choice in a number of utility sectors. From mobile phone operators to gas and electricity providers, choice of providers is relatively narrow. Also, the cost to switch providers either in terms of money, time or aggravation, or the perceived hassle to change, is relatively high in relation to most other consumer-facing verticals. These barriers are good for the companies but most definitely not good for the customer. For a number of utility services, you are often locked into a contract, sometimes for up to two years. For anyone who has moved broadband provider, you will know that this can open a whole can of worms with lost connectivity for a time. According to the Institute of Customer Service, customer service is improving within the utilities sector. However, it ranks twelfth out of the 13 sectors that are examined (UKCSI, 2017).

There are some new entrants with innovative models, including Utility Warehouse and Ovo Energy, who are attempting to address some of the stereotypes and issues that customers face when engaging with energy and utility companies. For example, OVO Energy enables customers to take more control over their energy with online account management that enables them to check their balance as well as submit meter readings. All of this helps the customer to have more control over their energy usage and costs. There is a corporate social responsibility (CSR) play, as 33 per cent of their electricity is renewable. They give a 3 per cent interest reward to customers who keep their balance in credit, and their customers save £120 on average. It is a strong customer value proposition.

Utility Warehouse enables customers to save on their electricity bills by, amongst other things, replacing all their light bulbs with LED bulbs. They also enable customers to take control of their complete energy and utility budget by providing one environment where customers can pay their bills and see all of their energy and utility services, including energy, home phone, broadband and mobile services, all together.

The pain in Spain falls mainly with your mobile phone bill

Until 2017 roaming charges have meant that using your phone while abroad was a fairly painful experience from a cost perspective. Using data for web access, social media and e-mail has been extremely expensive, as have calls and sending texts. It does seem that this has been a cash cow for a number of mobile operators. The mobile operator Three saw the opportunity to deliver a better customer experience by removing international roaming. Customers will not now be charged any extra fees for texts or data and can use their UK allowance instead.

Top practical customer experience tips

1 Walk through the customer's journey – regularly.

2 Rethink your customer value proposition.

3 Adopt customer-facing KPIs.

4 Learn from other verticals.

5 Train your colleagues to remove friction from the customer's path to purchase.

Expanded on below.

The following sections draw together a number of practical examples for different industries so that you can begin to brainstorm how these concepts can work for your own sector.

Walk through the customer's journey – regularly

You cannot beat putting yourself in the shoes of your customer. This will provide you with a huge amount of insight about where the barriers are to doing business with you.

Examples: automotive dealers

- Do you have a car configurator on the website? If not, you need one.

- What can you do remotely to enable me to experience the car I'm interested in buying? Can you send me a video of the car?

- How efficient are your sales associates at getting back to customers who have left phone messages? I've had many poor experiences here. Why not create a role specifically for a salesperson to call customers back?

- Most car dealers are understaffed at peak times: how do you deal with the overflow of customers who want to talk to a salesperson? Why not enable customers to book appointments on the website?

- If a customer is able to let you know what car they are interested in, how about you take the car to them at their convenience?

Rethink your customer value proposition

Examples: telco

Building loyalty is key. You can never start doing that early enough. That's where the customer value proposition comes in.

If you are a mobile phone operator or a retailer selling mobile phones, offering a risk-free package might be the way to go:

- Free phone replacement if you break yours.
- Temporary loan phone when yours is repaired.
- Free upgrade when the new model comes out.
- Global tariff: use your existing data package anywhere in the world at the same tariff.

I am not advocating that mobile phone operators lose money. I am advocating that they think through how to create a value proposition that is more customer-centric. At the very least, the proposition above would definitely increase the customer's lifetime value. Why would you go elsewhere?

Adopt customer-facing KPIs

If you want to understand where the friction is for customers, a good way to track and measure this is with the introduction of customer satisfaction-led KPIs:

- Examples would include measuring the Net Promoter Score (NPS).
- Customer satisfaction ratings of their experience.
- You would leverage ratings and reviews that customers have left in order to make better decisions around your product or services.

Learn from other verticals

Sometimes you might get your best learning from another vertical. The fact that most bars do not offer click and collect for your drinks order does not mean that there is not a market for it. It is already a learnt behaviour that customers demonstrate with ever-increasing propensity in the retail sector.

Train your colleagues to remove friction from the customer's path to purchase

- Train and empower them to resolve most issues without any escalation.
- Help them to understand where the pain points occur and how they can contribute positively to making it easier for customers to buy.

Over to Professor Malcolm McDonald

Moonpig was started by a Cranfield MBA. Cranfield University School of Management is a great incubator of disruptive business start-ups, so we know what works in this space. There is a potential problem, however, with disruptors such as Uber, Airbnb and the like, who are already having bad stories spread about disappointed customers. What seems to happen, inevitably, is that these companies become such a large threat that they fall into the trap of bureaucracy and start losing their 'start-up spark'. What great companies like this have to do is to keep the initial culture of creativity and passion of their founders in the same way that Amazon, Microsoft and Virgin have done.

This is merely a word of caution from an old, very experienced professor of marketing on the topic of value propositions; my own unpublished research at Cranfield University School of Management through our 21-year-old Key Account Management Research Club indicates that fewer than 5 per cent of companies have quantified value propositions, so I have just written *Malcolm McDonald on Value Propositions* with Grant Oliver, a Kogan Page book on the topic of how organizations that cannot quantify the value they create for their customers will not last long. Value, of course, is in the eye of the beholder (value in use) and consists of both tangible and intangible elements. For beer, for example, there is taste of course and other tangible elements, but prestige, self-display, aspiration, social reassurance, fashion, masculinity/femininity, and so on, also come into the equation and are usually much more important than the tangible aspects of the product.

All really successful brands, such as Johnson & Johnson, Procter & Gamble, General Electric, 3M and the like segment their market and appeal to specific needs. These are the long-term successful brands. They all have very clearly defined value propositions, which is why many of them have survived for hundreds of years. Getting the basics right in this way will smooth out the customer journey and achieve the results spelt out in this chapter.

References

Forbes.com (2016) [accessed 29 November 2017] Is the Direct Sales Model Critical for Tesla Motors? [Online] https://www.forbes.com/sites/greatspeculations/2016/03/03/is-the-direct-sales-model-critical-for-tesla-motors/#22e0a31f23b3

May, K (2014) [accessed 29 November 2017] How 25 Years of the Web Inspired the Travel Revolution [Online] https://www.theguardian.com/travel/2014/mar/12/how-25-years-of-the-web-inspired-travel-revolution

ONS (2017) [accessed 29 November 2017] Internet Access – Households and Individuals [Online] https://www.ons.gov.uk/peoplepopulationandcommunity/householdcharacteristics/homeinternetandsocialmediausage/bulletins/internetaccesshouseholdsandindividuals/2017

Retail Insider (2017) [accessed 29 November 2017] Digital Retail Innovations Report [Online] http://webloyalty.co.uk/Images/UK/Digital_Retail_Innovations_Report_2017.pdf

UKCSI (2017) [accessed 29 November 2017] UK Customer Satisfaction Index [Online] https://www.instituteofcustomerservice.com. Available at: http://ICS-ukcsi-exec-summary-july17-interactive-2078.pdf

How to be disruptive in your own business

04

WHAT YOU WILL LEARN IN THIS CHAPTER

- All verticals are being disrupted by new entrants that offer customers new and more relevant value propositions. This chapter will help you think through the options on how to become a disruptor in your own business – from creating and leveraging innovation labs to adopting a test-and-learn culture, all aimed at helping your business to evolve and compete effectively.

- There is a requirement to adopt agile business development to stay one step ahead of your competitors. If you need to be 100 per cent sure, you will be 100 per cent late – how do you innovate without requiring a business case for every new idea?

- While it is important to remember that, as the great Henry Ford famously said, 'If I had asked customers what they wanted, they would have said a faster horse!', I am an advocate of engaging customers in your business development plans.

Disrupt to improve

I'm not a huge fan of the term *disruption*. Primarily because I see the world through the lens of a customer and disruption tends to suggest a bad experience as opposed to a good one. However, I fully understand its definition in the context of the impact of new innovative, customer-facing businesses, most of which have created technology that has enabled them to offer a better, cheaper, quicker, more relevant customer proposition than was previously available in their chosen vertical. Think Uber, Airbnb, Instacart, Amazon, Alibaba, Crowdcube, PureGym, Purple Bricks (online fixed-fee estate agency) and many others. They have created better or alternative customer value propositions in their space and stolen a march on the established players in their market.

We live in a world where our expectations are to have or get 'everything now'. Our tolerance and patience is low, our expectations for efficiency are high. This drives the requirement for a fail-fast approach. You cannot stand still. You cannot take what you have for granted. Nor can you *ever think* that the business you have is fit for purpose for the medium to long term.

Top practical customer experience tips

1 Always start with ensuring you get the basics right.

2 Let customers help define how you might improve things for them.

3 Leverage disruptive thinking to drive innovation.

4 Become an agile business.

5 Create a culture of innovation.

Expanded on below.

Always start with ensuring you get the basics right

There are far too many businesses who jump straight to the sexy and exciting new things and forget the basics.

Whatever consumer-facing sector you operate in, whether it is automotive, casual dining, financial services or retail sectors such as fashion and electricals, there are certain basic fundamentals that will help to ensure you start on the right footing with customers. A few of these include:

- Engendering trust: customers may not have heard of your business before. Transparency is vital. Therefore, provide a phone number on your website along with some one-liners about your business such as how long you have been established, the fact you also have a bricks-and-mortar channel, how other customers rate you and so on.

- Reassuring me of the fact that if things go wrong, you will be there for me. In retail that would include returns and refund policies; in automotive it would include the warranty I get with the car I'm buying; in the travel sector it would include the fact that you are ATOL protected, so that if something goes wrong with my airline or hotel, I know I'll get my money back.

- Empowering me as a customer to have my order fulfilled where and when I want, eg delivered to my house or place of work, picked up in your store, delivered by bike from your restaurant to my house, click and collect, and so on.

- Letting me 'shop my way'. That means surfacing your range of products or services for me to purchase wherever and whenever I choose to do so.

Let customers help define how you might improve things for them

As I mentioned in Chapter 1, I firmly believe that businesses in all sectors need to behave like service providers and offer their customers far more than just a transactional experience. While customers are unlikely to be the source of your new ways of working, new technology or services, you can test which ideas are likely to make a difference to their lives. There is a host of new technology beginning to emerge that will make consumers' lives a little easier.

Amazon Dash

Amazon Dash Button is a Wi-Fi-connected device that reorders your favourite product with the press of a button. When the Dash button was introduced in 2015 there was some scepticism about its potential impact, and although sales-automated ordering buttons are relatively modest it is among Amazon's fastest-growing services. In 2016 there was a 650 per cent year-on-year increase in orders. For some brands Dash sales represent more than half of their total Amazon orders (Fortune, 2017). A new driver of Dash sales will be the introduction of one-click virtual Dash Buttons that can sit on Amazon's online marketplace or in its app. Ultimately it makes the customer's life easier as it empowers them to reorder a product without having to leave the house or even bother going online. It's the touch of a button. It couldn't get any easier or more convenient than that. There are retailers who sell commodity apparel such as underwear, business shirts etc. They can potentially also offer customers a similar convenient technology and experience to reorder their products. This sort of experience does not need to be exclusive to FMCG products.

Leverage disruptive thinking to drive innovation

Are you empowered to make a contribution to your business? To 'think differently'? To suggest ideas of how you can improve the customers' experience? You can do worse than simply encourage your colleagues to submit suggestions. You could even reward this with the best suggestions winning a cash bonus, holiday or some other incentive. You need a culture that fosters innovative thinking and not one that relies on a business case to prove the ROI from every initiative you think of undertaking.

Technology is moving so quickly, as are customer expectations of the type of experience they seek. If you have to prove the business case for every new initiative you will simply find that you are left behind by competitors who recognize that 'failing fast' is a strength and not a weakness – an opportunity to drive the business forward as opposed to something that was going to lose you money.

Imagine you had gone to your board and told them that you felt there was an opportunity to extend the reach of your brand and to open up click-and-collect order points in retail units on the high street, where the customer could come in and place an order, but not take away any products as there was no stock available to buy in the store. The first question would probably be, really? The second would be, what's the business case? There is only one answer to that: 'I don't know.' After all, it has never been done before by us or by anyone else. This is exactly what Andy Harding, former Chief Customer Officer of House of Fraser, told his board. House of Fraser's stores are huge. Therefore, opening a new store requires an enormous capital expenditure. In any case, they already have stores in nearly all of the major towns and cities in the UK. To this end, opening an order point, where customers can place an order and click and collect products is, in theory, a fairly good idea – it extends the reach of the brand and puts the customer in control of when and where they have their order fulfilled.

Retail banking

In my opinion, retail banking is also ripe for disruption. As I mentioned in Chapter 1, Metro Bank came into the market with new service levels around opening times that provide the customer with more flexibility. They also open branches in convenient locations such as retail parks. However, I'm not convinced anyone has yet worked out how to deliver the optimum experience across all touchpoints and accounting for all the micro moments of disruption that the customer faces in the retail banking space.

Cultural change to drive customer-centricity

Yes, you should have an innovation team, but if you also made innovation and customer-centricity part of everyone's job description, you would go a long way to creating the culture required to put the customer first.

Why not allow everyone the opportunity to contribute innovative ideas? Maybe offer a financial reward for any ideas contributed that improve customer service? You can also look to add KPIs and objectives such as 'make at least one customer service recommendation in the next quarter'. Every business also has internal customers. This is where organizations need to start in order to drive the right experience for external customers. Does the business have a can-do or cannot-do culture? Does it talk about its people as 'staff' or 'colleagues?' Does it celebrate success or penalize failure?

Become an agile business

The most forward-thinking brands have created innovation labs in their business. Lastminute.com, Shop Direct, John Lewis, Tesco and Walmart all have centres of innovation testing how to leverage artificial intelligence (AI), augmented reality, apps and many other new technologies that can improve the customer experience. This is not treated as a cost centre. It is a profit enhancement centre. It is the best opportunity for the brand to drive its business forward, to serve customers more effectively, to sell more, reduce customer churn, increase customer lifetime value, create a competitive advantage and so on. It is also the best opportunity for the brand to reinforce its relevance to its core customers – the value of which cannot be overstated.

Marriott – experimental lab hotel

According to the Retail Innovations Report, the Marriott Hotel chain has transformed one of its hotels into an experimental lab aimed at millennials and generation Z visitors who can give any innovations the thumbs-up or thumbs-down. Buttons and screens are located around the hotel allowing for guests to constantly vote on the success of new ideas. Among the innovations looking for approval are lofty common spaces where guests can congregate, independent coffee shops replacing large chains in the lobby, boutique gym classes taught at the gym by local teachers, and wooden floors rather than carpets. Reactions at the laboratory hotel will result in changes being made across the chain if approval ratings are high enough (Retail Insider, 2017).

Outside of Silicon Valley in the United States, much of the innovative technology, including AI, that is helping brands to deliver more customer-centric experiences is emanating from Israel. Shop Direct are amongst a host of other brands creating strategic partnerships with Israeli technology firms, enabling them to get first access to new solutions being developed.

Due to difficulties in recruiting people with the technology skills required to work in their existing head offices, some of the larger retailers who have their head offices outside of London, including Tesco, Argos and Shop Direct group, have set up London-based hubs, enabling them to tap into a broader pool of digital talent.

Create a culture of innovation

Leverage Table 4.1 to help define how to create an innovation culture within your business.

Table 4.1 The innovation culture framework

Business	Customers consulted or tested	Business case required	Fail fast mindset	Separate innovation lab or team	Innovation stopped when times are tough
Innovators	✔ Some innovators identify opportunities themselves, most at least test with customers before trialling	✗ Innovators don't ask for a business case every time	✔ Innovators welcome failing fast	✔ There is a separate team set up to develop new opportunities	✗ To the contrary, tough times are seen as opportunities
Many traditional organizations	✗ Too often products or services have not been researched	✔ A business case is required every time	✗ Failure might cost you your job!	✗ No innovation	✔ It didn't begin in the first place

Over to Professor Malcolm McDonald

Creativity and complacency are at different ends of the spectrum. We have always known this. Just listen to what the 18th-century poet Alexander Pope said:

Fixed like a plant on his peculiar spot,

To draw nutrition, propagate and rot,

Or meteor-like, flame lawless through the void,

Destroying others, by himself destroyed.

Alexander Pope, 'Essay on Criticism, Part 2'

Finding a balance between the two is recommended. As Charles Darwin (1809–82) said: 'It is not the strongest of the species that survive, nor the most intelligent, but the ones that are most responsive to change.' Also, the great Peter Drucker (1909–2005): 'If you are doing today what you did yesterday, you will not be in business tomorrow.'

Equally, be careful of innovation. One particular managing director did some research and set an objective that 40 per cent of all future sales should emanate from 'new' business every year. That became the target and people were rewarded for it financially. The problem was that in focusing on the future, they neglected the current business and went bankrupt! We cannot stress enough: never neglect the core business.

Some of the world's greatest companies are 3M, General Electric and the like. No one is going to take away their crowns, because they are creative and innovative in a very special way. They keep ahead of their competitors by working with their customers to uncover previously unknown needs. They then find ways to satisfy these needs and, in creating value for their customers, they continuously push forward the technical frontiers and stay ahead of the competitors.

Be careful not to fall into the trap of believing that your customers alone will have all the answers for you. Yes, you should engage with them, and solicit their feedback on ideas you have for improving your business, but remember that people did not ask Apple to invent iPods, iPads, easy music downloads and the like. Apple took the initiative, put in the analysis and invented ways of making life easier and more enjoyable.

It is also a good point to mention the hype around millennials and generation Z. Using millennials as the case example, arguably these classifications are not really relevant. They are spread evenly across different attitudinal groups. If you lined up five millennials and asked them a number of questions, each would disagree with the other, whilst older people are just as likely to agree with a millennial as disagree. This stereotyping is a completely inaccurate representation with which to frame your rationale, in the same way as it would be to group together a nationality or ethnic group. Marketers would do just as well targeting Aquarians or Librans! I must refer once again to the age-old and proven factor for commercial success – market segmentation.

References

Fortune (2017) [accessed 29 November 2017] Two Years After Launching, Amazon Dash Shows Promise [Online] http://fortune.com/2017/04/25/amazon-dash-button-growth/

Retail Insider (2017) [accessed 29 November 2017] Digital Retail Innovations Report [Online] http://webloyalty.co.uk/Images/UK/Digital_Retail_Innovations_Report_2017.pdf

The role of the store and its new footprint 05

WHAT YOU WILL LEARN IN THIS CHAPTER

- Retail stores are about to go through a revolution, a seismic shift in the experience they deliver. They have to. Otherwise, there are lots of customer segments who wouldn't bother going to a store.

- In this chapter, you will learn how to leverage digital instore to drive customer acquisition, conversion and retention. I'm not talking about gimmicks such as digital mirrors that don't add any value to the customer.

- I will clarify exactly how retailers leverage digital technology to remove friction from the customer's journey.

- I will bring to life why product and brand immersion are key components for customer engagement and what this means for the new store footprint.

- You will learn about how retailer space will be used differently.

According to UPS's 'Pulse of the Online Shopper' research from 2017, 84 per cent of customers still consider shopping in a store a major part of their shopping experience; 52 per cent said they wanted to touch and feel the products; 50 per cent went to the store to solve an immediate need; 47 per cent thought they would get superior customer service (although 53 per cent obviously didn't!); and 43 per cent thought they would see unique products. This all strongly suggests that stores still have a huge role to play in satisfying customer demand (UPS, 2017).

Retailers are also considering how many stores they need in the first place, particularly with a significant degree of channel shift. In the three months to the end of July 2017, Next saw a 0.7 per cent rise in sales against a predicted decline of 2.8 per cent. However, it is the contrast between Next's online sales (up 11.4 per cent) and instore (down 7.4 per cent) that is driving analysts to be cautious. Over the past 10 years, store revenues have risen by 2 per cent, while retail space has increased by 71 per cent. Next has far more stores than Debenhams and M&S (full-range stores) (543 versus 240 and 343 respectively). Coffee shops, nail bars and the like are all part of Next's inventive attempts to keep shoppers walking through its stores, but the reality is that Next just has excess retail space at its disposal and decided to balance the online/store formula (Meddings, 2017).

The role of the store

Many retailers are asking themselves what future role their stores can play in order to stay relevant to customers. This is a question that consumer product brands should also be asking. Yet I don't think they do. Or not as often as they should.

EXPERT VIEW

One example of a retailer who understands how to reinvent their stores to remain relevant is David Jones, one of Australia's leading department-store chains. In a move to create a real point of difference while also increasing visitation, dwell time, average order values and overall customer satisfaction, David Jones has created a fantastic instore food experience.

I spoke to Aaron Faraguna, Retail Director at David Jones. He told me that they started the development of their food proposition by talking to customers.

They ran numerous customer focus groups covering engaged customers, lapsed customers and a control group who don't shop with David Jones at all. Customers told them to make it a clean, quick and convenient experience and to develop something different, to make it interesting.

Their food department in key stores such as in the Westfield shopping centre at Bondi Junction has a proposition that not only drives sales of instore dining but also the food-to-go experience. All their food departments currently, or in the near future, have a fully localized proposition in terms of local expertise and product and strong community focus.

In Bondi, there is a semi-fine-dining experience and a cafe experience that includes food to go, pizzas and so on. The main restaurant is next to their instore butcher, with the proposition being that customers can have a steak then talk to the butcher to get another similar cut to take home to enjoy.

There is a sushi bar, a fresh bakery with the wonderful smell of fresh bread wafting through the food department, a fresh food-and-veg area, an oyster bar, a chocolatier and an open-plan kitchen for the main dining areas that bring the customer close to the action. Australian consumers want an authentic interaction and it is fair to say that David Jones is delivering this and, in doing so, delivering what the customer wants, therefore putting the customer first. To top it off, the food department is packed full of people with extensive experience and product knowledge that enable the retailer to bring the whole concept to life.

In their Bondi Junction store, the cheesemonger has been in cheese for 30 years, the butcher is a fully trained butcher and the fishmonger has been in the business for 40 years. They have a 'food concierge' desk where the customer can order food and wine, porterage, book a table for fine dining, arrange testing and demonstrations, take advantage of gift wrapping and gift cards, and where loyalty card members can engage.

They listened to customers, they created a fusion of relevant food experiences that engage and delight customers and they have a highly experienced team who will ensure that the customer experience is delivered consistently.

I'm an Apple man. Phone, laptop, iPad, desktop, watch, Air Pods et al. I've gone the whole nine yards. The Apple Store format is hugely innovative, and has to some extent become the benchmark for an instore environment. I visited Apple's flagship store in San Francisco in 2017. I had mixed emotions about the store. So, what's changed? Well there's a lovely line of trees in the store. They definitely help the ambience. The store feels more open than before. However, I wondered if instore merchandising could be made even more effective by creating an ecosystem of products and how they fit together. For example, I might want to see accessories next to products. Or a watch and all the different straps I can buy. Maybe show me some apps next to the watch. Sell me the watch and all the things I can do on it.

Apple arguably has one of the broadest, most connected range of products of all. Why not demonstrate the ecosystem and how all the various products can be used together?

Back in the day of the great man Steve Jobs, the stores were merchandised in a more integrated way. I could try different headphones on with the different phones. So, while Apple has changed their advertising to be much more driven by use cases rather than the product itself being the hero, they arguably have not yet delivered a use-case-driven experience instore. I fully understand the requirement for brands to showcase their products, the technical benefits and to create brand experiences that provide a halo effect for the brand. They make the brand more aspirational. Many do this extremely well, including Apple and Nike. However, it is important to remember that sometimes customers just want to buy something. Sometimes the focus on the new ranges or the instore experience might mean that core basics might not be available instore. Or that some products might not be as easy to find. You also need to cater for customers who simply have a desire to replenish products they purchase regularly. One example of this was in 2017 when I was walking around Nike's London flagship store and I enquired about sweatbands – I had to ask three different sales associates before finally being advised to head to the top floor to the tennis department. Sweatbands are an obvious cross-sell and, as such, could have been woven throughout the store in all key departments.

Another surprise for me is why many retailers do not leverage online data from product searches, cross-selling data, and customer journey analysis to inform instore merchandising decisions. There is a definite correlation in many categories between the online and offline experience.

From Apple to M&S: instore experiences are polarizing

Tim Kobe, founder of instore designers and customer experience architects Eight Inc, approached Steve Jobs with a white paper on the opportunity for Apple to create its own retail environment. He cannot possibly have foreseen the impact that Apple stores would have on customers and the general retail environment across the world. Fast-forward to today and many retailers are asking themselves what future role their stores can play in order to stay relevant to customers. Many retailers still have traditional if not outdated store environments. Think M&S women's fashion. The core female customer wants to feel special. My question is whether or not the core M&S environment is aspirational enough to maximize the sales opportunity for women's fashion. The concept of having umpteen sizes of the same product on one rail does seem contrary to what women really want. A woman wants to feel that she is buying something unique to her personal style, not a style that every second person walking down the street could be wearing. However, I appreciate that some women just want to pick what they want and pay for it, without having to ask someone to bring them their size. It's a difficult balance to get right – the marriage of convenience and aspiration.

Think Zara. Low-cost, fast fashion delivered in an aspirational environment. Zara stores feel higher end rather than value end. This in turn makes the consumer feel that they are getting even more bang for their buck. I genuinely believe that a more aspirational environment drives fashion sales for all brands, irrespective of their price point. Primark are continually improving their instore experience, with one of the best examples being their Madrid flagship. The store uses digital imagery to bring the store to life and deliver a very engaging environment.

Stores: to be or not to be, that is the question

Many have predicted the demise of the store, but I would argue it has actually taken on more importance. Customers in increasing numbers choose click and collect as a fulfilment method and continue to research online, but purchase offline, too. As an increasing percentage of customers migrate online, retailers need to think about how to leverage the digital opportunity. Digital also provides the potential for retailers to operate smaller stores, reduce operating costs and still deliver a good customer experience.

Sephora has opened a smaller-store format combining an edited instore range with virtual shopping baskets, allowing ordering from a broader online catalogue for collection or delivery. In the UK, as mentioned in Chapter 2, House of Fraser has done something similar, trialling small-footprint order points. Whatever your plans for stores and leveraging digital, my advice is always to start with the customer and work back to determine what experience is relevant in the context of your brand and product category.

The role of the store will certainly change. It will become much more about experience and true retail theatre. The store environment will seek to entertain, educate and engage. I cannot resist a good three-letter acronym, so you might call it the '3Es of instore'.

EXPERT VIEW

When I spoke to Mike Logue, CEO of Dreams, I asked him about what he thinks the role of the store is and how it will need to change to maintain its relevance for customers. This is what he told me:

Dreams are right at the forefront of this. We are moving to a showroom experience as opposed to a shop experience.

Mike told me that the role of the store is to support the digital experience, whether through a digital device or not.

Mike can see a time at some point in the future where there may be no physical presence of colleagues instore. You will get an automated digital experience while testing the comfort of the product you are selecting. Don't worry, this is not a near-term scenario! But it is a strong likelihood at some point.

Mike said that in the near term, the shop is supporting the digital experience and enhances the experience through exceptional service, testing the comfort of beds and mattresses, and that all of their stores will essentially run with web back of house: a linkage between what customers have been searching for online in their favourites and the experience the colleagues then provide the customer with in-house. This also provides the opportunity to more closely identify who buys or not and how they can follow up with customers who didn't buy in order to understand why. It is connecting the hard work that the customer has done in order to make the experience instore even more effective.

I also spoke to Julian Burnett, former CIO and Executive Director, Supply Chain, House of Fraser. He described the requirement for retailers to find a way of optimizing space, stock and labour – finding an algorithm for the right amount of space for the product with the right amount of labour to serve the local demographic of the customer. For example, House of Fraser's stores in Scunthorpe and Bath are very different, with different demographics, store footprint and range architecture. I thought this was a very effective way of thinking about the requirements not only to maximize the footprint and role of the store but to localize the proposition, even within the brand's domestic market.

Think acquisition, conversion and retention

Another way to think about how to leverage instore digital technology is in terms of customer acquisition, conversion and retention. Digital can help to pull more customers into the store environment, convert more than ever before and also capture their data and attention in order to drive retention. While still not that widely adopted by retailers, it seems fairly obvious that certain digital technologies will become ubiquitous over time. In particular, the mobile till, which for some retailers will also be used for clientelling so store colleagues can provide relevant personalized customer experiences. While Apple was the disruptor in this sense, a number of brands have designed stores with no fixed electronic point of sale, Victoria Beckham being just one.

EXPERT VIEW

I have had the privilege of meeting and getting to know Tim Kobe, Founder and CEO of Eight Inc and the man who designed the Apple stores. He kindly shared with me the white paper he presented to Steve Jobs in 1996 when trying to convince him to open Apple stores. The concept was simple: take control of a brand that was at that time only sold through other multibrand stores. Tim was already working with the North Face and Nike and had convinced them that they needed to take control of how their brand was presented and the best way to do so was to have their own stores. After all, some of the retailers selling their brands were discounting them or positioning them in a less than aspirational way. Therefore, by having their own stores, it enabled brands to control the conversation with the customer. Apple stores were created to provide a place where the experience instore reinforced the brand story. If the technology was easy to use, the stores should be too. They should be democratic and accessible to more people.

Back to removing friction: removing fixed electronic point of sale (EPOS) takes a barrier away and encourages customers to engage with store colleagues using iPads and other mobile devices. This in turn provides opportunities for cross-selling, better engagement and data capture, as well as creating more selling space where the tills would normally have been situated (something that the Dutch lingerie retailer Hunkemöller has done in a number of its stores). Mobile tills also lend themselves to offering customers e-receipts. E-receipts help retailers to overcome the age-old issue of how to capture customer data instore. I'm less sure about the role of self-service kiosks. They still seem to deliver inconsistent and clunky experiences. You only have to think of the phrase 'unexpected item in the bagging area' to know exactly what I mean by that!

Do iBeacon's have a role to play?

The jury has been out on iBeacons, Apple's technology that allows iOS- and Android-based apps to receive signals from instore beacons. This technology allows the app to understand the customer's position in the store at a micro-local level and deliver relevant content based on their location (iBeacon.com Insider, 2017). While iBeacons have still to gain real traction, in my opinion, proximity-led marketing will become far more prevalent and used for both customer acquisition and retention, by pushing offers to customers who are near or instore as well as learning instore customer behaviour and dwell time.

For example, Esprit used beacons in their Austrian flagship stores, which connected to the app and triggered messages to provide an enhanced shopping experience through store navigation, discounts and loyalty points (Proximity Directory, 2017). Also French multichannel retail group Auchan implemented beacons to gain a deeper understanding of their customer behaviour by calculating time spent in each aisle and allowing special offers to be sent through to their app as they walk through the store (Proximity Directory, 2017).

Stores are here to stay

In conclusion, stores are not going anywhere as retail theatre and digital innovation only make them more relevant. After all, Amazon is opening dozens of book stores for a reason. Who would have imagined this a couple of years ago when everyone thought book stores were a dying entity? Not only that but the largest online business in the world is going head-first into multichannel retail in grocery.

There are new retail concepts emerging such as Wolf & Badger, who have stores in London and New York whereby they don't own the stock. They provide the space for emerging brands to sell through their brick-and-mortar and online stores. They drive traffic and footfall and manage customer service; when an order is placed instore the customer can take the product away as they would in a traditional retail environment but when it is procured online the brand is notified of the purchase and they send the order out directly to the customer.

Top practical customer experience tips

1 Continually review how you might remove friction for the customer through all channels and touchpoints.

2 Think about how you merchandise and provide discovery and access to products.

3 Leverage digital technology in the changing room to drive sales.

4 Use mobile tills to remove friction and drive engagement at the point of sale.

5 Capture Net Promoter Scores instore (and through all channels).

6 Drive product and brand immersion.

7 Extend your range and offer through the endless aisle.

8 Add more benefits to customers above simple points-based loyalty.

Expanded on below.

Continually review how you might remove friction for the customer through all channels and touchpoints

In this scenario, friction means disruption for the customer. It is where something gets in the way of them being able to purchase what they want, when they want it. In retail stores this can cover various micro-moments in the customer's instore path to purchase – from product discovery, through trial to acquisition. The same applies to any other consumer-facing vertical, be that automotive, financial services, travel and so on. Where are the barriers that stop customers from purchasing and how can you remove them?

Think about how you merchandise and provide discovery and access to products

I recently visited a shop in the wonderful Emporium shopping centre in Melbourne, where their major issue was that the product was inaccessible. Lovely leather bags on a high shelf out of the reach of all but the local basketball team. The apparel on offer was all neatly folded into small, tight cubby holes. The issue with that is that human nature dictates that we don't like to pick up a product in that scenario as we are unsure how we can put it back in the correct state (Derbyshire, 2017). So we don't bother. This is a huge point of friction.

Leverage digital technology in the changing room to drive sales

Another example of when the customer is not empowered is the standard changing-room experience in most retail outlets. You try on a dress, a suit, a shirt, a jumper etc, and often it doesn't fit. In that instance, you will be open to asking the sales assistant to find you another size. However, if you don't like what you have tried on, you are highly unlikely to ask the assistant to bring you something else. After all, you cannot remember what other styles are available and the sales assistant doesn't know your taste. You certainly cannot be bothered to get dressed, go out to the shop floor to find something else you might like to try on and then go through the whole getting undressed changing-room experience again. It's another example of when the customer is not empowered.

The New York-based high-end fashion and accessories brand Rebecca Minkoff have recognized this and have created highly innovative and effective interactive digital mirrors in their changing rooms. The customer can pre-select different items to try on, which are then brought to the changing room. If they don't like what they have tried on, they can swipe through and view all the other styles and sizes available. While they are waiting for these products to be brought to them, they can also request a drink – a coffee, cup of tea or even a glass of Moët! Nice. More importantly, due to the customer empowerment that this has driven, sales in their Soho store in New York have increased by 30 per cent. I got that from the horse's mouth, so to speak, when I visited their store in New York in January 2017 (Milnes, 2017).

Use mobile tills to remove friction and drive engagement at the point of sale

One might argue that the cash desk, till or fixed point of sale is in a way a barrier between the retailer and the customer. It certainly doesn't encourage interaction. It doesn't play to a conversation about what other associated products might work well with what you are buying. Nor does it lend itself to capturing the customer's data. Possibly the biggest issue of all is that you may have just spent half an hour or more trying to find the right product, only to reach the till area and find that there are 20 people in front of you and that it will be another 10–15 minutes before you can get out of there! This is often why consumers abandon their basket instore, particularly in environments that have long queues such as fast-fashion outlets. Mobile POS addresses all of the above.

Just to be clear, I'm not advocating that you remove tills altogether, as some customers who are purchasing multiple items will have a challenging time checking out by mobile till. Ideally retailers should have both fixed POS and mobile POS.

Capture Net Promoter Scores instore (and through all channels)

Surprisingly, very few retailers capture customer sentiment instore. Yet for almost all multichannel retailers, most of their sales still take place in the physical environment. The Adidas store in Soho, New York has Net Promoter Score kiosks. If you truly want to be customer-centric, then you must give customers the opportunity to provide you with candid feedback at all stages of their journey. This doesn't just apply to retailers. This would be the same for banks, travel companies, restaurants and the automotive sector. As a restaurant, wouldn't you like to know what customers thought of their meal? What they thought of the service, the overall experience? I don't think I have ever been to a restaurant that formally captured my thoughts on the experience I'd just had. Imagine what they could learn. Pizza Hut used to encourage customers with messages on their receipts to fill out online surveys about their experience in the restaurant. The customer then received a free garlic bread next time they visited the restaurant.

Drive product and brand immersion

In this case I visited the Nike flagship store in Soho. They have a very strong service proposition. The minute you walk into the store there is very clear messaging about same-day delivery, ship from store and click and collect, all of which puts the customer in control and removes all doubt about why you wouldn't buy. There are lockers to leave your bags in; after all, it's a four-floor store. Then there is the most impressive aspect of the instore experience – there was a group of very athletic-looking staff who, when I asked them how they might help me, told me that they could spend up to an hour with me instore helping to find the right product for me. That's taking personal shopping to a new level. Normally this type of experience is only available in luxury-brand environments.

Extend your range and offer through the endless aisle

Every retailer has limited shelf and floor space in their stores. As a result, sales and demand are continually being lost due to the retailer being out of stock of a size, style, colourway, sku etc. That is why an instore kiosk, also known as the endless aisle, is a great opportunity to ensure this demand is not lost by extending their retail instore shelf, allowing customers to make orders online and collect them from the physical stores. In my experience, store-assisted sales through an endless aisle work far better than just providing a kiosk that customers can scroll through. However, store colleagues need to be incentivized to help place these orders for customers, otherwise there is a risk that they won't bother helping or, even worse, will try to sell the customer something else they don't really want, simply to generate their commission.

Add more benefits to customers above simple points-based loyalty

Loyalty cards absolutely have a role to play in encouraging repeat purchases and reducing customer churn. However, some brands only provide added value when you spend more money. The idea that consumers will continue to spend more with one business, just to accrue some points or discount is, in my opinion, flawed. That is because for many consumers, in this multichannel world, their convenience is more important than getting a discount. I talk in detail about what good looks like around loyalty and CRM in Chapter 17.

Over to Professor Malcolm McDonald

Let's take a moment to consider stock-outs in retail outlets. Everyone on planet earth knows that the average size of a woman, as an example, is 16–18 (Tali, 2016). Yet almost every store quickly runs out of size 12, the most popular size in clothes, causing untold inconvenience to shoppers and, even worse, resulting in lost sales. It is exactly the same with supermarkets. Once a popular item is sold out, the HQ system no longer registers sales, often resulting in even fewer items of stock reappearing on shelves – a totally self-defeating exercise in what this chapter has advised against – being technology driven rather than being customer-need driven.

At this point, let me return to the issue of market segmentation. In any market, there will be at least 7–10 segments, a segment being a group of customers with the same or similar needs. One example is from the consumer travel industry, which I discuss in my 2018 book on value propositions (McDonald and Oliver, 2018). This major international travel agent uncovered 10 different segments of travellers and we show only two of them here in Table 5.1 and Table 5.2 (disguised for confidentiality reasons).

Table 5.1 The Sunworshippers

	Internet	Mobile telephone	iTV	Broadcast TV	Traditional channels
• Recognize					
Exchange potential					
• Initiate dialogue					
• Exchange information					
Negotiate/tailor					
Commit					
• Exchange value					
• Monitor					

Table 5.2 John and Mary Lively

	Internet	Mobile telephone	iTV	Broadcast TV	Traditional channels
• Recognize				▊	▊
Exchange potential					
• Initiate dialogue		▊			
• Exchange information		▊			
Negotiate/tailor					
Commit		▊			▊
• Exchange value		▊		▊	
• Monitor		▊		▊	

Down the left of each diagram is the Cranfield sales process. It will be observed that this is an interactive dyadic process involving both supplier and consumer. Along the top are the channels used by the consumers in each segment, represented by the shaded areas against each step.

Even a quick glance reveals the very different ACTUAL behaviours of consumers in each segment. From this it can be readily appreciated that without such knowledge of actual consumer behaviour and preferences, any kind of offer development and communication programme is likely to be hit and miss, at best. Indeed, to summarize a survey by Marketo (2017) only a small percentage of consumers believe marketers are aligning their communication with how they prefer to engage.

So, whilst everything spelt out in this chapter is valid and powerful, with correct, needs-based segmentation it will be even more effective.

References

Derbyshire, D (2017) [accessed 29 November 2017] They Have Ways of Making You Spend [Online] http://www.telegraph.co.uk/culture/3634141/They-have-ways-of-making-you-spend.html

iBeacon.com Insider (2017) [accessed 29 November 2017] What is iBeacon? A Guide to iBeacons [Online] http://www.ibeacon.com/what-is-ibeacon-a-guide-to-beacons/

Marketo (2017) [accessed 29 November 2017] The State of Engagement [Online] https://uk.marketo.com/analyst-and-other-reports/the-state-of-engagement/

McDonald, M and Oliver, G (2018) *Malcolm McDonald on Value Propositions: How to develop them, how to quantify them*, Kogan Page, London

Meddings, S (2017) [accessed 29 November 2017] Wolfson Needs Less Space For Next [Online] https://www.thetimes.co.uk/article/wolfson-needs-less-space-for-next-tnvqrnp52

Milnes, H (2017) [accessed 29 November 2017] How Tech In Rebecca Minkoff's Fitting Rooms Tripled Expected Clothing Sales [Online] https://digiday.com/marketing/rebecca-minkoff-digital-store/

Proximity Directory (2017) [accessed 1 December 2017] Proximity Marketing In Retail [Online] https://unacast.s3.amazonaws.com/Proximity.Directory_Q117_Report.pdf

Tali, D (2016) [accessed 5 December 2017] The 'Average' Woman Is Now Size 16 Or 18. Why Do Retailers Keep Failing Her? [Online] https://www.forbes.com/sites/didemtali/2016/09/30/the-average-woman-size/#447ee8262791

UPS (2017) [accessed 12 December 2017] Pulse of the Online Shopper [Online] https://solutions.ups.com/ups-pulse-of-the-online-shopper-LP.html?WT.mc_id=VAN701693

We live in a hyper-local world where mobile is key

06

WHAT YOU WILL LEARN IN THIS CHAPTER

- The move to voice activation and what 'conversational commerce' actually entails.
- Developing a mobile-first strategy and why that is vital.
- Mobile versus app or do you need both? I examine the options and recommend the right approach.
- I provide a link to a detailed mobile and app usability framework, prepared by Amanda David, a true mobile expert at Practicology.
- I provide recommendations for the role of mobile instore.

Alexa

Alexa, play Oasis Wonderwall.

Alexa, what time is my dental appointment tomorrow?

Alexa, can you order me a cab for 4.30 pm on Friday?

Alexa, can you order me some apples please?

Specifically, this signifies that we are moving into a voice-activated world. Yes, we have had Siri on our iPhones for some time. But let's be honest, not many of us have had the courage to talk to our phones in public, giving them instructions on what we want to do at that moment! It feels a bit embarrassing, primarily because it hasn't become a learnt human behaviour yet. It hasn't been widely adopted. But believe me, it will. Within a few years, we will not even be touching the screens of our smartphones, we will be giving them voice-activated instructions. We will be getting into our cars and telling them how we want the air conditioning to be, what music to play, what position our seat needs to be and, of course, where we want to go! It's the internet of things, artificial intelligence, augmented reality and every other shiny new (ish) terminology for new technology mashed into one all-new, customer-empowering world. Yes, it's all about customer empowerment.

Customers expect to be served where and when is most convenient for them. Mobile and apps are the drivers for this. A good example of best practice is where Net-a-Porter's personal stylists engage with customers on the WhatsApp platform in what has proven to be a valuable one-to-one relationship builder, which the company says has led to some of its biggest sales. The seamless customer experience on mobile when moving from the Net-a-Porter site to having conversations with stylists on WhatsApp has led the luxury fashion company to work on developing a *conversational commerce* capability that enables actual purchases to be made directly through WhatsApp. It is another sign of the value of mobile in retail (Retail Insider, 2017).

Top practical customer experience tips

1 Always think mobile first.

2 Balance the approach to apps versus mobile web.

3 Leverage iBeacons and free Wi-Fi to drive engagement instore.

4 Review our best-practice checklist for apps.

5 Plan for conversational commerce.

Expanded on below.

Always think mobile first

Think about it, if you were starting a new business today, you may not even want to consider developing a desktop version of your website. After all, whether you are a restaurant, a hotel, a retail bank, an insurer, a retailer, a car dealer or whatever sector you happen to be in, the majority of your customers will engage with you on their mobile device, not only when they are researching you but, in the case of a multichannel business, when they are in the vicinity of your location.

Balance the approach to apps versus mobile web

How many apps can any one person be expected to have? Or more importantly, be expected to engage with on a regular basis? Frequency and engagement are key drivers. Therefore, there is no question that some brands and some sectors lend themselves well to having customer-facing apps, such as banks, travel companies and media titles. Some retailers also have the potential to engage through apps.

Amanda David from Practicology studied the benefits that a mobile app offers and decided whether all retailers need one. With the recent announcement that the Apple App Store receives 500 million weekly customer visits and has had 180 billion downloads, it appears that consumer demand and prospects for apps are stronger than ever. It is not just apps in general, but retail apps specifically (David, 2017). A worldwide survey by UPS revealed that 64 per cent of consumers have used retailer apps, but 53 per cent preferred using a retailer's mobile site. This begs the question: is developing an app the right move for every brand and how should retailers make this decision? (UPS, 2016).

Start by listening to, and understanding, your customer

Remember, the customer is king and should dictate your channel strategy. Whether it is via social media, a post-purchase survey, instore or through a focus group, talk to your customers. This feedback is invaluable, and you will invariably get a return on the investment. Womenswear retailer Missguided presents a fantastic example of this. Their customers made it clear that they wanted a shoppable app and Missguided duly listened, building a 'swipe-to-hype' tinder-style app and ultimately reaping the rewards. In the four months after launching on iOS, Missguided made £30 million in sales from purchases on the app (Poq Commerce, 2017).

The demographics of your customer base should also influence your decision. For example, 'millennial generation' customers within the 18–34 age bracket are more likely to utilize an app as long as it provides a good user experience and fulfils customer needs.

Your audience will also dictate whether you need both iOS and Android versions of your app. Although it is preferential to have both, retailers often 'soft launch' on one operating system to gauge reception. Location is also a determining factor in this decision. An international brand may prioritize Android as it has 75 per cent market share in Europe, while a solely UK-based retailer may look to launch on iOS first (David, 2017).

What is your product?

Evaluating customer demand is paramount, but the product also has a major part to play. Apps are great for retaining customers by encouraging engagement, loyalty and repeat purchases. However, for a couture fashion retailer producing a small catalogue each season, with prices upwards of £20,000, or a high-end furniture retailer specializing in quality, long-lasting products, a transactional app will probably add little value. In these instances, it may be worth investigating a content-focused app.

What is the USP?

There is little point in developing an app that exactly mimics the functionality of your mobile site. Apps offer additional USPs and can be fantastic tools for bridging the gap between online and offline. For retailers with a bricks-and-mortar store presence, consider how the utilization of an app could shape the instore experience. For example, an in-app barcode scanner could enable the customer shopping instore to place an order for an out-of-stock product for delivery later that day. This would utilize the app's key advantage over mobile sites: access to the device camera. John Lewis's app includes a 'Kitchen Drawer' of stored receipts enabling quick and easy returns and exchanges, meaning no more fishing around for paper receipts in your wallet or order confirmations cluttering your inbox.

We have seen retailers successfully launch apps that include exclusive features such as:

- A superior user interface that includes clearly defined calls-to-action with no need to zoom to enter field details.

- Push notifications that can be used to engage customers, rather than bombard them with irrelevant information. Compelling strategies include alerting customers to promotions on their favourite brand and using instore beacons to push relevant offers.

- Loyalty dashboards that enable easy point collection, tracking and spending instore and online. ASOS and Starbucks have particularly good examples of this.

- Touch ID for account login and payment.

- Gamification and augmented reality. Strong examples of this include Net-a-Porter's *Porter* magazine app, John Lewis's use of visual search in their iPad app, Grabble's swipe-to-like functionality, and Topshop's 'My Wardrobe' quiz.
- Interactive content including shop-from-the-page look books.
- Persistent login and account sync across all online channels.

Does every business need an app?

To put it simply: no. But if there is sufficient demand and it is beneficial to the customer's omnichannel experience then it must be considered. Whatever the decision, you must recognize that success should not be measured purely by revenue uplift. Apps also function as showrooming and customer engagement tools, and the sales uplift will often be seen across multiple channels – online and instore.

Leverage iBeacons and free Wi-Fi to drive engagement instore

Beacons and Wi-Fi enable a business to recognize where the customer is within their physical environment and, to some extent, what behaviour they are displaying. On the subject of Wi-Fi, please, please, please always ensure it works for customers. There is nothing more frustrating than not being able to take advantage of free Wi-Fi. Not only that, when you travel on trains in the UK, even if you have previously signed up for Wi-Fi, not only does it often ask for re-registration/login, but it interferes with your own data network on your phone, rendering you unable to download or send e-mails or access the web.

Review our best-practice checklist for apps

At www.koganpage.com/100-practical-ways-CX and at www.100practicalways.com/customerexperience

The framework was created by my colleague Amanda David from Practicology to help clients optimize their mobile proposition. Although aimed primarily at retailers, it can be applied to any consumer-facing business.

Plan for conversational commerce

Before you know it, we will not be pinching and scrolling. Our behaviour is being changed by technology. Many of us now own Amazon Echo (Alexa), Tmall Genie and Google Home devices. Our ability to now ask an AI-driven device to tell us the answer to something or to buy a product will see us also doing this on our mobile phones.

With this in mind, you need to start planning now for how you ensure your products or services are the ones that are promoted first when a consumer asks for 'top-rated hotels in New York', 'best Italian restaurants near me', or 'where to buy my new kitchen'.

Over to Professor Malcolm McDonald

Let us also never forget the human touch. Technology is the key driver of engagement for consumers but not everyone will feel empowered by technology. Some may feel so immersed in gadgets and tech noise to their pocket that they will be refreshed by a genuine smile and a helpful attitude – even a personal invitation through the door for a unique marketing promotion rather than it getting disregarded as a mobile notification to their inbox.

The new advances are of course a novelty now, and rightly so as this is the current differentiator. However, don't forget to look ahead and consider when it all becomes the norm that reverting back to the customer basics may become your mark of differentiation. Everything said in this chapter should be implemented as well as, not instead of, a real personal service.

Let us also remember that AI has its limitations, the biggest being the ultimate lack of empathy and human judgement. No one, for example, would ever trust a robot to decide whether or not to switch off someone's life support system. They are programmed to run on logic and may subsequently miss valuable opportunities to go above and beyond pleasing the customer with the genuine, heartfelt service that leaves its mark.

There will always be customers who want to lead a quality of life away from technology and – when they do want it – simplicity and smooth integration across the multiple touchpoints and devices will be key. Do not expect them to have a degree in computer science to make it work!

To round off here, customer service and customer-centricity will always be largely dependent on people.

References

David, A (2017) [accessed 13 December 2017] Does Every Retailer Need an App [Blog] *Practicology* [Online] https://www.practicology.com/thinking/blog/does-every-retailer-need-app

Poq Commerce (2017) [accessed 29 November 2017] Missguided App Case Study [Online] https://poqcommerce.com/missguided-case-study/

Retail Insider (2017) [accessed 29 November 2017] Digital Retail Innovations Report [Online] http://webloyalty.co.uk/Images/UK/Digital_Retail_Innovations_Report_2017.pdf

UPS (2016) [accessed 29 November 2017] UPS Pulse of the Online Shopper [Online] https://solvers.ups.com/assets/2016_UPS_Pulse_of_the_Online_Shopper.pdf

Organizational design to put the customer first

WHAT YOU WILL LEARN IN THIS CHAPTER

- Where the gaps are in traditional organizational structures and the implications this has for customer-centricity.
- New capabilities required in order to meet the new normal customer expectations.
- New roles that help to deliver customer-first cultural change (chief customer officer etc).
- This chapter provides a framework that can be used to determine the level of digital maturity in your business across the team, talent and skills and to understand better what good looks like.
- How operating models are adapting to a customer-first approach.

Sharing the stage with the man who invented the world wide web

I once had the great honour of sharing a stage with the man who invented the world wide web, Sir Tim Berners-Lee, at the World Retail Congress in Rome. During this session, some important points came out regarding retail. The moderator for our session, BBC presenter Babita Sharma, asked me the first question: 'Martin, you do a lot of work in retail, what's next for the web, and what does it mean for retailers?' I answered as follows:

> It's not about the web, as we live in a multichannel world. The problem with that is that we have structured our businesses around channels and not around the customer and that these siloed operating models and structures do not lend themselves well to putting the customer first.

I then proceeded to provide some anecdotes from when I was head of e-commerce at brands including Burberry, Harrods and Ted Baker as to the issues that this caused and the impact it had upon the customer experience. I'll talk a lot more about this shortly and how retailers can integrate their organizational structure to deliver a seamless customer experience across all channels and touchpoints.

So, who actually owns the customer?

There is a lot of debate about who owns the customer in a consumer-facing organization. To follow are the job titles that I have come across at a customer experience event in the UK:

- Director CRM, Loyalty and Customer Insight
- Customer Service Director
- Chief Operating Officer
- Customer Propositions Director
- Insight and Marketing Strategy Director
- Premier Design Director
- Creative Director of Digital
- Transformation Director
- Global Chief Actuary and Director of Data and Analytics
- Operations Director
- Director of Consumer Insight
- Client Experience Director
- Commercial Director
- Director of Customer Experience
- Retail Director
- Chief Operating Officer
- Chief Commercial Officer
- Chief Marketing Officer
- Group Director of Customer Experience and Marketing
- Director of Digital Marketing
- Co-Founder and Chief Operating Officer
- Retail and Service Proposition Director
- Business Transformation and Governance Director

- Strategic Communications, Brand and Campaigns Director
- Chief Customer Officer
- Customer Service Director
- Retail Distribution Director
- Group Customer Experience and Operations Director

While not all of these stakeholders necessarily have ownership of the customer within their respective organizations, it does provide a view of who sees customer experience as a core part of their role. Interestingly, not one of the above job titles has the word 'retention' in it. No, not one customer retention director. Almost every consumer-facing business I know is entirely skewed towards customer acquisition. The lack of focus on customer retention is remarkable. There really lies the challenge at the heart of putting the customer first. I have heard CEOs talk about the fact that they own the customer. Or that the whole business does. As an intent, that's fine. As a model for execution, it is deeply flawed – as the reality is that the business can only truly put the customer first when it has a culture and a strategy that promotes this across the entire organization. The key to success is that someone has to have a clear mandate for delivering the transformation required to achieve this.

I am privileged to have been on the same stage as some amazing leaders and one is the former CEO of Walgreens, Greg Wasson, who presented at Shop.org in the United States in 2013. His view was as follows: 'I see myself as a B52 bomber providing cover for Sona and her team, removing the roadblocks to enable her to leverage digital to help us achieve our business objectives.' Now that is a leader who recognized that he didn't have the best view of what the new customer journey looks like, nor the digital smarts to deliver it. However, he knew that his digital leader, Sona Chawla, did have what it took to deliver the new, joined-up, customer experience. Therefore, he did the best thing he could and cleared the path for her to effectively deliver this.

EXPERT VIEW

I spoke to Mike Logue, the CEO of Dreams, the leading bed and mattress retailer. What makes a good CEO in this multichannel, digital and customer-first era? Mike told me that 'If you're not truly interested in the business and the customer, you won't follow things through internally and deliver the right experience. It's about being passionate about the consumers.'

Mike said that the reason why it is more important now is that their ability to see the customer journey earlier is there, and if you are passionate about why a customer is joining the journey or not, the visibility is so much greater than before. Without this passion for the customer you will fail, because the potential to lose the customer now during their journey is so much greater in terms of competition and the proliferation of choice the consumer has:

'It comes back to the drive of he or she as a CEO being truly interested and passionate. If you're not, your colleagues will see through it and the customer will see through it. If you're not bothered and you're simply turning up for a wage then you're toast. If not truly passionate about being customer first, you won't beat the competition.'

You should not expect colleagues to always know how to delight customers if they have not been empowered to do so in the first place. Customer-centricity requires cultural change and has to be driven from the top down and the bottom up. The CEO has to have the mindset and own the responsibility for delivering a culture and a way of working that is truly customer obsessed. Accordingly, new employees have to be told the importance of this and, more importantly, how they can play their part in delivering the appropriate customer experience when they are being inducted into the business.

The case for change

The reality is that old functional organizational structures fail to properly address the diverse customer behaviour we see today, let alone anticipate and prepare for how consumers will want to shop and engage with them in the future.

EXPERT VIEW

Craig Smith, Digital Commerce Director at Ted Baker, talked to me about the old world versus the new world and what that means to an organization's structure and capabilities. He sees the requirement to remove both blockers in thinking and in some cases also 'legacy people'. He described how the Football Association (FA) runs a programme to define whether or not someone is fit for purpose to run a football club, and that maybe we now require something similar in retail – a scorecard to evaluate relevancy of skills and capabilities.

By 2023, successful, high-growth retail businesses will bear little resemblance to today's organizations. Within five years, I predict retailers will organize themselves much more specifically around the customer, requiring a step change from many retailers' current goals of merely acquiring a single view of their customers. They will need one-to-one customer engagement strategies, focused on delivering a deeply personalized experience through all touchpoints and experiences the customer has with the brand. We can already see the beginnings of this in play today with instore clientelling, CRM programmes and online personalization. However, much like the organizational structure challenges facing retailers, these approaches are not joined up and do not deliver the 360-degree customer-centricity required.

The period between 2018 and 2023 will be a time of significant organizational evolution for retailers as they work towards the transition to an integrated customer-first business with all operations re-engineered around the needs of the customer. While each retailer will develop the structure that is right for them, the key to this transition will be developing core competencies and areas of expertise in customer engagement and experience, brand and operations, each of which integrate elements of 2018-era marketing, merchandising, IT, store operations, and other functional areas. Businesses are understandably structured around business as usual (BAU). The challenge with that is, as I referenced in Chapter 1, without a focus also on the medium to long term you might find that, 18 months to three years down the line, your business is irrelevant. The traditional organizational structure intended to deliver BAU is not geared up to looking far enough down the line to deliver the experience customers will demand. The drivers to deliver this will touch your entire value chain and include: technology, people, structure, processes, service levels, range, pricing, content, marketing, supply chain, the last mile and so on.

How embedded in the business does digital need to become?

Retailers will need to digitally upskill from the boardroom to the shop floor. They need to take their organizations to a level where all employees are experts in all channels, and are capable of delivering the experience demanded by the customer and at the same time promoting the organization's multichannel customer journey. This requires a significant cultural shift in the business, and it is no understatement to say that huge barriers to change will need to be overcome.

The C suite

Many existing CEOs across consumer-facing verticals progressed to the top job at a time when their business held the balance of power, rather than the customer. That was in the 1990s. There lies a large part of the challenge.

I was lucky. I saw the opportunity that e-commerce and digital had, early in the advent of this new channel. I was also not yet at the level of an organization where I could afford not to worry about this new-fangled thing and where I could employ someone like me to get to grips with it. My career was still developing. I was early to digital but, in my opinion, also late to find my calling. So, I felt that I had no choice but to throw myself into this space. That is certainly a decision I've been grateful I made, ever since. Most CEOs did not have this opportunity. They had already progressed far higher up the career ladder than I had, and therefore didn't get their hands dirty in the introduction and early growth stages of e-commerce. Only once the sales coming from online got to 10 per cent plus, have most taken it upon themselves to understand more about what it entails to be successful in digital. To this day, many have not even got this far.

While most CEOs have a high-level understanding of how the customer journey is evolving, some struggle to envisage the proposition they must deliver to address this and to effectively challenge and guide the digital leaders within their business to leverage digital to deliver the right experience for the customer.

Digital experience really helps, but it is not a pre-requisite to being an effective CEO. However, I absolutely do believe that having a very strong customer focus and customer orientation is. Therefore, my overarching question is: 'are the majority of incumbent CEOs fit for purpose to lead their organization into the next decade?' Some are. Many are not. It is also likely that these CEOs will lead the beginning of the transition of the business; but unlikely that they will be the right people to deliver the joined-up, customer-centric business of 2023, providing what customers want, where and when they want it.

EXPERT VIEW

One CEO from a bricks-and-mortar background who has firmly embraced digital and clearly understands what it means to put customers first is Philip Mountford, CEO of lingerie brand Hunkemöller. I asked Philip about what makes a great leader in this day and age. This was his response:

Philip responded quite humbly by saying that he was fortunate that he had been given a blank piece of paper by the PE owner of the business to determine how to shape and scale the business. Very few CEOs get to rewrite the history of a business. Most are baton holders; very few are able to reinvent the business. Philip has broken down barriers between e-commerce and stores, partly by incentivizing all senior management teams and colleagues so that everyone benefits from multichannel sales. In addition, he has also developed a more integrated structure that is firmly anchored in delivering the right product in the right channel and at the right time, supported by integrated marketing communications.

There have been encouraging signs that some retailers are recognizing that digital and customer-facing skills are required in their CEOs, for example Sur La Table, the leading North American kitchenware retailer, appointing Billy May. I spoke to Billy. He is one of the most experienced digital and e-commerce practitioners in the United States. He is also one of the very first to make the transition to the top job of retail CEO, moving from Abercrombie & Fitch to Sur La Table, a leading experiential kitchen and culinary retailer. I asked Billy what were the skills that he thought gave him the tools to move to the top job. This is what he told me: 'When you talk about being customer-centric, digital executives tend to start with the customer and work backwards. They have an orientation towards resolving and developing solutions to consumer problems. Digital executives, whether marketing or trading, focus on metrics, track interactions with scorecards, and are generally focused on outcomes. They strive to meet and exceed customer expectations. They also tend to be more collaborative and cross-functional, willing to test, learn and scale.'

Billy used a good example of the fact that commercial digital executives do not code, therefore they need to work collaboratively with engineers and developers. They are often dependent upon other parts of the business such as stores/omnichannel, buyers and merchandisers, content creators and so on, in order to deliver the required financial performance. Those who were digital executives in the early stages of digital and e-commerce had to work hard in order to get themselves heard. This required them to become more collaborative and ensure stakeholder engagement from across the business.

Unlike many other executives, those from a digital background tend to focus equally on longer-term strategic planning and shorter-term execution capabilities.

Another CEO with a digital pedigree, Mothercare's Mark Newton-Jones, is also in place. In the United States, Kohl's has appointed their former Chief Customer Officer, Michelle Gass, as CEO – another sign that businesses are recognizing that customer-centricity will be at the heart of the organization's success. However, these are still the exceptions. With most retail CEOs unlikely to be unseated by a customer or digital leader any time soon, they must work with their customer, multichannel and e-commerce directors of today to deliver what is required.

The models below highlight how I see the evolution of organizations from being siloed to customer-centric.

Digital transformation of the organization

Phase 1: forming

Figure 7.1   Phase 1: forming

The typical owner of the first phase of digital transformation is the head of e-commerce or the head of multichannel. This phase would typically have a digital maturity score (DMI) of 25–45 per cent; DMI is a 25-point weighted scorecard against key criteria.

This stage usually marks standalone e-commerce to early-stage multi-channel operations. The hallmarks of this phase are:

- It is quite siloed and operates as a business within a business.
- The P&L focus is on online only.
- Digital skills sit in one team.
- Specialist digital skills develop.
- Trading teams are high performing.

Phase 2: growing

The growing phase will usually be led by the multichannel director. This is where the multichannel functions would begin to integrate, thus providing a DMI score of around 45–65 per cent. These would be the markers of this stage:

Figure 7.2   Phase 2: growing

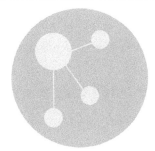

- Customers interact through digital instore, on mobile devices, on desktops.
- Cross-channel experiences are implemented such as click and collect, store stock online, endless aisle instore.
- Online is the digital heartbeat of the business.
- P&Ls are channel specific.
- Some functions may be integrated.

Phase 3: flourishing

Figure 7.3   Phase 3: flourishing

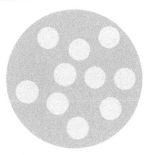

The final phase is flourishing, where you would find the organization to be truly customer-centric. This stage would have no single owner and accountability, for multichannel experience is shared across the board. This stage would have a DMI score of over 65 per cent with hallmarks such as:

- Decision making is driven by insight.
- The organizational structure and operating model is structured around the customer.

- There is a focus on 'revenue per customer' and 'customer lifetime value' rather than just a channel P&L.
- Digital skills are distributed throughout the organization.
- Job titles do not contain any qualifiers such as 'multichannel' or 'omnichannel'.

How the digital maturity index is scored

Figure 7.4   Digital maturity index for team, talent and skills template

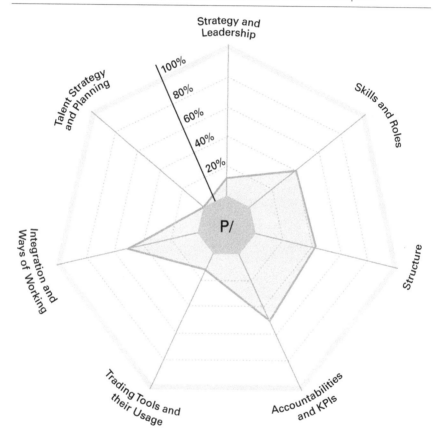

SOURCE Practicology

Strategy and leadership

1   With a customer and digital focus, the company has digital leadership from the top down.

2   The definition of a digital leader is someone who has a depth of understanding of digital that goes way beyond the superficial. They are likely to have worked in an e-commerce or digital role for much of their career.

3   Customer-centricity is a strategic pillar of growth and digital is recognized as a means to deliver this.

4   The digitally enabled customer-centric vision and strategy for the company are well communicated and understood.

Multichannel skills and roles

1   e-Commerce and multichannel roles are specialized within functions.

2   Skills and roles exist that cover all the e-commerce and multichannel disciplines that are relevant and appropriate.

3   Trading skills: e-commerce trading teams are commercially focused.

4   Depth of experience: people filling digital roles are experienced and have a good grasp of best practice in their function to continually drive growth.

Multichannel skills and roles: breakdown by discipline

The right skills and roles exist to adequately cover strategy *and* implementation in each of the following areas:

1   Leadership.

2   Customer acquisition: skills and roles can cover all biddable media channels including PPC; retargeting; search engine optimization (SEO); affiliates; display; paid social; marketing analysis.

3   Customer retention and engagement: skills and roles can cover social media; e-mail marketing; CRM and loyalty; copywriting and editorial.

4   Site management and content: skills and roles can cover campaign calendar management; content planning; photography management; web design and artwork; web production; ratings and reviews.

5   Site merchandising: skills and roles can cover online merchandising; stock management; product enrichment; categorization and publishing; search-merch management and merch analysis.

6   Site analytics and conversion-rate optimization (CRO): skills and roles can cover web analytics; multivariate testing; reporting.

7   Development and programme or project management: skills and roles cover product ownership; programme and project management; business analysis; front-end development. If outsourced, skills exist to manage third party.

8 Digitization of the store: skills and roles exist to manage click and collect and lead other initiatives.

9 Logistics and customer services: skills and roles exist to manage web logistics and customer service (this category refers to management roles rather than warehouse staff or CSRs).

10 Customer insight: skills and roles exist to manage data science; data analysis; data manipulation; CRM strategy; CRM campaign management.

Structure

1 The e-commerce or multichannel roles sit within a structure with clear reporting lines and responsibilities, regardless of whether they are in integrated or standalone teams. The structure follows and supports the company strategy.

2 Ownership of the e-commerce or multichannel P&L comprises control over all relevant trading levers, either through structure or accountabilities.

Accountabilities and KPIs

1 There are clear role descriptions that are well understood and articulated by individual team members.

2 Roles have clear, measurable objectives linked to commercial KPIs and metrics. KPIs branch down through the team layers, so the whole team contributes to common goals. KPIs are reviewed at an appropriate frequency and used to hold teams to account.

Trading tools and their usage

1 The team is fluent and conversant in web analytics, marketing performance and other tools. Most team members have access to relevant tools, check performance daily and conduct their own analysis. Insight, rather than data, forms the backbone of the trading process. Actions are taken off the back of using insight.

2 There are agreed definitions and standards for KPIs, metrics and other performance measures.

Integration and ways of working

1 e-Commerce or multichannel disciplines are well integrated into the rest of business, either structurally or through ways of working.

Talent strategy and planning

1 The organization understands what future skills will be required in the business as the digital environment and consumer behaviour continue to mature. Digital capabilities required of all roles are recognized and backed by an action plan and road map.

2 The business recognizes the importance of digital upskilling and actively promotes and invests in an L&D programme.

Prioritizing teams for digital upskilling

The demand of consumer-facing businesses for digital talent is outstripping supply, and the talent pool is limited. This means that good candidates can command high salaries, often significantly higher than other directorates within the organization. Therefore, upskilling your existing teams is a must-have requirement for anyone wishing to retain their talent. It would be recommended to develop L&D programmes for the three groups shown in Figure 7.5.

Figure 7.5　Learning and development

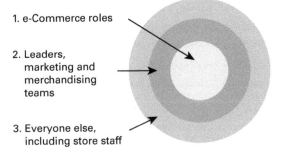

1. e-Commerce roles

2. Leaders, marketing and merchandising teams

3. Everyone else, including store staff

The siloed state of play

To be truly customer-centric we need to break down the siloes that still exist in most businesses. We have structured around channels and not around customers.

Most retail organizations are not structured to serve today's customer and their cross-channel, cross-device, socially infused behaviour. Why? Fundamentally, today's retail organizations are set up first and foremost to serve the brand, not the customer. As retailers, we ask the customer to buy from us and thereby deliver margin, sales and a return on investment.

Figure 7.6 highlights the challenge with most retailers still operating in siloed channels. There are no economies of scale. There is much duplication. But, most importantly, the customer loses out due to inconsistent assortment and marketing communications across channels, as both are being driven by different teams.

Merchandising teams are divided by channel. Some parts of the team are focused on 'drive aisles' and 'floor sets' instore, while others focus on how to present products online (where the customer purchase process often starts) – all while trying to serve the same customer. Few retailers to date have organized their merchandising experts into teams that are focused on customer segments or needs groupings. Wouldn't that be a truly customer-centric way to plan the range?

Also, merchants still often define merchandising or product categorization in terms of how the merchant buys the product, rather than how customers shop and expect to find product. Fashion and luxury brands are particularly guilty of this, creating inward-looking terminology to represent 'collections' that customers have never heard of.

All too often, online and offline buying and merchandising teams are siloed by channel. In extreme cases, buyers for stores and online have little, if any, contact with one another, and essentially are in competition in terms of delighting customers and supplier relationships.

We still see differential pricing for the same products across different channels in many businesses. Customers do not understand this, even if retailers have credible commercial reasons for doing so such as differential costs of sale or trying to be price-competitive against online-only peers. Channel proliferation has made this more difficult to manage for brands in particular.

> In my opinion, we need to move from 'omnichannel' to 'unichannel' where the customer enjoys not only a consistent experience but consistent pricing.

Customers of a fashion brand with a wholesale channel may find that the same item is on sale at different prices not only at the brand's own site and stores, but at a different price on a department store's website or a flash sale site such as Vente-privee or Brand Alley. Similarly, merchandisers for different channels often find themselves unable to make optimal decisions due to the constraints of the stock pools they are working with. Refusing to hand over stock to a website that could sell it three times over, in order to maintain a full range instore where it is not selling, is still an all too common complaint.

The marketing function is often divided and disjointed and split by channel or areas, which ultimately creates disparate views of the same customer or, at the very least, renders the organization incapable of having a single view of the customer. Current organizational approaches exacerbate the issue. Defining teams and departments as 'brand/direct/CRM' and 'offline/online' perpetuates a divided view of any single customer. Additionally, few marketing teams are juggling both the emotional (brand/story) and analytical ends of the marketing spectrum – most brands today are generally good at one or the other, but rarely good at both.

The IT organization's first thought is of managing risk rather than the impact to the customer. As a result, many IT organizations are more focused on employee and internal analysis tools than they are on customer experience. Furthermore, many IT teams continue to be independent, rather than living within each area in an organization to be stronger partners in delivering on customer needs. Imagine how much more effective IT would be if there was an agile development team with a fail-fast approach attached to key customer-facing areas of the business!

A digital team that is too often standalone with a patchwork of connections to other organizational teams – unsure of what to do with all things digital, many retailers have done with digital exactly what they do with other functions: created a silo. As with all silos, this situation sets up internal competition for budget, resources, and attention from yet another area within the organization without serving their customers' needs.

A distribution and supply chain function that in many cases still segregates stock for different channels – to this end, there is not a single pool or even a single view of stock, and so products are not being sent to the channel where the demand is. In addition to these organizational obstacles the reality is that many retailers today simply are not customer-led in the first place. How many retailers truly put the customer front and centre of all they do?

The various models we see in today's market include companies led by merchants ('product first' strategy); by brand (leveraging the aspiration and emotional engagement of the 'label' versus specifically their product or service); and technology (focused on how technology can provide a better experience and differentiation). All too few have genuinely adopted a customer-led ('customer service first') strategy. To be successful, retailers in the short, medium and long term need to restructure from the ground up,

Figure 7.6   Customer channels

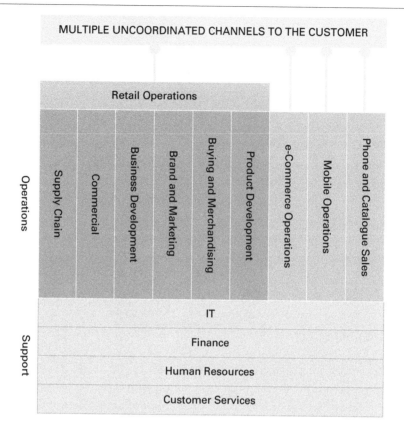

MULTIPLE UNCOORDINATED CHANNELS TO THE CUSTOMER

Retail Operations

Operations

Supply Chain

Commercial

Business Development

Brand and Marketing

Buying and Merchandising

Product Development

e-Commerce Operations

Mobile Operations

Phone and Catalogue Sales

IT

Finance

Human Resources

Customer Services

Support

using the customer as the focal point for how they set up functional teams to optimally serve that customer.

Figure 7.6 shows an established retail organizational model built around channel silos. The customer experience within each channel is often good, but begins to fray as the customers move from one channel to another.

Multiple channel retailers with little or no integration

The customer is mobile-savvy and expects all of a retailer's touchpoints to work together (why wouldn't they?). As retailers, however, we know that current hierarchies, reporting relationships, even profit and loss, and incentive structures are simply not designed to deliver on what the customer assumes is an entirely logical – if largely invisible – infrastructure to support how he or she shops now.

Figure 7.7 represents a focus on serving the customer and aligning all of the business functions and operations to achieve this goal.

Figure 7.7   Customer-centric business functions

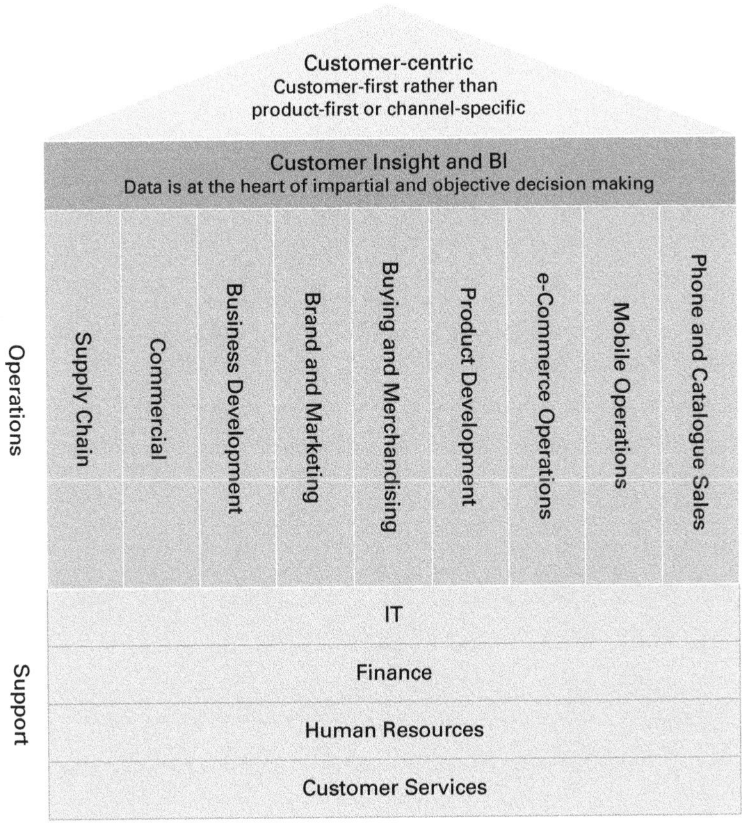

Customer-centric
Customer-first rather than
product-first or channel-specific

Customer Insight and BI
Data is at the heart of impartial and objective decision making

Operations

Supply Chain

Commercial

Business Development

Brand and Marketing

Buying and Merchandising

Product Development

e-Commerce Operations

Mobile Operations

Phone and Catalogue Sales

IT

Support

Finance

Human Resources

Customer Services

Organizing around the customer requires new models for structures, accountabilities, ways of working and talent. It also needs insight and business intelligence to play a central role in evidence-led decision making. This means investing in insight will need to be a core, strategic focus for any business.

Each company will tailor its 2023 structure to its particular customer, product and brand. Some will employ organizational change models such as RACI (responsible, accountable, consulted, informed) (Jacka and Keller, 2009) to frame the resource plan and realign accountabilities.

R – Responsible: person working on activity.

A – Accountable: person with decision authority.

C – Consult: key stakeholder who should be included in decision or work activity.

I – Inform: needs to know of decision or action.

The RACI change model can help to realign responsibilities (Jacka and Keller, 2009). In 2023 the key difference will be that consumer-facing businesses will be focused on one thing: **delivering on customer needs and expectations** rather than focusing on marketing goals versus merchandising goals versus IT goals.

Whatever your structure, agility is key

I spoke to Jonathan Wall, Chief Digital Officer of leading fashion retailer Missguided, and asked him, 'How do you set up a business in an agile way?'

He has a very innovative approach to organizational design that he has implemented both in his previous role at Shop Direct Group as well as at Missguided. Jonathan described thinking about the customer journey and building the business in this way. For example:

- a digital marketing team driving traffic;
- a customer onboarding team;
- a team whose role is to help customers to find the product to add to basket and so on.

All of this was built in an agile way. Shop Direct will have eight product teams to manage the end-to-end journey.

I asked Jonathan, 'How can you do this in a multichannel business?'

Jonathan likes to take an evidence-based approach: 'Building the business in an evidence-based approach to deliver a hypothesis to then iterate' is how he described it.

Think about problems you have, eg 'We're really busy on a Saturday: is it because people like to try things on more on a Saturday?' In which case, you would staff accordingly.

Jonathan likes to remove opinions and base structure and staffing on evidence.

The roles required to drive change

A change agent!

While the current multichannel or e-commerce director may well have the vision for what the multichannel customer experience should be, do they have the skills and experience required to drive the change programme to re-engineer the business in order to deliver the vision? Or does the business need to bring someone in or engage an external supplier to support the change management and transformation of the business? Some retailers have split this role in two, with a trading e-commerce director and technical/development e-commerce director. Doing this allows a retailer to retain maximum focus on revenues and profitability from multichannel retailing today, while at the same time addressing the road map and business change agenda.

One new role emerging is that of the chief customer officer or customer director

This is someone whose responsibility it is to ensure the customer experience is consistent through all touchpoints. However, customer experience on its own will never be enough to deliver the fully rounded experience required by the customer, as marketing communications is a key component and therefore in our opinion should also sit with the chief customer officer (CCO).

The next big battleground is around personalization and engagement, and the CCO should be the person most capable of delivering a more engaging and personalized experience with the brand. What background should this person have? It requires a mix of skills and experience:

- multichannel, with a bias towards online;
- digital expertise so they have the vision and practical tools to deliver the store experience;
- ideally marketing experience, both brand- and performance-based so that they can ensure consistent and joined-up communications with the customer.

CIO (chief insight officer)

Retailers have masses of data but not insight – and they often lack the skills in the business to effectively interpret data and turn it into actionable insight. To this end, we are likely to see a new role emerge that focuses on surfacing actionable insight from across the value chain of a multichannel business. This will have both an internal and an external focus. From cause-and-effect perspectives, the internal factors are the cause and the effect is the impact on customer experience.

Digital/multichannel CTOs

There will be continual demand for chief technology officers (CTOs) with a strong digital bent and core multichannel backgrounds who have owned the road map for digital and multichannel transformation.

Digital CEOs

For those of you not there already, this is where you are all headed! Who better to lead the retail business of tomorrow than those responsible for reshaping the customer proposition and leading the transformation to a more integrated multichannel business – and who put the customer at the heart of all they do?

Let's not forget about the 'gig economy'

The term 'gig economy' is increasingly being used to refer to low-paid, flexible work whereby people are working for any one of a multitude of the new disruptive businesses and can include those such as Uber, or delivery services like Hermes or Deliveroo. These people are not employees, hence the term 'gig economy', which infers that people are offered one-off pieces of work. There has been increasing scrutiny of these players and many who have increasingly raised concerns about rates of pay, complexity of working hours and of relatively poor job security. Nonetheless, it is not going away. Technology has been the enabler to driving these new business models, and the flexible workforce or 'gig economy' is required to enable these services to be delivered profitably.

EXPERT VIEW

Finding the right technology skills is not always that easy

I spoke to Julian Burnett, former CIO, Executive Director, Supply Chain, House of Fraser, about some of the challenges he and other CIOs were facing when it came to skills and structure around technology. He told me that technology-vendor road maps are not keeping up with customer and retailer demands. This in turn forces retailers to build solutions in-house. He also has the same challenge with system integrators – they cannot find relevant skills. Julian described how digital is the way of transforming by using technology, and is not the same thing as e-commerce.

One challenge of this is that in the technology-vendor market, very few vendors are addressing the digital and physical requirements in a channel-agnostic way. When you add this to House of Fraser's desire to be more agile and analytical, it led to Julian building his own engineering and data science team within the business.

House of Fraser are leveraging their data science team and third-party tools to ensure that they have more control over the marketing of products and pricing to reflect competitor activity. They are able to either reduce their prices or spend less on marketing.

Top practical customer experience tips

1 Develop new roles that can help drive customer-centricity.

2 Give someone ownership of the customer and their experience, and crucially the mandate to deliver the change required to become a customer-first business.

3 Create a customer-first culture throughout the entire business.

4 Create a cross-functional team with accountability for delivering customer first.

5 Adopt a two-tier organizational structure in areas such as IT – one focused on BAU, one on the road map for new developments.

6 Ensure you have a leader who understands what putting the customer first really means.

Expanded on below.

Develop new roles that can help drive customer-centricity

Without these specific roles, an organization will not truly be able to drive the transformation required across the business to truly put the customer first. Most businesses lack actionable insight. The key role required to surface this is a data scientist, someone who can interrogate the date and determine actions required. For example: which customer segments shop across more than one of your channels? Who are your most profitable customer segments? How do you find more of them? Who responds to your marketing activity and incentives?

Give someone ownership of the customer and their experience, and crucially the mandate to deliver the change required to become a customer-first business

If you fail to do this, you will never become a truly customer-centric business. It takes a considerable degree of change and transformation to get the whole organization aligned and delivering the appropriate customer experience. Someone has to drive this change. It won't happen on its own. It won't happen if the CEO assumes responsibility for it, as they will be far too busy running the business and all its constituent parts.

Even once you have given someone this responsibility, you need to clear the path for them. In any organization, there is always resistance to change. Most people don't like change. Therefore, it is the role of the CEO and the board to ensure that the individual given the mandate to drive the transformation towards a customer-centric business has all the support they require to deliver this. That will include ensuring that all directors and directorates within the business are on board.

Create a customer-first culture throughout the entire business

A business's culture, its values and what it stands for are crucial in so many ways. Not least when it comes to the people you want to bring into the business, as you need to engage people who have a natural propensity towards great customer service. In Chapter 8 I expand upon culture in detail and the areas to focus on to drive cultural change.

Create a cross-functional team with accountability for delivering customer first

Create accountability for the change towards a customer-first business across your organization through a cross-functional team. This is such a monumental change to your organization that you cannot hold one person to account for its successful delivery. If you make people across the whole value chain accountable then you have a far greater chance of getting it right.

Adopt a two-tier organizational structure in areas such as IT – one focused on BAU, one on the road map for new developments

You cannot possibly expect a team who already have a day job to also take on business development/new initiatives. In my experience, this happens far too frequently. When this approach is adopted, something has to give. Either your existing systems and business suffer because the focus has moved to the 'shiny new things' the team have been asked to develop, or the new developments will be late, overbudget and most likely poorly implemented as a result of having to spend so much time just keeping the existing systems working.

I would recommend having a core team in each operational area, whose job is to maintain business as usual (BAU), and a separate team to develop the new ways of working. When you are ready, you swap out the old for the new. In any case, it often requires a different skill set and a different mindset for each area.

Ensure you have a leader who understands what putting the customer first really means

The transformation to a truly customer-centric organization has to be a top-down and bottom-up approach. The CEO sets the tone. They have to lead by example. The fact that the founder and former CEO of AO.com John Roberts spent 40 minutes every day signing customer letters would not have been lost on his colleagues. He was setting the tone for how the business had to deal with customers. I know a number of other CEOs and former CEOs who would do likewise – Sir Charles Dunstone, Chairman of Dixons Carphone, being just one of them.

Over to Professor Malcolm McDonald

Whilst this chapter has focused on building organizational structure in retail, there can be little doubt that in all sectors the future is going to be very different, given the accelerating pace of technology, requiring totally new skills, mindsets and organizational structure.

Companies are already doing many of the things spelt out in this chapter and heads of digital strategy are binning their business cards after a decade during which they lost touch with the fundamentals of their business. These people were not out of touch with digital, it is just that they lost sight of the basic needs of their consumers and the underlying long-term drivers of their business.

They realize that today we have fabulous digital tools at our disposal, but they also realize that the same age-old issues of marketing strategy remain – market understanding, market segmentation, insight, branding, positioning and engagement. But let's get back to the role of digital in all this. McKinsey provided a useful definition of digital as follows: 'Consumer-controlled electronic interactions or cross-platform usage. Digital is shorthand for all things "non-traditional" that flow from online and mobile usage' (Duncan, Hazan and Roche, 2013).

The same article then went on to say: 'Digital takes segmentation several steps further to strengthen sales, operations, product development and all other key customer-facing business processes. Incorporating product and brand-specific usage, spending, attitudes and needs can make developing a far more nuanced segmentation possible. This highly segmented approach will be needed to win and maintain customer relationships.'

But as stated in this chapter, this has not happened yet, particularly in retail. It would indeed be truly wonderful and energizing for consumers if we could have a seamless experience across all touchpoints, particularly one that indicates that they know who we are and what our preferences are.

I should like to make one final point here about the importance of customer retention, referred to at the beginning of this chapter, as it is indeed a major weakness in most organizations, something discussed in more depth in my recent publication on marketing planning (McDonald, 2016). First, P&L accounts usually have only one line for revenue and most of the others are for costs. The problem with this is exactly as spelt out in this chapter. There is no indication of how many customers have been lost during the reporting period. There is another problem, however, which is cultural. Customer acquisition is like hunting. Retail is more like farming. Hunting is exciting.

Farming is boring. The consequences, however, of the widespread failure to measure and record customer retention/loss can be devastating. The bottom line is that a 5 per cent increase in customer retention can increase profits by up to 95 per cent unless, of course, HBR, Bain and Company, Forrester and the like are telling lies (Stillwagon, 2014)!

The following is an example from a real company that was operating in a growth market. Its P&L account showed sales growth, but they were unaware that their underlying market performance was extremely poor and that all it would take for the financials to deteriorate would be a slowing down of market growth, which eventually happened, with disastrous consequences. Although there were other competitive indicators, the most serious was their customer retention performances, as shown in Figure 7.8.

From this, it can be seen that there were six segments in this market. Of particular interest are segments 3 and 6. The biggest segment is segment 3, accounting for 27.1 per cent of industry sales, but for only 14.7 per cent of industry profits. Segment 6 represents only 11 per cent of industry sales, but almost one-quarter of industry profits.

This particular company's best performance (a 15 per cent customer defection rate) was in the worst segment, and even here a 15 per cent defection rate is a very poor performance. In segment 6, however, the best segment by far, its defection rate was 35 per cent, meaning they were losing over one-third of these customers every year. Their performance in the very profitable segment 5 was almost as bad and it is truly damaging when companies don't do this kind of crucial analysis, having, of course, carried out proper needs-based segmentation in the first place.

Figure 7.8   Measurement of segment profitability

	Total Market	Segment 1	Segment 2	Segment 3	Segment 4	Segment 5	Segment 6
Percentage of market represented by segment	100.0	14.8	9.5	27.1	18.8	18.8	11.0
Percentage of all profits in total market produced by segment	100.0	7.1	4.9	14.7	21.8	28.5	23.0
Ratio of profit produced by segment to weight of segment in total population	1.00	0.48	0.52	0.54	1.16	1.52	2.09
Defection rate	23%	20%	17%	15%	28%	30%	35%

To conclude my comments, the principal author of this book, Martin, is totally correct in his predictions about the future, and I complement this with a single point. A new generation of digital experts will indeed take over the running of our business, but we need to remember that digital is not strategy. If it is used the way Martin has suggested in this chapter, the strategic game will improve, with better targeting, positioning and branding, but above all, improved customer satisfaction.

So, whilst you cannot have a successful digital strategy without a robust strategy for what you sell, who you sell it to and why they should buy from you rather than from someone else with something similar, you most definitely DO need a digital strategy now to catch these new consumers so they can grow with you.

References

Duncan, E, Hazan, E and Roche, K (2013) [accessed 19 December 2017] IConsumer: Digital Consumers Altering the Value Chain [Online] https://www.mckinsey.com/~/media/mckinsey/industries/telecommunications/our%20insights/developing%20a%20fine%20grained%20look%20at%20how%20digital%20consumers%20behave/iconsumervaluechain.ashx

Jacka, J M and Keller, P J (2009) *Business Process Mapping: Improving customer satisfaction*, John Wiley & Sons, Chichester

McDonald, M (2016) *Malcolm McDonald on Marketing Planning*, Kogan Page, London

Stillwagon, A (2014) [accessed 5 December 2017] Did You Know: A 5% Increase in Retention Increases Profits by Up to 95% [Online] https://smallbiztrends.com/2014/09/increase-in-customer-retention-increases-profits.html

Cultural change – must be top down and bottom up

08

WHAT YOU WILL LEARN IN THIS CHAPTER

- You will learn that the CEO must be the one person obsessed more than anyone else with putting the customer first. Otherwise the business will not have a truly customer-centric culture, nor will its people be empowered to do the right thing for the customer.

- I will highlight a framework and approach that you can leverage to drive customer-centric cultural change.

- I will discuss how to empower staff to put the customer first.

- The importance of transparency in all customer interactions.

The importance of culture

As the great Peter Drucker said, 'Culture eats strategy for breakfast!'

I couldn't agree more. Does your organization invest more time and effort in thinking about its strategy or its culture? I'm confident that in 90 per cent of cases, the focus is on strategy. The company's culture is often forgotten about – when it is one of the key building blocks for success.

Richards, a high-end fashion retailer in Greenwich, Connecticut, and with stores across the United States (includes Mitchells and Marios fascias), are the epitome of a truly customer-centric business. They know most, if not all, of their customers by name. Their staff have been with them for decades. Jack Mitchell, the son of the founder, has himself written a book about 'hugging your customer' – a metaphor for being customer-centric. This tells you all you need to know about the culture.

To have a business as customer focused as Jack's you might find it more effective to adopt an approach of recruiting for attitude and training for skills.

Defining culture

I felt it worthwhile to paint a picture of what constitutes an organization's culture. I have come up with a framework involving the letter v! So, to follow are the 6Vs of culture:

1 Vision

An effective organizational culture should emanate from a clear vision, or mission statement that the business creates to describe its purpose and direction of travel. This in turn provides purpose for the culture of the business. One of the greatest marketing campaigns of all time was in the vehicle rental sector when the number-two challenger brand Avis, who wanted to gain market share from Hertz, said, 'We're second but we try harder.' It's not too much of a leap from there to imagine how a service culture would have been required to permeate Avis's business in order to deliver this and implement the vision (Richards, 2017).

2 Values

The values of a company are very much at the heart of its culture. They are what the business stands for. The authenticity of the organization's values is paramount. Values would normally describe how the business treats its employees, customers and so on. It is critical that these are implemented and adhered to on a daily basis. This is not something to pay lip service to. Values also play a big part in defining the type of people you need in your organization. Your values should permeate the business and also be a core component of you becoming a more customer-centric business. Corporate social responsibility (CSR) should also form part of your set of values. In Chapter 9 I talk about CSR in detail. Your values might include having integrity, caring for your community and giving something back, putting customers front and centre of all that you do.

3 Verbalize

You need to relentlessly communicate and support your colleagues as you drive cultural change in the business. Share good and bad examples of how your colleagues have implemented your cultural values. Things that went well, and those that didn't, and the corrective actions taken to improve. You should also share examples of other businesses and how they have been successful in driving through cultural change and specific scenarios of where this has had a positive impact.

The tone and how you talk to both customers and colleagues is also hugely important. This comes from the top and is often a reflection upon how people are managed and general behaviour. As I mentioned in Chapter 7, the CEO has to have the mindset and own the responsibility for delivering a culture and a way of working that is truly customer obsessed. Jack Mitchell, whom I mention on page 110, has written a book called *Hug Your People* (Mitchell, 2009).

The most effective CEOs walk the floor, and want to hear directly from customers about what they could do better. I call this listening to the voice of the customer.

4 Vested interest

You cannot beat having some skin in the game. Think about how the performance of your people is measured and how they are incentivized. For example, if you only have commercial KPIs that relate to sales, profit, volumes and so on, then you can expect colleagues to focus on those. If on the other hand you had KPIs such as customer satisfaction, and Net Promoter Score (NPS) that you used to measure performance, then those have a better chance of driving the right outcome for the customer. They also lend themselves better to a more thoughtful, customer-centric culture.

You will only be able to drive cultural change in your business if you make people accountable. It may be that not everyone in the organization can adapt to the new culture you wish to implement across the business, and that in itself may lead to the requirement to restructure or, at the very least, to remove individuals whom you feel are incapable of adapting to the new culture.

5 Virality

The web by nature has a viral impact. Think about businesses you know that have either gone out of business, or been impacted significantly by negative sentiment online on social channels. The reverse can be said of when a brand does something positive. It can generate a huge amount of goodwill and end up with thousands of advocates as opposed to detractors. With this in mind, it is worth giving thought to your culture and the positive implications it can have in terms of people talking about your business, both customers and colleagues. Bad news travels fast, so does good news.

6 Verification

Having the right culture is something that has to be maintained. Defining it then forgetting about it will, at best, over time ensure that your people forget what the business stands for and how it behaves – and at worst can lead to a breakdown of customer trust. Therefore, it is vital that someone has responsibility for ensuring that the culture of the business is not something stated on an annual report or strategic document, but that it is delivered day-in, day-out.

Often responsibility will sit with the HR director and their team. My advice would be to appoint a cross-functional team to keep an eye on your culture and customer-centricity. That way, you have the best chance of ensuring it is continually and consistently delivered across the entire organization. Metro Bank in the UK, for example, has a very open culture and a system whereby its colleagues are able to call out any senseless rules that get in the way of delivering the right experience to its customers (FinTech Futures, 2013).

The cultural shift from a digital perspective

For most retailers, the move towards an embedded digital business requires significant cultural change. So, what is a digital culture? It has to be all-encompassing. It is far more than simply creating digital tools or leveraging technology.

Customer engagement

The customer has to be at the heart of this. After all, it is their experience across different channels and touchpoints and their ability to 'shop and engage how they want' that determine the success of multichannel businesses. Digital is the enabler to deliver this experience. With the emphasis on customer service, retailers will be putting customers at the front and centre of everything they do and leveraging digital to deliver the optimal experience. Metro Bank has a general policy that 'if it's right for the customer, it's the right thing to do' (FinTech Futures, 2013). Their focus is on creating fans as opposed to customers. Can you think of a traditional bank, anywhere in the world, that could even begin to think this way?

Commercial imperatives

There are many issues that supress the commercial performance of multi-channel consumer-facing businesses. Too many e-commerce teams are technically sound but commercially ineffective. They are not traders. Also, too many retailers struggle to evaluate the halo effect of multichannel and therefore have not joined up their channels to deliver the experience customers require. Working in siloes – whether it is with a separate e-commerce team or disjointed range planning and merchandising – means the customer is not presented with what they want to buy, where and when they want to buy it.

Actionable insight

Big data, small data, whatever-you-want-to-call-it-data, we have more of it than we ever had before. However, data is not insight, and therefore we need to ensure we instil a culture of wanting to understand what the data is telling us and the actions required to improve performance. Wouldn't we all feel a lot better about our roles if we were able to take decisions supported by insight?

Empowering your teams

Is your team across all touchpoints empowered to deliver the experience demanded by customers? Previously the Chief Digital and Marketing Officer, Sainsbury's and Argos (Post Acquisition), Bertrand Bodson, spoke about its store team providing the biggest potential digital army in the country. Think about it, most retailers' store teams are of an average age below 30, almost all of whom are early digital adopters. Enabling them to leverage digital technology instore such as clientelling solutions or mobile tills is second nature.

Innovation and matching the pace of change

The ability to fail fast and to innovate in order to stay ahead of the game is crucial. Yet most retailers still work with a fairly fixed annual road map. This also talks to the organization's view of investment. The space we're in is changing so quickly, every day new developments ensure that customer expectations of their experience are changing constantly and therefore we require a culture that ensures we keep up with the pace of change the customer is experiencing.

A truly customer-centric culture and ethos

Culture is hugely important and significant as a driver of change and transformation to deliver a customer-facing business. One of the best examples of a business with a truly customer-facing culture is Zappos, the largest online footwear retailer in the world, which was acquired by Amazon in 2009. Tony Hsieh is the CEO. They offer new hires $2,000 to quit – the thinking being that they are only interested in retaining those who are truly customer obsessed (Felloni, 2015).

CASE STUDY AO.com

AO.com (formerly AppliancesOnline.com) have a very strong customer-facing culture. Staff in the call centre can compensate customers whether it costs 50p or £5,000. They are not under financial restraints and can do what is 'fair and reasonable' in order to fix issues. They treat every customer as if they were their own family – and how they would fix it for them. They can dispatch a new product on the same day and also send a bunch of flowers as an apology without needing approval. They employ people who care and are passionate about the business and their customers. They have the 'and' not 'or' approach. You cannot pay people to care. Their goal is to recruit people who are 'ambitious AND humble' – it is usually the case that you get one or the other (Mulquiney, 2016).

As I have outlined already, culture is driven from the top. To this end, John Roberts, AO.com founder, used to spend 40 minutes a day signing customer letters when he was still involved day to day. Customers got a response from him, whether they had written to complain or to compliment the business. This also creates a closed feedback loop. How many CEOs do you know who take the time to do this?

Drivers beware! AO.com also have a publication of Facebook feedback of their drivers; customer feedback on the quality of customer service provided. The bimonthly publication is sent to the drivers and also to the founder. It includes both positive and negative feedback with the aim to show the effect their drivers can have on the customer experience (Mulquiney, 2016).

CASE STUDY   Luxury products, delivered unluxuriously

With my 20th wedding anniversary looming, and on a holiday in the United States with my family, we happened 'purely by chance' to stumble upon a boutique/high-end handbag store that I hadn't heard of. My wife and daughters remarked on how beautiful a certain little treasure was: the seed was planted. Landing back in the UK with two days to go, I had few options to secure this perfect gift. So, I Googled it. Up popped Matches Fashion offering next-day delivery, a brand I knew but had not purchased from before. Great! The only issue was it would arrive between 6 pm and 9 pm. My wife would be in, but I might not be for the whole delivery window. Of course, I didn't want my wife to be the one to take in the box as the game would be up at that point!

I called, explained the circumstances and asked if they could schedule the delivery for a one-hour time slot. 'Sorry sir, our delivery company cannot do that.' Despite the luxury price tag, I was incredibly surprised that they could not offer more flexibility. After further discussion, I was left with the promise of being called back, but did not hear from them again. I bought the bag and hoped for the best.

Whilst my wife was very happy with it, my disappointment in the customer experience was shared in a later conversation with the co-founder of Matches Fashion, Ruth Chapman. She promptly addressed the issue and it is fair to say that Matches Fashion is now arguably one of the most customer-centric retailers out there. Everyone who works in the business, from the mail room to buyers, from the packers in the distribution centre to the marketing team, has the customer front and centre in their minds at all times. This drives the appropriate processes and proposition to deliver the optimal customer experience.

In the e-commerce world, talk of personalization usually refers to how websites display to different customers, which products are promoted, and maybe pricing. Service and fulfilment tend not to be discussed in such depth. While fulfilment options such as next-day evening delivery are good, when you go into a luxury retail store you expect personal service; increasingly luxury retailers – and indeed other retail sectors – will find that their online customers expect such personal service too.

The aim is to know what the customer wants before they even know they want it. This is driven by a combination of customer data on behaviour, where the customer is travelling to, what outfits they prefer in different situations. The good news is that Matches Fashion addressed this issue and have built a phenomenally successful business, culminating in their sale to a leading PE house in 2017 for £400 million (Butler and Wood, 2017).

Top practical customer experience tips

1 Use the 6Vs framework to develop your customer-first business culture.

2 Surprise and delight customers.

3 Lead by example: culture comes from the top.

4 Create a cross-functional team to ensure your culture is maintained.

5 Always be fully transparent with customers.

6 Develop a marketing plan to communicate your culture to both external and internal customers

7 Culture eats strategy for breakfast – never forget that.

Expanded on below.

Use the 6Vs framework to develop your customer-first business culture

Use the 6Vs. If you don't document it, and don't follow a process and communicate it widely across the business, it will not happen. Your culture and values will not be effectively delivered.

Surprise and delight customers

A great example of this is at Pret A Manger (Pret). Their store colleagues are empowered to offer the customer a free coffee when something goes wrong – or other random acts of kindness. Often this is unexpected and therefore has a big impact on how the customer feels about Pret. However, this is also about staff being empowered to do the right thing; it is not about customer entitlement and expectation to always get something when they want it.

Lead by example: culture comes from the top

As I stated earlier, culture comes from the top. It is fine for HR to define this, but for culture to permeate the business it has to be lived and breathed by the board, by the CEO, the COO, the CFO et al. Does the CEO sit in a palatial office, with all the trimmings of being at the top, or do they place themselves amongst their colleagues? Being at the heart of the business has lots of advantages. I'm not advocating this as something that all CEOs should do. But it tells you everything you need to know about the CEO and their view of colleagues and culture – and the importance of being visible in the business.

Create a cross-functional team to ensure your culture is maintained

As stated in Chapter 7, you need someone or some people who have the mandate to determine and deliver a customer-obsessed culture and business. A cross-functional team will also help to ensure alignment across the business.

Always be fully transparent with customers

Customers can sense when they are being taken for a ride and they are very quick to call it out and amplify it on social media channels. So, be smart, don't ever try to pull the wool over your customers' eyes.

In Chapter 14 I talk about the electrical retailer AO.com, who are amongst a rare breed of businesses that understand the importance of full transparency with customers. As already mentioned above, their founder and former CEO John Roberts spent 40 minutes a day writing back to customers, irrespective of whether they had written to the business about a good or bad experience. This is what I call 'a closed feedback loop'. Subsequently this led to customers going straight back on to social media to praise the business.

Develop a marketing plan to communicate your culture to both external and internal customers

Your external customers will need to know what is different about your business now and why they should believe in you. Your internal customers will need to know why you are changing and what that change means for them.

Culture eats strategy for breakfast – never forget that

Make sure yours is relevant. This is the heartbeat of your business. Your culture courses through every part of your business both internally and externally. If your colleagues don't like the culture then your customers most certainly will not.

Over to Professor Malcolm McDonald

I should like to concentrate my comments for this chapter on the importance of mission statements. As Martin has stressed, these are crucial to help immerse both staff and customers in your brand values and ethos. Getting this aspect of business right can change your business for the good for ever.

Let me, however, start by dismissing the majority of what passes for mission statements in many organizations: a collection of generic, meaningless pronouncements about being 'customer-led', 'customer-centric'. These are often popularized in offices and openly mocked by employees who don't buy into the concept after observing the internal day-to-day company ethos.

The world is full of what I call generic mission statements, such as the following:

The generic mission statement: 'Our organization's primary mission is to protect and increase the value of its owner's investments while efficiently and fairly serving the needs of its customers. (Insert organization name…) seeks to accomplish this in a manner that contributes to the development and growth of its employees, and to the goals of the countries and communities in which it operates.'

The clichéd generic mission statement: 'To maximize shareholder wealth by exceeding customer expectations and providing opportunities for our employees to lead fulfilling lives whilst respecting the environment and the communities within which we operate.'

Is there any organization in the world, I ask, to which this would not be equally applicable? There are three types of mission statement, as set out below.

Types of mission statement

- *Type 1*: 'motherhood' – usually found inside annual reports. Designed to appease shareholders, otherwise of no practical use.

- *Type 2*: the real thing. A meaningful statement, unique to the organization concerned, which 'impacts' on the behaviours of the executives at all levels.
- *Type 3*: this is a 'purpose' statement (or lower-level mission statement). It is appropriate at the country/branch/departmental level of the organization.

Let me, then, explain where they fit in and why they are so important.

Why are mission statements important?

If the organization has no clear notion about its vision and values, it may be in a quandary regarding the way forward. You will understand from this that I am including vision and value in this discussion and explanation of mission statements.

The process of business strategy formulation should commence with a review and articulation of the company's mission. The mission (or vision) encapsulates the company's identity in terms of what it is, what makes it special, what it stands for, and where it is heading. It should explicitly reflect the basic beliefs, values and aspirations of the organization, providing an enduring statement of purpose that distinguishes the organization from its competitors and an important device for coordinating internal activity.

Although our research has uncovered several different formats, we have summarized the best in terms of the ideal format, as follows.

The contents of a mission statement

1   *Role or contribution*: for example, charity, profit seeker, innovator, opportunity seeker.

2   *Business definition*: this should be done in terms of benefits provided or needs satisfied, rather than the services offered.

3   *Distinctive competences*: these are the essential skills, capabilities or resources that underpin whatever success has been achieved to date. Competence can consist of one particular item or the possession of a number of skills compared with competitors. All should be considered in terms of how they confer differential advantages, ie if you could equally well put a competitor's name to these distinctive competences, then they are *not* distinctive competences.

4   *Indications for the future*: this will briefly refer to what the firm *will* do, what it *might* do and what it will *never* do.

The nature of corporate missions

An examination of what has been written about missions suggests that a number of key issues are important and need to be taken into consideration. They are:

- It is unwise to define the mission too narrowly or too broadly.
- The audience for the mission should be considered carefully.
- It is crucial to understand the business one is in.
- The mission should be unique to the organization preparing it.
- The mission should be need-oriented, rather than offer-oriented.
- Within any organization, there will need to be a hierarchy of mission statements.

The mission statement must provide some focus to the activities of an organization. However, just as there are dangers in defining the business too narrowly, as in the case of IBM in the 1980s and Kodak more recently, to have no bounds can be equally damaging.

Indeed, this might be the more common of the two faults. For example, the deregulation of the financial services sector in many countries led to banks diversifying away from their core business into stockbroking and investment banking, with disastrous results. Similarly, retailers have undertaken diversification away from what customers perceived to be their traditional realms. Finding they were unprofitable in these areas, they struggled to get back to their core retailing business.

Sometimes, their identity gets lost in the process. For example, the UK brand of Woolworths – although it attempted to diversify it threw away its old strengths of identity and was unable to fill the vacuum. Another example is the US energy services company Enron. This company entered into deals and projects that were beyond the scope of its core mission and went on to be reported for irrevocable accounting and fraud issues in the early 2000s (BBC, 2002). In these cases, if *effective* missions had been formulated, with the requisite strategic focus that this implies, they may have found alternative methods of diversification that avoided loss of profitability and lack of business-wide integration.

DHL WORLD EXPRESS – WORLDWIDE MISSION STATEMENT

DHL will become the acknowledged global leader in the express delivery of documents and packages. Leadership will be achieved by establishing the industry standards of excellence for quality of service and by maintaining the lowest-cost position relative to our service commitment in all markets of the world. Achievement of the mission requires:

- Absolute dedication to understanding and fulfilling our customers' needs with the appropriate mix of service, reliability, products and price for each customer.

- An environment that rewards achievement, enthusiasm and team spirit, and which offers each person in DHL superior opportunities for personal development and growth.

- A state-of-the art worldwide information network for customer billing, tracking, tracing and management information/communications.

- Allocation of resources consistent with the recognition that we are one worldwide business.

- A professional organization able to maintain local initiative and local decision making while working together within a centrally managed network.

The evolution of our business into new services, markets or products will be completely driven by our single-minded commitment to anticipating and meeting the changing needs of our customers.

SOURCE McDonald, Payne and Frow (2011)

The mission for DHL as stated above focuses on many of the key issues we consider should be addressed in a mission statement for such a firm. It also illustrates the need to develop corporate objectives that are highly integrated with the mission statement. Without a strong linkage, which provides a means of measuring whether the mission can be achieved, much of the potential value of a mission can be dissipated. The relationship between corporate objectives and mission has been well summed up by the Chairman and CEO of General Mills:

We would agree that, unless our mission statement is backed up with specific objectives and strategies, the words become meaningless, but I also believe that our objectives and strategies are far more likely to be acted upon where there exists a prior statement of belief (ie a mission) from which specific plans and actions flow.

To summarize, mission statements can sometimes be an empty statement on a piece of paper, or can reflect and underpin fundamental values of an organization in pursuit of its strategy. It is important for all companies to encapsulate this into a brief, highly personal and meaningful statement. It gives the various stakeholders in the service organization a clear purpose and sense of direction.

The service mission statement is an important device that can provide an understanding for staff working in different parts of the organization, enabling them to pull together and uphold the corporate value and philosophy. However, it is essential that the mission statement is communicated clearly to all stakeholders and is perceived to be both relevant and realistic. Unless these requirements are met, the mission statement is unlikely to have any real impact on the organization, staff empowerment and cultural change.

References

BBC (2002) [accessed 14 December 2017] Business/Enron Scandal At-a-Glance [Online] http://news.bbc.co.uk/1/hi/business/1780075.stm

Butler, S and Wood, Z (2017) [accessed 29 November 2017] Husband and Wife Bank £400m From Sale of Matchesfashion.com [Online] https://www.theguardian.com/technology/2017/sep/01/husband-wife-chapman-bank-400m-sale-matches-fashion

Felloni (2015) [accessed 29 November 2017] Zappos' Sneaky Strategy For Hiring the Best People Involves a Van Ride From the Airport to the Interview [Online] http://uk.businessinsider.com/zappos-sneaky-strategy-for-hiring-the-best-people-2015-12

FinTech Futures (2013) [accessed 29 November 2017] Metro Bank All About Customer Care, Says Donaldson [Online] http://www.bankingtech.com/184801/metro-bank-all-about-customer-care-says-donaldson/

McDonald, M, Payne, A and Frow, P (2011) *Marketing Plans For Services: A complete guide*, John Wiley & Sons, Chichester

Mitchell, J (2009) *Hug Your People: The proven way to hire, inspire, and recognize your team and achieve remarkable results*, Random House, London

Mulquiney, A (2016) [accessed 2 May 2018] 5 Customer Service Lessons from AO.com [Online] https://www.maginus.com/news/blog/5-customer-service-lessons-from-ao.com/

Richards, K (2017) [accessed 29 November 2017] How Avis Brilliantly Pioneered Underdog Advertising With 'We Try Harder' [Online] http://www.adweek.com/creativity/how-avis-brilliantly-pioneered-underdog-advertising-with-we-try-harder/#/

Less about corporate, more about social responsibility

WHAT YOU WILL LEARN IN THIS CHAPTER

- Cause and effect: social responsibility and sustainability.
- What you stand for really counts.
- I demonstrate brands whose social responsibility has had serious cut-through with customers. Examples include Kering Group (Gucci, Balenciaga and others); Kathmandu, the outdoor retailer; Toms, the shoe retailer; Warby Parker and Magrabi, the prescription eyewear retailers.
- I will provide practical examples of how to ensure your supply chain helps you to achieve your goals for sustainability.

In a way sustainability suffers from the same challenge as the core subject of this book – putting customers first – in that many businesses see this as a cost rather than a benefit. They have a fundamental lack of understanding of sustainability, of its growing importance to their customer base and, of course, to the environment. They don't see the reputational and commercial risk of not addressing it head on.

EXPERT VIEW

I spoke to one of the world's thought leaders in this field, Livia Firth.

Livia is the Founder and Creative Director of Eco-Age, which is a brand/ marketing consultancy that helps businesses to grow by creating, implementing and communicating sustainability solutions. Over the past 10 years, Eco-Age has developed considerable connections with the world's most influential voices in sustainability, and is able to drive global debate, focusing on positive social and environmental impact.

I began by asking Livia what she thought that retailers should do that they don't now, when it comes to corporate social responsibility (CSR). This is what she told me: 'They don't tell the stories of the products they sell – where it was made, by whom, what materials were used. Sometimes this is an oversight on their part, for many it is because they don't have a positive story to tell!'

This really resonated with me. I am a marketer by trade, and the brand builder in me says that telling stories about how products are manufactured, including what materials are used, is potentially an incredibly powerful message to impart on customers. To Livia's point, however; if the brand has no focus on sustainability and the environment, they may well not have anything positive to shout about! Millennials in particular, more than any other age group, are hugely focused on sustainability. Many of them want to know up-front what the approach is to sustainability of the brand they are thinking of buying. Therefore, to ignore this and to continue to focus only on margin and to have products manufactured in a way that harms the environment or the people who are producing them on your behalf is taking a very narrow and short-term perspective. Over time, these businesses will lose sales and market share as their customers migrate to brands who can demonstrate that they genuinely care about the environment and who have taken steps to ensure they are adopting the best approach to sustainability.

With this point in mind, I was keen to understand what consumer-facing brands could do to move from sustainability and CSR just being a tick-box exercise to something much more meaningful and impactful.

Livia told me that CSR is an old word. In most people's minds a box to tick. However, we're now moving towards purpose-led initiatives. Companies need to realize that they are responsible for the impact they create and should want to do it in a better way, better for the environment, for customers and for their colleagues.'

To substantiate this point, Livia used the example of Kering Group, who own multiple luxury brands including Stella McCartney, Gucci and Balenciaga. She told me that Kering started many years ago with a department dedicated to sustainability and that they then started an environmental P&L, which they call an EP&L.

This is a highly effective development as an environmental profit and loss account (EP&L) allows a company to measure in monetary value the costs and benefits it generates for the environment, and in turn make more sustainable business decisions. It moves the business away from a tick-box scenario to one where sustainability becomes a core part of business strategy and everyday life. Kering describe their EP&L as facilitating a better way of thinking. It measures the environmental footprint in their own operations and across their entire supply chain and then calculates its monetary value.

This is a great example of a business that clearly puts sustainability and social responsibilities at the heart of what they do, but that also recognizes the commercial benefits of doing so. Livia also cited Unilever as a business that has sustainability at its core. She told me that 'they launched the first-ever human rights report on their supply chain. They have also done a lot of work on what a fair wage looks like and how to address the issue of poverty in the supply chain.'

Livia told me that customers have more information now than they have ever had previously. Some of this information is also driven by employees in the supplier's business. An example of this comes from Turkey, where factory staff sewed a label into the jacket saying Zara were not paying them enough (Business of Fashion, 2017). Sadly, there are also many supply chain-related tragedies that have occurred over the years in a number of Third World countries including Bangladesh, where workers have died or been badly injured in factories that were poorly constructed or, as Livia points out in her documentary, *The True Cost*, where the factory only had one door and no exits for workers to escape and therefore workers have perished in fires or other traumatic events.

These events, and the information that is now available, have heightened awareness amongst consumers and therefore there is a far higher focus than ever before on how brands ensure that factory workers and others in the supply chain are being treated. There is massive reputational risk associated with getting this wrong.

Livia and her team work with many leading retailers around the world, just one of which is the multichannel luxury retailer Matches Fashion. They wanted to educate their suppliers and brands about the impact of social responsibility and Eco-Age helped to develop this as well as a code of conduct for the brands, for the team internally, for shipping and packaging and other elements of their value chain. What a great way of ensuring that both your colleagues and your partners are bought into what you are trying to achieve – and with a code of conduct in place, you have something to leverage when it comes to holding people to account. It is a good example of a business that understands the importance of social responsibility and the impact it has on its customers.

Livia told me that unless you address the human capital (social) in your own business and natural capital (environmental), raw materials will become scarcer and scarcer. In other words, unless you secure both the rights of your workers and the sustainability and supply of your raw materials your profits will drop. There are clear tangible commercial benefits to sustainability and being focused on both human capital and natural capital. The key is that these commercial benefits are driven by integrating social responsibility and sustainability into the core of your business. It simply does not help anyone when it is merely treated as a tick-box exercise.

If you want to know more on the subject of social responsibility, sustainability and the impact of the supply chain on the environment, and if you are serious about sustainability, the environment and the impact upon your customers, then I highly recommend you watch Livia's documentary *The True Cost*. https://truecostmovie.com

Even if millennials are not your core customer of today, they will be in the future.

Millennials care about sustainability, therefore it is vital that you position yourself with authenticity and credibility. Millennials are those born between 1982 and 2002 (Howe and Strauss, 2009). Millennials are a hugely important customer segment. Not only as individuals, but for their influence over others and for the fact that they are the young families and empty-nesters of tomorrow. There is an opportunity for brands to be with millennials throughout their journey, providing they demonstrate what it means to truly understand what social responsibility means and how to implement this throughout their business.

Retailers must get their act together

Consumers care about the world we live in. We are increasingly influenced by global warming and other related events that drive us towards brands that genuinely demonstrate that they too care and have created a business that is socially responsible in some shape or form.

For some time, my wife has taken her own bags when she goes shopping, whether to a supermarket or a fashion mall, and will no longer accept plastic bags for any of her shopping. She does not want to feel as though she is contributing to the build-up of plastics in our oceans. While retailers in the UK are now required to charge for plastic bags, this does not fundamentally address the issue. Bunnings, the Australian DIY retailer that also has a presence in the UK, banned single-use plastic bags, whereby most retailers in Australia and other western markets have moved to a more durable and more expensive plastic bag. While this helps to reduce the issue, it clearly does not go far enough towards eradicating it.

Unfortunately for retailers, according to Annie Leonard, an expert in over-consumption, the retail manufacturing industry is the second most polluting industry on earth, second only to oil. According to Ms Leonard, only 1 per cent of the materials used to produce our consumer goods are still in use six months after sale (Leonard, 2007). This issue has to be addressed otherwise it will continue to turn millennials off those retailers who fail to reverse this trend. Increasing awareness around these issues has seen the birth of conscious consumption. It represents a mindset whereby consumers actively seek out ways to make positive decisions about what to buy and look for a solution to the negative impact that consumerism is having on the world.

A study found that people would pay 5 per cent more for their clothes if it were guaranteed that workers were being paid and treated fairly, in safe working conditions. The fashion industry could take people out of poverty by adding even 1 per cent of their profits to their worker wages (Baker, 2015). This has also been found to be prevalent with younger consumers. The 2015 Cone Communications Millennial CSR study found that nine out of ten millennials would change brands to one that is associated with a cause and two-thirds engage in CSR through social media. The study also found that millennials would make personal sacrifices in order to have an impact on issues they care about, for example, paying more for a product, sharing instead of buying and being paid less to work for a responsible company (Cone Communications, 2015).

Millennials' priorities and how big brands are meeting them

For example, millennials care about social impact:

- 83 per cent are active citizens and believe businesses should be involved in societal issues.

- 79 per cent wish it were easier to know what companies are doing and that they would talk about it.

- 82 per cent believe businesses can make an impact in addressing societal issues.

- 69 per cent want businesses to involve consumers in societal issues.

(Rudominer, 2016)

Cone Communications' survey also found that 87 per cent of Americans will purchase a product because a company is supporting an issue they care about, and millennials have shown that they are more likely than other generations to research to see what a company cares about and what they contribute to (Cone Communications, 2015).

It's not all about profit

Let's return to Matches Fashion, a highly successful multichannel luxury retailer that brought in Eco-Age to review their supply chain and to give them a view of how they could be more socially responsible as a business – whether that meant using dyes that are made from vegetables as opposed to synthetic dyes, or packaging that is made from recycled material, to how the brands they stock look after their manufacturers. From a cultural perspective, Matches Fashion has integrity and therefore it is hugely important to them that they are also giving back to their community. Yes, they are in business to make a profit, but as their co-founder Ruth Chapman told me, they are determined to leave their mark from a CSR perspective.

Leverage your community

Brands including Zady, Toms, Worby Parker and Kathmandu have all recognized the power of creating business strategies and cultures that place at their heart the idea that the community can give something back and they can give something to less well-off communities, as below:

- Toms and Worby Parker both promote the fact that for every pair of shoes or glasses purchased respectively, they give away a free pair to those in need.

- Zady, a clothing and consumer goods e-commerce company, positions itself as a lifestyle destination for conscious consumers.

- Magrabi, the Middle East and North Africa's leading optical chain, goes even further. While it does not seek to take advantage of the marketing opportunity of promoting what it does, it is working to try to cure blindness within Cameroon and other countries.

- Kathmandu, the New Zealand-headquartered outdoor retailer, puts people first, and places human rights as their number one material issue. They also support projects that have positive impacts on their local communities as well as contributing to measurable social improvements in Nepal, from where the inspiration for their brand derives.

All of these approaches are less about logos and making the brand look good through a single campaign, and more about making consumers feel empowered to make socially conscious buying decisions by developing a relationship with that brand. By buying from Toms, or encouraging friends to do so, consumers are actively supporting a cause. However, they are also buying a product that is desirable in its own right; Toms is making it easy for consumers to demonstrate their social credentials. This approach can resonate for many consumers, but particularly millennials. They will Instagram or Snapchat pictures of their latest pair of Toms, because they look great and because they know they have bought a child in a developing country a new pair of shoes to wear too.

Brands that appear to put the responsibility into the hands of their consumers can create engaged and loyal consumer audiences, who are also more likely to become valuable customers over the longer term.

Giving back: get one, give one

As per the example above with Toms, the 'get one give one' (G1G1) model was made famous in the first instance in 1995 by Nicholas Negroponte's launch of the not-for-profit 'One Laptop Per Child' project. It has since become a strategy employed by many start-ups such as Toms and Warby Parker (Joyner, 2014).

Create a long-term plan and clear objectives

One of the earlier adopters of an integrated CSR strategy is Marks & Spencer with Plan A, which is their commitment to make their business more environmentally and socially sustainable. Unfortunately, there are too few businesses that currently have such an integrated and focused approach to CSR.

This is not all they do. Last year, M&S pledged to raise £25 million for mental health, heart and cancer charities, and halve food waste across its operations by 2025, as it steps up its ethical commitments under its chief executive, Steve Rowe. Rowe said the fashion, food and homewares retailer was also 'determined to play a leading role' in social change by supporting community projects in 10 cities, including Rochdale, Glasgow, Liverpool and Middlesbrough. M&S's initiatives include cutting carbon emissions and giving grants of up to £50,000 for community businesses, careers advice for young people, and 10,000 pairs of plimsolls to children starting school (Butler, 2017).

Other retailers and service providers are also thinking about how to 'give back' by supporting those in need. The food industry has always had a challenge with wastage, and when there are so many people who struggle to make ends meet, providing meals and sustenance is an incredibly important CSR initiative.

A good example of this is Sainsbury's and the Olio app. After a successful six-week trial in two stores, Sainsbury's widened its initiative with Olio. The initial trial saw 10,000 items of food shared out, which would otherwise have been wasted. Local residents download the Olio app, which informs them when surplus food is available from local branches of Sainsbury's. Volunteers upload pictures of the food items onto the app, which users can then select before picking up from one of the participating local branches. Olio works independently in some large UK cities but the Sainsbury's tie-up is the first of its kind with a major retailer (Retail Insider, 2017).

Tesco – winner of the Experian Award for Building Stronger Communities in 2017 – focused on food poverty. The company launched Community Food Connection, which uses an app to connect stores that have surplus food with local charities. Creating a culture of sustainability can be difficult when employees are also juggling demands ranging from pressure to cut costs, to meeting sales targets. 'It's making the linkage to the strategy and thinking about how that relates to the nature of the business', says David Grayson, Director of the Doughty Centre for Corporate Responsibility at Cranfield School of Management. 'Then it is the hard slog of aligning that with compensation, executive development, training and communications messages' (*Financial Times*, 2017).

Solar City put energy into their CSR

Another great example of 'caring for the community' and 'giving back' is Solar City, a leading US-based solar power provider. They produce and distribute solar power systems to power homes, schools and businesses. There are 1.4 billion people in the world who have no access to electricity. This is approximately 20 per cent of the population of our planet. Therefore, solar power can be even more valuable to communities in Third World and developing countries who have limited or no access to electricity.

For these countries, having no electricity often means school, work, leisure/social environments stop at sunset.

Solar City created its 'Give Power Foundation', which in turn donates solar power systems to schools in South America and Africa. This allows the schools to operate at night and offer classes for adults and children. These classes can improve both the short- and long-term prospects of the communities served (Gauss, 2017).

Inauthenticity can destroy a brand

'People can smell inauthenticity', says David Grayson. 'If business is claiming one thing and is operating in another way, that is a dangerous position to be in' (*Financial Times*, 2017).

One group of brands that are clearly authentic in their approach to sustainability and CSR is Kering. They own a number of brands including Gucci, Stella McCartney and Balenciaga. Figure 9.1 highlights their approach to CSR, which is something that is very much at the heart of their strategy.

Figure 9.1   Kering's EP&L

Understand
where impacts
are

Develop a
knowledgeable
decision-making
process

Steer our business
strategy in a
responsible way

**WHAT IS
THE PURPOSE
OF THE EP&L?**

Strengthen our business
and manage risks for the
future

Be transparent
with stakeholders

SOURCE Kering (2017)

Top practical customer experience tips

1 Drop the word corporate and focus on social responsibility.

2 Implement a code of conduct for colleagues, suppliers and partners.

3 Make purchasing decisions that put sustainable products first.

4 Support your local community.

5 Encourage your customers to take part in your CSR initiatives.

6 Implement an EP&L – be clear about the value of being socially responsible.

Expanded on below.

Drop the word corporate and focus on social responsibility

If you don't, consumers will not engage with your initiatives.

Implement a code of conduct for colleagues, suppliers and partners

Walk across your business and consider the implications of social responsibility, your carbon footprint, your packaging, your sourcing policy and so on. Talk to your customers. Get them to tell you what is important to them. These should be the starting points for the creation of your CSR charter. You can now implement a code of conduct for all of your colleagues, suppliers and partners to ensure that people are held to account for the ongoing implementation and delivery of your sustainability and social responsibility approach.

Make purchasing decisions that put sustainable products first

Be that fair-trade coffee, or recyclable paper, this helps to engender the right mindset amongst your colleagues and sets the tone for your business focus on being socially responsible.

Support your local community

Can you become an active supporter of local businesses and the local economy? Is it better to pay a little more to source locally than to save a few dollars/pounds by sourcing from another country?

Encourage your customers to take part in your CSR initiatives

How can your customers play a role in supporting your CSR policy? Can they recycle packaging? Or even send it back to you to reuse?

Implement an EP&L – be clear about the value of being socially responsible

While being socially responsible is a virtue, it will prove to be an unsuccessful strategy if you don't understand the value of doing so. Adopt the approach that Kering takes and implement an EP&L. Measure the environmental footprint of your own operations and across your entire supply chain.

Over to Professor Malcolm McDonald

For CSR to work, we must first produce shareholder value added for investors. Remember ICI (Imperial Chemical Industries, the former bellwether share on the FTSE)? They were brilliant to their employees, local communities, charities and so on. But, they didn't make as much money as Du Pont, Siemens and the like and went out of business, so now there are hundreds of thousands of former employees without a job, and local communities and charities are left with nothing!

CSR should not be tackled as an add-on or management initiative, but as an underlying management ethos. It is also interesting to note that these companies, apart from being 'good citizens', driving the circular economy and so on, were also extremely profitable. In other words, not only did they satisfy all other stakeholders, they also satisfied their own shareholders.

This reminds me of a proposal from one of my senior colleagues on an advisory board I sat on at one of our top business schools. The suggestion was that 'ethics' should be added as an elective on the master's programmes. I pointed out that ethics should be an integral part of the curriculum for Finance, HR, Economics, IT and so on, not an afterthought, or add-on to a series of production-orientated lectures about a particular discipline.

In order to do so in practice, the ability to understand the circular economy can be invaluable, as an integral part of the corporate strategy. It can then be tailored individually to your organization as a source of differential advantage for growth in sales and profits.

Pioneering innovators, however, have realized the circular economy is not only about resource supply, but more about evolving the business model to transform the nature of resource demand from the customer's point of view.

An Accenture report (Accenture, 2014) identified more than 100 truly disruptive companies applying circular-economy thinking and new technology to transform in ways that seriously threaten incumbents, so creating what Accenture call 'circular advantage'. This advantage comes from innovating for both resource efficiency and customer value – delivery at the heart of a company's strategy, technology and operations!

One such example is Nike, who have for many years worked hard to balance the dual demands of resource productivity and customer value. For example Nike's FlyKnit™ technology, which enables the company to create a shoe upper out of a few single threads. The result is a less wasteful (by 80 per cent) production process that renders a better-fitting and lighter shoe that can help boost an athlete's performance. This in turn can be used to support the environment and gain their customer's respect.

Nike's Vice-President of Sustainable Innovation is quoted in the Accenture report as saying: 'This isn't our sustainability strategy. It is integral to our business strategy.'

Let me summarize the Accenture report on the topic of the circular economy. The 'Take, Make, Waste' model of the past 250 years is no longer sustainable. The availability of resources such as land, forests, water, metals and mineral fuels cannot keep up with demand. The world is already using 1.5 planet's worth of resources every year. Based on current trends (growing population, expanding global middle class), we will consume three planets by 2050. This will translate into US \$1 trillion in losses for companies and countries whose growth remains tied to the use of scarce and virgin natural resources. Economic development and resource scarcity are on a collision course.

The same report spells out many case examples of companies that have already adopted circular principles to close the loop on energy and material. There are many other examples given in the Accenture report and I recommend it to readers who are interested not only in the whole CSR/ sustainability domain, but also in creating competitive advantage.

For more details on this topic, see Catherine Weetman's 2016 book, *A Circular Economy Handbook for Business and Supply Chains.*

References

Accenture (2014) [accessed 13 December 2017] Circular Advantage [Online] https:// www.accenture.com/t20150523T053139__w__/us-en/_acnmedia/Accenture/ Conversion-Assets/DotCom/Documents/Global/PDF/Strategy_6/Accenture-Circular-Advantage-Innovative-Business-Models-Technologies-Value-Growth.pdf

Baker, J (2015) [accessed 29 November 2017] The Rise of the Conscious Consumer: Why Businesses Need to Open Up [Online] https://www. theguardian.com/women-in-leadership/2015/apr/02/the-rise-of-the-conscious-consumer-why-businesses-need-to-open-up

Business of Fashion (2017) [accessed 18 December 2017] Unpaid Turkish Garment Workers Tag Zara Items to Seek Help [Online] https://www. businessoffashion.com/articles/news-analysis/unpaid-turkish-garment-workers-tag-zara-items-to-seek-help

Butler, S (2017) [accessed 30 November 2017] M&S Offers Cash Grants to Community Businesses in Ethical Relaunch [Online] https://www.theguardian. com/business/2017/jun/01/ms-targets-food-waste-and-social-change-in-sustainability-plan

Cone Communications (2015) [accessed 30 November 2017] 2015 Cone Communications Millennial CSR Study [Online] http://www.conecomm.com/ research-blog/2015-cone-communications-millennial-csr-study

Financial Times (2017) [accessed 13 December 2017] The 2017 Responsible Business Awards Winners [Online] https://www.ft.com/content/68b26566-5bf7-11e7-b553-e2df1b0c3220

Gauss, A (2017) [accessed 13 December 2017] 6 Socially Responsible Companies to Applaud [Blog] *Classy* [Online] https://www.classy.org/blog/6-socially-responsible-companies-applaud/

Howe, N and Strauss, W (2009) *Millennials Rising: The next great generation,* Vintage, London

Joyner, A (2014) [accessed 30 November 2017] Beyond Buy-One-Give-One Retail [Online]. [Online] https://www.newyorker.com/business/currency/ beyond-buy-one-give-one-retail

Kering.com (2017) [accessed 29 December 2017] What Is An EP&L?, *Kering* [Online] http://www.kering.com/en/sustainability/whatisepl

Leonard, A (2007) Story of stuff, referenced and annotated script, *Journal of Occupational and Environmental Health,* **13** (1)

Retail Insider (2017) [accessed 29 November 2017] Digital Retail Innovations Report [Online] http://webloyalty.co.uk/Images/UK/Digital_Retail_ Innovations_Report_2017.pdf

Rudominer, R (2016) [accessed 30 November 2017] Corporate Social Responsibility Matters: Ignore Millennials at Your Peril [Online] https://www.huffingtonpost.com/ryan-rudominer/corporate-social-responsi_9_b_9155670.html

Weetman, C (2016) *A Circular Economy Handbook for Business and Supply Chains: Repair, remake, redesign, rethink*, Kogan Page, London

Retail as a service

10

WHAT YOU WILL LEARN IN THIS CHAPTER

- You will learn why consumer-facing businesses need to become service providers and what that means in practical terms.
- The types of services they can offer that put the customer first and add value to their experience and therefore strengthen their relationship with the customer.

Why become a service provider?

As I have outlined throughout the book, 'selling stuff' to customers is no longer enough. Particularly not in the age of Amazon, Alibaba and the other marketplaces who provide superior customer value propositions. Nor is it enough with the proliferation of choice consumers have as to where they buy their goods or services. There is also the high likelihood that these marketplaces will look to broaden their ecosystem and start to add services. How long before Amazon has a pharmacy and sells over-the-counter medicine? Or starts selling prescription frames/glasses?

In the UK, John Lewis has taken the bold step to launch a home solutions proposition where you can book an accredited tradesperson to carry out repairs, install electrical appliances, even decorate your house. They also revealed that they are sending their partners to theatre school in order to be able to deliver the appropriate level of service to different customer types. Its new store in Oxford has an experience manager dedicated to organizing instore events every day of the trading year.

Meanwhile, Ikea has acquired Task Rabbit. So, if assembling flat-packed furniture is not high up on your bucket list of things to do, then they can provide a tasker to do this for you. These moves to provide services to consumers are not only a defensive play against the rise of marketplaces and other disruptors, but also recognize the growth of the DIFM (do it for me) segment.

There is an entire generation of digital natives who appear to be more aligned with sharing and renting than owning. Some of this is driven by economics, some by their attitudes, values and beliefs. This segment of customers may still be more prone to doing it themselves, while for many other segments they fall into the DIFM requirement. Think of Dixons Carphone and Best Buy's 'Geek squad'. Why waste time trying to install sometimes complicated technology when someone else can do it for you?

Enjoy.com, a US-based pureplay selling technology products, provides free experts who come to install products and provide advice on how to get the most out of your new acquisition:

- If you were a DIY retailer selling garden sheds, would I expect to build the shed myself or you to do it for me?
- If I bought a holiday from you, might I be interested in any other services you could procure on my behalf that would mean I didn't have to spend precious holiday time renting a car, looking for places to go, arranging a tour, or asking the concierge about good restaurants?
- If you were a car dealer, once I'd purchased a new car, would it be more convenient for me if when the car required a service, you picked it up from my house and dropped it off afterwards?
- If you were a bank or insurance company, would my lifetime value and your retention rates increase if you proactively told me about more relevant policies that I could benefit from that genuinely added value to me and my family?

I think you know the answer to all of the above.

Maintain your relevance by providing services

As I outlined in Chapter 2, it is my firm belief that in order to remain relevant to their customers and to provide something more than simply selling a product, over time, retailers will need to become service providers.

M&S partnered with West End shopping platform Dropit in two of its London stores, allowing customers to have their shopping picked up by courier. Customers can now choose to leave their shopping behind once they have paid for it, rather than carrying it with them during the rest of their shopping trip. Dropit then teams up with courier companies and selects the best option for the delivery address based on price and availability. A one-day Dropit pass costs £10. Dropit claims that its users spend an average 150 per cent more than shoppers not using its service (Waller-Davis, 2017).

Providing services can take many forms, from walking into the Nike store in Soho in New York where you are greeted by the sight of an athletic bunch of personal shoppers who can spend up to an hour with you in the store helping you to find the right products – to the grocery store that has packing staff to help elderly customers or those with a very large shop, who also help take the groceries to the customer's car. If retailers don't understand what it means to also provide a service in addition to selling their products, they are highly likely to find their sector disrupted.

In niche sectors such as car tyres, this has also happened. One of the major inconveniences of having a flat tyre on your car is that you may not have a spare wheel and are therefore forced to drive to the nearest tyre-fitting garage. This is where 'Tyres On The Drive' come in. They come to you, wherever you are, at a time of your choosing. Therefore, it puts you as the customer completely in control.

Subscription is delivering a service

If you can pre-order something – you may want to think of it as 'setting and forgetting' – then that is hugely convenient. No need to have to remember when to reorder your shampoo or household cleaning products, your mois-turiser or bottles of water. It can apply to so many different product categories.

Birchbox was one of the first UK subscription services. They send subscribers a selection of five or six beauty samples every month. Product selections are tailored to suit the customer's preferences. They are charged a set fee that varies depending upon the length of commitment the customer has made. Customers can then head to Birchbox's website if they want to order full-sized versions of any samples. There are a huge number of other subscription-based US retailers, from Dollar Shave Club, which sells razors, to Loot Crate, which provides gaming merchandise, to Barkbox, which provides toys and treats for dogs.

In the fashion space, US brand Stitch Fix curates a selection of products and sends customers boxes filled with surprise content. There is no monthly commitment. They charge customers a $20 fee for styling each box, and the fee can then be put towards the purchase of any item in the box that the customer wants to purchase. They are given three days to decide what they want to buy.

Table 10.1 Customer service framework

| What aspect do the services cover? | | | | |
How do they help consumers?	Product	Delivery and returns	Marketing	After-sales and customer service
Convenience	'Bundle it up for me' – if you're booking a flight, the airline offers you car hire and other relevant extra services	I can choose the most convenient delivery method and you enable me to return for no cost I can return to your stores if I want to	I receive incentives that I can use across all channels There is messaging in all channels to let me know that I can 'shop my way'	The customer service team starts from a 'can do' mindset and tries to resolve my issues first time I am able to interact with live chat or over the phone if I choose to
Value creation		I can choose a Prime-type delivery proposition where I pre-pay for unlimited deliveries	I get first access to the sale and to discounted products	
Peace of mind	'Set and forget' – a subscription service whereby I can ask a retailer to send me the same product every so many weeks	If something isn't right, there is a free, easy-to-use returns service		I'm offered appropriate reassurance of what happens if thing go wrong, eg ATOL covering my flight costs if my airline goes out of business or a warranty for a product

(continued)

Table 10.1 *(Continued)*

What aspect do the services cover? → How do they help consumers? ↓	Product	Delivery and returns	Marketing	After-sales and customer service
Remind me	'Let me not forget' – when a retailer reminds a customer, when they are checking out, of products they bought the last time that they haven't added to their bag		You send me reminders about events, birthdays/ when I need to send gifts, when I'm likely to be running low on a product or when I'm due to renew a service	
Personalization	You offer me the option of personalizing gifts or products or services I've procured		You only ever send me marketing communication that reflects what I buy or what I like doing – nothing generic	When I contact the call centre they have all of my history, what I bought, what I like etc

Also, it's great to contact a customer after a purchase to find out how they are getting on with their new acquisition |

Which service would work best for you?

I have created a framework in Table 10.1 to help you think about the services you might want to offer and why these add value to the customer.

CASE STUDY Hotel – motel – Holiday Inn

On a visit to Hong Kong, I had the most fantastic customer experience and thought I would share it, as there are many little touchpoints to learn from.

I had the very good fortune to be put up at the Mandarin Oriental Hotel by an event organizer for a conference I was presenting at. From the minute I arrived, the experience was fantastic. It was clear to me that they had thought through all the potential touchpoints and how to deliver the most relevant customer experience.

The person who checked me in then took me to my room and explained how everything worked. Having just flown for 11 hours, the first thing I wanted was a shower. It may seem like a small thing but while the mirror steamed up, a space the size of my body in the middle didn't, it remained clear. Too much information I'm sure, but I thought it was great, and I've still no idea how they did it.

The little touches in the hotel were great. From showerheads being turned away so you didn't scald yourself or have a coronary due to the cold water when you turned it on, to fresh ice in my champagne bucket every day. One evening I couldn't get my TV to work. I called reception and they said they would sort it out straight away. After returning from dinner, there was a letter from the person who had fixed my TV, with an apology and their contact details should I have any further problems.

Of course, every good hotel has a turn-down service. But not like this:

- A nice soft pair of slippers were left by my bed along with some oil to apply to help me sleep.

- The maid/cleaner knew my name – in fact everyone in the hotel seemed to know my name. Compare that to Practicology's (2017) e-mail comms report where 15 per cent of retailers don't even send a welcome e-mail.

- The gym was open 24/7, none of this only opening at 7 am malarkey.

- They put branded cable ties on my phone and laptop cables for chargers.

- The toilet paper was folded, no need to fumble around trying to find the start of the roll.
- Light buttons were all clearly marked and illuminated when the room was dark.
- More sockets than you could shake a stick at.
- I finally found someone who could tie my shoelaces… They tied them every night!
- They folded my clothes.
- There was a hook for my bath towel.
- Sweets in the basket.
- They put the receipts and business cards I'd been collating in a little box.

And so it goes on… My checkout was extended (without charge) until 4.30 pm as I was not flying until 11 pm.

This is a business that clearly understands what it takes to put their customers first, and a business that does not just look at cost, but looks at the cost benefit of delivering such a great experience. In all cases, staff are well trained and empowered to deliver the right experience, right down to the last minute when I left the hotel, and both the receptionist and the bell boy asked if I'd left anything behind in the room or in the safe and that I had my passport.

Top practical customer experience tips

1 Can you make customers' lives easier by enabling them to pay a subscription or for auto-replenishment of big, bulky or frequently used products?

2 Enable customers to interact with a live chat service online.

3 What services can you offer that enhance the experience of the customer buying from you?

4 Ensure that there is clear 'shop my way' messaging on all channels and touchpoints.

5 Use the service framework created.

Expanded on below.

Can you make customers' lives easier by enabling them to pay a subscription or for auto-replenishment of big, bulky or frequently used products?

This can apply to anything from pet food to household cleaning products, from beauty and personal care to non-perishable foods.

The beauty of this is that it locks customers in. It guarantees and secures their business. It maximizes their lifetime value to you. It is also highly likely that they will spend more with you over time due to the fact they already buy from you.

Enable customers to interact with a live chat service online

I was one of the first e-commerce practitioners to implement live chat in the UK when I did so at Ted Baker in 2007. Live chat is a great way to drive sales, increase conversion, and drive up average order values and units per transaction. It works for some segments of customers who need more technical information than the site offers on products such as televisions or computers, or it can just be for reassurance for a customer buying a new suit or dress.

It is your virtual sales assistant. Some businesses are delivering this service through their call-centre team and increasingly businesses are using chat bots to deliver live chat. I will talk about AI in detail in Chapter 15 and give you my thoughts on the effectiveness of this.

What services can you offer that enhance the experience of the customer buying from you? Can you help them build, install and maintain what they have purchased?

Ensure you cater for the ever-increasing 'do it for me' (DIFM) segment of customers. What services can you offer that enhance the experience of the customer buying from you? We live in a task-rich, time-poor world, therefore customers will increasingly look to engage with businesses that can help them build, install and maintain what they have purchased. This is probably the quickest-growing segment of customers in terms of their buying need. We have seen a plethora of both new entrants in this space as well as acquisitions. Ikea bought Task Rabbit. John Lewis offers an online directory of service providers for customers to search and choose from.

Ensure that there is clear 'shop my way' messaging in all channels and touchpoints

Don't take for granted that customers know you have a website, or that they can click and collect. You need to ensure that all channels promote the others. That way there will be no ambiguity with regards to how customers can procure your products or services.

Use the service framework created

Think about how your products/services, aftersales/customer service and your overarching customer value proposition can support your different customer segments.

Over to Professor Malcolm McDonald

Service brands as customer services

I should like to expand on these with some comments about service companies and the importance of their brand names.

It is recognized by all the world's leading brand valuation companies that brands per se account for at least 25 per cent of all intangible assets. These intangible assets might include the personality of the brand, the ethos, the personalized service – aspects that cannot be directly identified as driving profit, but of course make up the holistic brand and service experience. In fact, in reality I believe it is much more than this, because everything an organization does across all its disciplines manifests itself in the offers made in the marketplace and, of course, all of these have the organization's brand name on them.

The purpose of this introduction is to point out the fact that brands have come to dominate the commercial landscape, yet in the service sector, brand management is still a somewhat confused, black art. Many traditional service-sector brands around the world are little more than suppliers' labels, are 'me too', have poor positioning, poor quality and poor support. Such service organizations do not understand the consumer and are frequently forced to trade on price.

A successful brand conforms to the following criteria

1 A successful brand has a name, symbol or design (or source combination) that identifies the 'product' of an organization as having sustainable competitive advantage, such as Coca-Cola, Microsoft, Marks & Spencer.

2 A successful brand results in superior profit and market performance.

3 A successful brand is only an asset if it leads to sustainable competitive advantage.

4 A successful brand, like other assets, will depreciate without further investment in the satisfaction of consumer needs.

The term 'brand' encompasses not only consumer products, but a whole host of offerings that include people (such as pop stars and politicians), places (such as Paris), ships (such as the *Queen Mary*), industrial service and retail products. Translating this over to service brands and brands as a service, we must initially recognize that the definition and challenges outlined here are broad, expanding and evolving according to the individual needs of each.

The challenges of services branding

The increased competition in services industries has made many companies realize that a strong service brand is an essential part of their competitive advantage. Unfortunately, the understanding of service branding has not kept pace with the growth of the service sector. Service-based brands such as Virgin, as opposed to product-based brands such as washing powder or breakfast cereals, involve a multiple interface with the consumer, where the consumer experiences the brand at various levels. The initial response of service marketers to the new challenges was based on the assumption that the principles of product branding would equally apply to service branding. They soon discovered, however, that the specific nature of services requires tailored concepts and approaches and that product branding is unlikely to be effective if its principles are transferred to services without any adaptation.

In the financial and insurance sectors, for example, very few brands have managed to create a complete set of perceptions in people's minds. A question such as 'What does Barclays Bank offer that is different from Lloyds?' would probably lead to a puzzled silence, in spite of the billions of pounds spent each year on advertising. However, the airline industry has demonstrated that it is possible to achieve a clear differentiation of service brands. If travellers were asked to rank Virgin, Lufthansa or Singapore Airlines according to punctuality, in-flight entertainment and attentive cabin staff, they are very likely to give similar answers without hesitation.

Consistent service brands through staff

First of all, a service brand is based entirely on 'the way the company does things' and on the company's values and culture. This means that a brand personality cannot just be designed by a marketing department, but depends on the whole company, from the chief executive to anyone who has contact with the customers. This is because customers' perceptions of the brand depend highly on individual interactions with the staff of the company, as in the case of the hotel example described in this chapter, so particular emphasis has to be placed on the consistent delivery of the service. Brand building needs to be undertaken from the bottom up and involves a profound analysis of every aspect of the interaction between the customer and the company.

Branding to make tangible the intangible

One of the most problematic aspects associated with service brands is that consumers have to deal with intangible offerings. An effective way to make brands tangible is to use as many physical elements as possible that can be associated with the brand, such as staff uniforms, office décor and the type of music played to customers waiting on the telephone. A service brand can project its values through physical symbols and representations, as Virgin airlines has so successfully done with its vibrant red colour reflecting the dynamic, challenging position being adopted. Package design plays an important role for branded goods, and in service brands this likewise represents an opportunity for more effective differentiation, as in the case of McDonald's boxes for children's meals. The yellow and blue stripes in Ikea stores, for example, not only allude to the Scandinavian tradition of the company but also guide consumers through the different sections. Finally, the design of the physical facilities may be used to *differentiate* the service brand from its competition. The polished steel interiors of Pret A Manger restaurants allow consumers to distinguish them clearly from other sandwich bars and bistros.

One way in which consumers evaluate a service brand depends largely on the extent to which they participate in the delivery of the service. If the service performance requires a high degree of consumer involvement, it is vitally important that consumers understand their roles, and are willing and able to participate, otherwise their inevitable frustration will weaken the brand. For example, large, easy-to-read signs and displays at the entrance of Ikea stores inform consumers how they are supposed to take measurements, select pieces of furniture and collect them. The Ikea brand is built on the principle that consumers are willing to be involved in 'creating' the service, not just in consuming it, tapping into the very personal experience and desire to 'build' your own home, rather than just purchase it.

In conclusion, there are some exciting disruptors emerging such as Airbnb and ZipCar, but on the whole, the service sector still illustrates the overall challenges with service branding and the need for a new mindset. A service brand has to be based on a clear competitive position, which in turn has to be derived from the corporate strategy. This requires a holistic approach and the involvement of the entire company. The brand positioning and benefits should then be communicated to the target market segments and real evidence has to be delivered of the brand's ability to satisfy customer needs.

To summarize

- Branding as customer service.
- Great brands do not differentiate just for the sake of differentiation.
- They innovate around core service benefits.
- They make the brand distinctive and famous (easy to recognize).
- The whole organization lives the brand at all touchpoints.
- They make it easy to buy.

In other words, they get the basics right.

References

Practicology (2015) [accessed 1 December 2017] Practicology Customer Communications Report 2015 [Online] https://www.practicology.com/files/3114/4017/0408/Practicology_Customer_Communications_report_2015.pdf

Waller-Davies, B (2017) [accessed 13 December 2017] M&S Stores Sign Up For Hands-Free Shopping, *Retail Week* [Online] https://www.retail-week.com/topics/technology/ms-stores-sign-up-for-hands-free-shopping/7021404.article

Winning the hearts and minds of customers in international markets

11

WHAT YOU WILL LEARN IN THIS CHAPTER

- Customers in international markets have different elements that matter more to them. Take Germany for example, where paying by direct debit or bank transfer is key. Free returns are also very important in Germany as it has a strong catalogue heritage and propensity to return products.
- How to win the trust of customers in new geographical markets.
- China and the opportunity there.
- Options for structure and operating models.

Consumers are happy to buy across borders

Internationalization is very much on most business's agendas, irrespective of the consumer sector that they operate in. In fact, one could argue that game changers like Brexit, the UK's 2016 vote to leave the European Union, have almost forced businesses to look to expand their reach in other geographies. In the United States, many retailers are faced with the perfect storm of having too many stores, as more and more customers move online, as well as losing market share to marketplaces such as Amazon.

According to UPS's European 'Pulse of the Online Shopper' survey in 2017, 73 per cent of consumers had purchased from an international retailer within Europe and 57 per cent had purchased from an international retailer outside of Europe (UPS, 2017).

EXPERT VIEW

Billy May, CEO of Sur La Table in the United States, has extensive experience of internationalization. Previously, he was Senior Vice-President, Marketing, Direct-to-Consumer, Omnichannel and Corporate Development for Abercrombie & Fitch (A&F), and before that, Global Vice-President of Digital and e-Commerce at adidas Group. Whereas adidas has localized operations around the world, A&F utilizes a centralized operating model. All the decisions around internationalization and localization are made from Columbus, Ohio.

When the company made the decision to expand internationally in the mid-2000s, it decided to do so by going direct and internationalizing on its own, without utilizing third parties or licensees.

As the company opened physical stores, it also decided to launch localized websites at the same time. Unlike the physical experience, however, Billy said that 'you cannot assume that international markets behave like your own market'. While experiences are shared globally, consumer behaviour is very different digitally, country to country, especially within Europe.

You have to be relevant to those local markets: pricing and promotions, payments and payment options (one of the most overlooked considerations), fulfilment, shipping and returns. For example, Billy May highlighted the UK as one of the most advanced omnichannel markets globally and therefore customer expectations around fulfilment and availability are very clear. If you want to be relevant in this market, five to seven days shipping is not acceptable.

Equally important in an era of customer-centricity, if not more so, marketing has to be relevant for the end customer. It has to be localized beyond just language, creative and content – but on price and promotion as well, taking into account local holidays and events that you don't have visibility of back in the United States. From both resource and local market requirements, it is good to work with a local partner, including a marketing agency, who can provide the insight and support required to connect with the customer and drive a brand forward.

What are the opportunities offered up by internationalization?

Driving growth/revenue streams:

- Wholesale opportunities:
  - local market offline;
  - local market pureplays;
  - international pureplays;
  - international stores shipping worldwide;
  - franchise partners.
- Retail opportunities:
  - stores;
  - online;
  - showrooms;
  - pop-ups;
  - drop ship and partners (ie Amazon, eBay or local versions).
- Instore opportunities to drive loyalty to localized sites:
  - multilingual store staff;
  - buy instore for home delivery to home country;
  - multi-currency payment gateway on tills;
  - e-mail capture.

Current approaches to internationalization

Table 11.1 Current approaches to internationalization

Strategy	Pros	Cons
1. **Do nothing**: don't allow anyone to buy from overseas	• Not many! • Potentially reduce fraudulent orders	• A very poor customer experience • Limits potential demand and impacts sales and profitability • Lose opportunity to take market share from new markets

(continued)

Table 11.1 *(Continued)*

Strategy	Pros	Cons
2. **Standardization**: switch on the buy button only	• Get some indication of potential demand from other markets	• With no localization, the demand will be suppressed
3. **Adaptation**: localize some aspects	• You start to get a better indication of potential demand from other markets • You drive conversion (payment or currency is often the first element to be localized)	• It doesn't provide a true perspective of what the demand could be
4. **Localization**: fully localize the customer proposition online (payment, currency, language, service)	• The best customer experience • You will maximize demand generation from local markets	• It's the most expensive route to go
5. **Dipping toes**: marketplace presence	• It's a cost-effective way to discover potential demand for your brand	• You don't own the customer or their data, the marketplace does
6. **Multichannel market entry**: lead with online, open stores	• The best potential customer experience as it enables the customer to 'shop their way'	• It's expensive to open stores in other markets
7. **Lead with stores**: then localize online	• You can get closer to your customers and bring your brand to life	• It's expensive and also limits the reach of the brand

EXPERT VIEW

I spoke to Dave Elston who was previously Digital Director Europe for Clarks. I asked him the question, if he had his time again, what would he have done differently having had the experience of localizing Clarks in various markets. These are the key lessons learnt:

• He said that he saw things through a British lens too much to begin with.

• Germans and other nationalities have a very different mentality to shopping online and what they like and don't like.

- He would have had someone in the team who had sold online in Germany right from the off.

- He would have implemented payment by invoice for Germany, which, having not done so, limited the scope of opportunity, but also being very conscious of the balance between increased basket size versus increased returns.

- He felt that he underestimated the importance of corporate social responsibility – particularly to German customers. For example, consumers would contact the call centre asking about how leathers were produced.

- He would have looked into how best to manage returns in Germany more closely before launching. However, you need to help executives see other markets through consumers' eyes – they were looking at high returns rates, in excess of UK levels, thinking there was something wrong when these are the norm in Germany.

- He would urge retailers to look into how you enable the best returns process for the consumer and understand their expectations, eg how to implement quicker refunds back to the consumer.

- Dave would look more closely at how consumers across the EU shop in different ways and at different times, eg Northern EU versus Southern EU and the understanding of these variances. For example, the French are very focused on inspiration, the Germans on end use and therefore merchandising needs to reflect these variances in consumer behaviour.

- Dave also believes that fulfilment expectations will increase in the EU and consumers will not be prepared to wait more than a day or two for their orders.

Figure 11.1 demonstrates the most common approach to localization and steps prioritized along the way, and the fact the all the building blocks need to be in place to maximize the return from marketing activity.

The impact of language alone on conversions and sales is significant, as shown in Figure 11.2.

For example, Germany is a highly attractive market due to is sheer scale and size; however, it is a complicated market to succeed in due to:

- The biggest EU market.
- Population of 81 million.
- Germany is a country of 5,700 towns and cities but only three have populations of more than 1 million.
- Only 81 conurbations have more than 100,000 inhabitants.

(*continued on page 158*)

Figure 11.1 Localization transition process

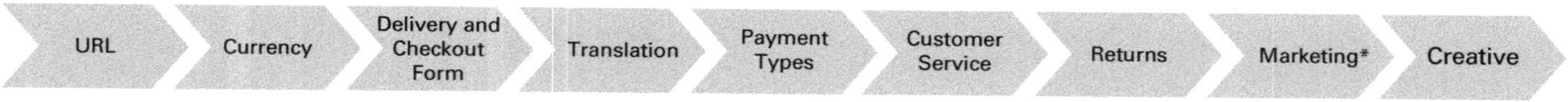

| URL | Currency | Delivery and Checkout Form | Translation | Payment Types | Customer Service | Returns | Marketing* | Creative |

*Marketing will have limited returns, prior to the other building blocks being put in place

Figure 11.2 Conversion through translation

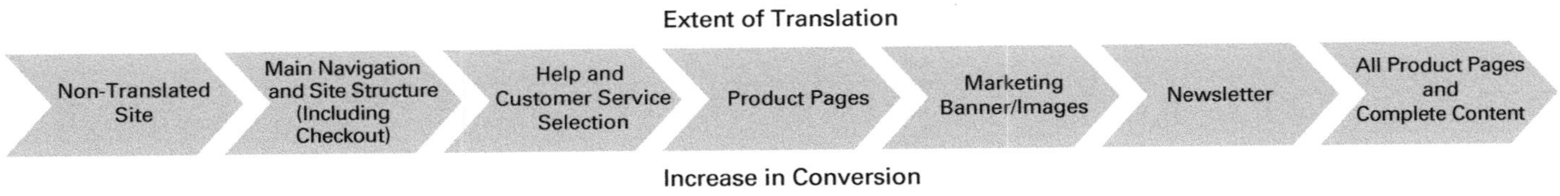

Extent of Translation

Non-Translated Site → Main Navigation and Site Structure (Including Checkout) → Help and Customer Service Selection → Product Pages → Marketing Banner/Images → Newsletter → All Product Pages and Complete Content

Increase in Conversion

- 37 million people (45 per cent of the total population) live in 300 cities.
- 75 per cent of Germans have made an online purchase.
- Returns rates can exceed 40 per cent.

(Hughes, 2016)

Often when brands from English-speaking countries internationalize, they go for English-language markets initially – the UK, United States, South Africa, Australia, New Zealand etc. However, it is far more complex than they perceive:

- Size guides are different.
- Terminology is different.
- Marketing channels behave differently.
- Payment methods are different.

Key drivers for success

- Visitors:
  - store presence;
  - existing partnerships;
  - marketing activities, including PR;
  - brand awareness;
  - internet penetration;
  - size of population;
  - trading history in market.
- Conversion:
  - user experiences;
  - localization, including translation;
  - payment methods;
  - delivery costs;
  - service proposition;
  - product offerings and suitability to market;
  - competition: wholesale, partners and local competitors.

- Average order values (AOVs):
  - items per order;
  - disposable income;
  - pricing strategy;
  - payment types (invoicing);
  - cost of shipping and promotional thresholds.

- Returns:
  - reliability of shipping partners;
  - customer habits;
  - sizing guides and clarity of product information;
  - payment types (invoicing drives high returns).

- Abandoned baskets:
  - delivery charges;
  - payment types;
  - fraud screening;
  - security and privacy concerns;
  - checkout options (guest checkout versus forced registration);
  - checkout information, processes and ease of use to market standard.

The great mall of China

China is on everyone's radar. The scale and size of the market makes it very attractive. However, it is quite possibly the most complicated international market to expand into.

While direct to consumer (D2C) has not historically been a large portion of the overall market, there are a growing number of brands launching their own direct channels in the market. WeChat, the Chinese social media mobile application, is also the game changer for driving D2C sales. D2C is also a driver for consumer engagement and the ability for businesses to showcase their brand effectively, which is impossible on crowded marketplace sites.

The Tmall marketplace is the dominant player in the Chinese market and should be the first channel for any brand that wants reach and exposure. It has around 56 per cent of the total market. JD.com is another with around 22 per cent of the market and this should be considered, along with a direct online offer in China, to reinforce the brand proposition (Chadha, 2017). Margins have been a challenge as marketplaces have generally been discount driven.

However, according to a 2016 KPMG report, Chinese consumers are now more likely to be loyal to a company that has excellent customer support (51.8 per cent) compared to those who offer special promotions to loyal customers (43.7 per cent). Trustworthiness and customer service are more important drivers. An ongoing issue for brand owners is counterfeit goods. In the past two years, the government has led a crackdown on fakes and counterfeit products in order to prop up the local market confidence in buying products domestically.

There are key trading peaks in online:

Singles Day 11/11 This is the single biggest trading day in China, generating US $25.3 billion sales in 2017; 90 per cent of the sales were made on a mobile device (Russell, 2017).

Double 12 Day 12/12 This is another big e-commerce day and the autumn moon festival, mid-September is another important holiday for small gift giving (CIW, 2016).

With 70.1 per cent buying online because they trust global brands more than smaller or local brands, there may never have been a better time for international retailers to add China to their road map (KPMG, 2016).

US brands need to travel better

US brands definitely have an opportunity, if not a necessity, to extend their reach into new geographical markets. However, in a general sense, they must get smarter at how they localize their propositions.

Many go for English-language markets to begin with, the UK and Australia being prime targets. Effective entry digitally is not as easy as it first appears. A few of the key considerations that US brands need to get right are:

- Do they have brand awareness? They might have hundreds of stores in their domestic US market, but do customers in the new markets know who they are, what they stand for and what their customer value proposition is?

- Best Buy attempted to replicate its big-box proposition from its domestic US market. They ended up closing their stores in China, Turkey and Europe. In China, one of the challenges was failing to differentiate its product lines from local retailers (International Business Guide, 2013).

- Size matters – US apparel sizes are different from the UK, which in turn are different from Europe. You must get these right otherwise you will negatively impact conversion rates and drive a significant percentage of returns.

- Mind your language – American English is not the same as UK or Australian English. In fact, Australians also have terms unique to them. For example, a thong in the UK is underwear/knickers, in Australia it is a pair of flip flops! Fall in the US, which in the UK is the autumn season, means to fall down in the UK!

- Australia is counter-seasonal. They are in the southern hemisphere. Their summer is winter in the UK and in the United States. So, you need a very different range of products than those for sale in your domestic market.

- Do you expect UK or Australian consumers to pay duties and taxes on top of the cost of the product, when they will often be able to buy comparable products in their own market without these costs added?

- Do you think UK and Australian consumers want to pay in $US or £GBP and $AUS?

- How will you manage customer service? You are in a very different time zone from both of these countries.

When it goes wrong and why

Expectations can be too high on the financial return. It takes time to build up, particularly if you have no or limited brand awareness. Therefore, you need patience and the backing of the board to stay with it.

Underestimation of investment cost – internationalization online is not cheap. You have a whole host of things to think about that will require investment. These include:

- resource/head count;
- translation (ongoing);
- adapting your technology to support local payment types;
- changing the front-end customer experience where necessary;

- marketing: both acquisition and retention costs;
- managing reverse logistics (returns);
- fulfilment;
- customer service.

Key blockers

- Lack of localization: this is the main cause and effect of underperformance.
- Marketing in the wrong areas: you need to test and learn quickly.
- Not enough resource – as outlined above.
- Weak brand recognition – it takes investment to build a brand in a new market, often in above-the-line advertising and more traditional media.
- Lack of buy-in at all levels – along with marketing budgets, international is often the thing that suffers from a reduction in investment when the business is having to 'cut its cloth'. Not everyone buys into the opportunity in the first place. Therefore, it is vital that you ensure that you engage with a broad set of stakeholders across the business to take them on the journey with you, and for them to understand what the opportunity is.

Top practical customer experience tips

The 11Cs of internationalization:

1 Choose the right *country* to expand into.

2 Understand local market *consumer behaviour*.

3 Localize customer *communication*.

4 Localize for *culture and climate*.

5 Offer localized *customer service*.

6 Understand the value chain and proposition of your *competitors*.

7 Offer the appropriate *currency and payment types*.

8 Know what good *conversion* looks like and how to deliver it.

9 Consider the most appropriate *channels to market*.

10 Think localized *content*.

11 *Crew*: consider staff resourcing and structure for internationalization.

Additional tip: determine how you will gain trust in new markets. These points are expanded on below.

The 11Cs of internationalization

I created a framework for internationalization a number of years ago that still holds good today to consider the opportunity and challenges for internationalization. It also works well when considering what the customer experience should be. Published with kind permission of Econsultancy (January 2012), the full article, titled 'The internationalization of e-commerce: a best practice guide', can be accessed here: https://econsultancy.com/reports/the-internationalisation-of-e-commerce. It is called the 11Cs of internationalization (see 'Top practical customer experience tips' box above, and see the expanded details below).

Choose the right *country* to expand into

Table 11.2 Country prioritization framework

For Review	Considerations
Competitor analysis	Size of opportunity: local market brands and foreign companies with marketshare
Pricing strategy	Look at similar products in market for customer price point expectations
Distribution and logistics	Shipping costs, import duties, returns facilities, local partners
Language expectations	Cost of fully translated sites vs countries trading in English
Existing awareness	Number of visitors to site currently, existing wholesale partners
Marketing costs	Review by territory for PR costs, PPC costs etc
Case studies	Review of like brands and their experiences vs paving the way
Size of opportunity and need	Review suitability of product to market.

Understand local market *consumer behaviour*

Market analysis has to be clear about customer segmentation, and how relevant and closely aligned your product or service offer is with local customers:

- broadband/mobile penetration;
- credit card/PayPal usage;
- fulfilment/delivery expectations;
- demographic, lifestyle factors, behaviour.

Localize customer *communication*

- Marketing, customer service and content.
- Is local language content necessary? If so, users will likely expect local-language customer service too.
- Will you use internal local language resource or third parties only? The costs for different countries will affect ROI.
- Even with in-house resource you will likely need in-country marketing/PR support to ensure the plan is optimized.

Localize for *culture and climate*

- In Sweden, functionality and speed are the most important features. In France, the focus is on design.
- There are basic operational issues to consider too – public holidays, working hours etc.
- There are bigger strategic questions about whether you need to localize the product range too.

Offer localized *customer service*

- How will you handle customer orders and queries from multiple time zones?
- The hours of operation might be affected by going into markets in different time zones.

- How many languages can your own customer service team support?
- Shipping and the last mile of delivery.

Understand the value chain and proposition of your *competitors*

Consider marketing, market share and positioning in order to understand how to gain a competitive advantage against:

- local competitors;
- other international online competitors.

Offer the appropriate *currency and payment types*

- Germans pay by ELV or direct debit.
- Scandinavians like cash on delivery (COD).
- The Chinese used to favour COD but this is changing fast.
- Can your payment service provider cater for all the methods customers will wish to use?

Know what good *conversion* looks like and how to deliver it

- What KPIs should you expect in different countries? Do the KPIs themselves differ?
- How do you reassure customers that you are a trustworthy business to buy from?

Consider the most appropriate *channels to market*

- If you have stores in the country, will you provide cross-channel services?
- How will direct selling online impact your relationship with local wholesalers and franchise partners?

- What kind of mobile proposition should you provide? In the Netherlands, for example, smartphone penetration is high, but mobile transactions low.
- Marketplaces.

Think localized *content*

- It is not just language that needs changing – you will also need a content strategy appropriate to each market you wish to target.
- Your CMS should allow you appropriate levels of access and control over the content created.

Crew: consider staff resourcing and structure for internationalization

- How are you going to resource the team?
- Can you do it all from your central office?
- Localized language/service.
- Localized marketing.

Determine how you will gain trust in new markets

- Tell them how long you have been established.
- If you have got stores in your home market, shout about them. They provide credibility.
- Provide a contact number on the homepage of your website.

Over to Professor Malcolm McDonald

The following considerations are relevant to any organization thinking about international marketing:

- Whether to market abroad.
- How to choose where to market abroad.
- How to succeed, once there.

The first of these questions is the most important and is represented by box three of the well-known Ansoff Matrix (1980): Market Extension. As mentioned in this chapter, it is riskier to enter new markets than to introduce new products to markets where customers know you and where your brand name is trusted. But assuming you have decided to enter new international markets, the next question concerns where to market abroad.

This should be an easy question to answer, as there will be some countries where the opportunities for success are greater than others and where you have more opportunities to be competitive. But it is prudent to be totally logical about this question and, as Martin has pointed out, if you are an international brand, it would be foolhardy to ignore markets such as China. Once there, success will depend entirely on traditional marketing processes, which I will now spell out.

International marketing, at its simplest, is the performance of the marketing task across national boundaries. The basic approach, however, is no different from domestic marketing and the principles involved remain the same. Thus, a supplier has to perform market research, identify a target market, develop appropriate products, adopt a suitable pricing policy, promote sales, and so on. In spite of this, whenever organizations begin to operate outside their domestic markets, mainly otherwise successful enterprises seem to suffer.

This has led both academics and practitioners to wonder why. On examination, what becomes clear is that although the principles are the same, the context is different and adopting a similar mindset for the international marketplace as for a domestic market can create problems. What emerges, then, is the significance of the differences rather than the similarities involved when marketing abroad. Within this, it becomes important to recognize that the control it is possible to exercise over the marketing mix is reduced, depending on how the supplier enters the market. Let me start by summarizing just some of the environmental factors that have to be taken account of, shown in Table 11.3.

Table 11.3 Environmental factors affecting global marketing

Environmental factor	Example
Legal systems	Contrast between common law, civil law and law based on religious systems
Political ideology of the government	Ranging from totalitarian dictatorships to liberal democracies

(continued)

Table 11.3   (*Continued*)

Environmental factor	Example
Historical links	Can be both positive and negative. Former colonies often have beneficial links, whilst long-standing national rivalries can create difficulties
Attitude towards foreign investment	Some counties encourage it with financial inducements while others make it conditional requiring, say, technological exchange
North/South cultural divide	Most areas of the world see differences in attitude and behaviour and consumption
Technological infrastructure	Can include transport, telecommunications, research establishments, access to sources of power and so on
Economic development	The degree of industrialization will usually affect levels of prosperity, infrastructure development, public health and so on
Role and influence of government	Some governments legislate widely, such as Singapore, while others have low levels of state enterprise and intervention, such as the United States

As one example, the United States is a highly developed free market economy that has a strong car culture and distinctive shopping habits. Tesco moved into this market in spite of a similar move having proved a nightmare for both Marks & Spencer and Sainsbury's before it. They introduced a new brand, Fresh and Easy stores, modelled on the Tesco Express stores in Britain, and majored on a limited range of 'wholesome food that doesn't cost your whole pay cheque'. However, local stores for major grocery shopping were counter-culture: highly competitive markets promoted choice as an expectation for the US consumer, and focusing on price and convenience is what Americans do better than anyone else. Tesco eventually withdrew with losses approaching £1 billion. Listed below are some other factors making marketing internationally more complex:

- language;
- tastes and fashions;
- packaging requirements;
- physical environment (temperature, humidity);

- power supplies;
- security arrangements;
- family structure and size;
- business hours;
- what is polite and impolite;
- social niceties;
- literacy levels;
- communications infrastructure;
- distribution practices;
- methods of transaction.

Nonetheless, the principles for success are always the same and are as follows:

- Understand the market in depth.
- Target needs-based segments.
- Make a specific offer to each segment.
- Have clear differentiation, positioning and branding.

With these rules, wherever you trade in the world, you will be successful.

References

Ansoff, H I (1980) Strategic issue management, *Strategic Management Journal*, **1** (2), pp 131–48

Chadha, R (2017) [accessed 1 December 2017] Alibaba's Tmall Maintains Reign Over China's Retail e-Commerce [Online] https://retail. emarketer.com/article/alibabas-tmall-maintains-reign-over-chinas-retail-ecommerce/58ada2369c13e50c186f6f32

CIW (2016) [accessed 1 December 2017] Alibaba Double 12 Promotion Focuses on Social Commerce in 2016 [Online] https://www.chinainternetwatch. com/19392/alibaba-double-12-2016/

Hughes, I (2016) [accessed 1 December 2017] Key Considerations for Targeting the German eCommerce Market [Online] https://www.salesoptimize.com/ german-ecommerce-market/

International Business Guide (2013) [accessed 19 December 2017] 10 Successful American Businesses That Have Failed Overseas [Online] https://www. internationalbusinessguide.org/10-successful-american-businesses-that-have-failed-overseas/

KPMG (2016) [accessed 1 December 2017] China's Connected Consumers 2016 [Online] https://assets.kpmg.com/content/dam/kpmg/cn/pdf/en/2016/11/china-s-connected-consumer-2016.pdf

Newman, M (2012) [accessed 15 June 2018] The Internationalisation of E-commerce: A best practice guide. London: Econsultancy [Online] https://econsultancy.com/reports/the-internationalisation-of-e-commerce

Russell, J (2017) [accessed 2 May 2018] Alibaba Smashes Its Single's Day Record Once Again as Sales Cross $25 Billion, *TechCrunch* [Online] https://techcrunch.com/2017/11/11/alibaba-smashes-its-singles-day-record/

UPS (2017) [accessed 12 December 2017] Pulse of the Online Shopper [Online] https://solutions.ups.com/ups-pulse-of-the-online-shopper-LP.html?WT.mc_id=VAN701693

Customer-centric 12 marketing communications

WHAT YOU WILL LEARN IN THIS CHAPTER

- How the mix of marketing communications has changed and what that means for skill sets and activity.
- Growth hacking explained, and the opportunity it offers.
- The opportunities presented by proximity marketing.
- The evolving customer journey, and what that means for acquisition activity.
- The owned, bought/paid and earned touchpoints on the customer journey.

How times have changed. In 2005, above-the-line advertising would still be the first thing you thought of when it came to acquiring new customers. Google AdWords was still relatively nascent. While above the line still has an important role to play, primarily from a brand awareness perspective, digital marketing channels are the key drivers for customer acquisition and retention.

Loyalty by default involves focusing on a narrower set of existing customers. However, I fundamentally disagree with the core point I keep hearing about loyalty – that somehow loyalty is dead, it doesn't deliver value any more. The notion that somehow loyalty has run its course. I disagree because consumers have never really been that loyal. Not because they do not want to be, but because they have not seen the value of being loyal to one brand or another.

Retailers, CPG brands, travel companies, financial services providers and key players in other verticals have struggled to understand what drives loyalty. It must be more than some crude points-based programme. It also must add value in more ways than simply offering an incentive off the next purchase. I would argue that loyalty has yet to deliver the value that consumers seek; therefore, in terms of cause and effect, it has underdelivered and as a result consumer behaviour has aligned itself with this, whereby consumers have become inherently disloyal.

Will better, more rounded, well-thought-through loyalty and CRM programmes make a difference? Yes, they will. But businesses need to go further. They need to stop thinking of themselves in the traditional context that they 'sell stuff' and 'sell services' and move to a model whereby they behave like a customer service business that just happens to sell stuff or sell services. That is an entirely different way of working and behaving. It is one that both existing and new customers would take far more seriously, as they would begin to realize how much they really like the business in question and how much that business cares about them. It is a whole new customer value proposition.

Let's not forget the value of loyal customers. It is what we call the Pareto effect. Most businesses generate a sizable percentage of their sales from a small percentage of the customer base. If I were a consumer-facing business generating 70–80 per cent of my sales from 20–25 per cent of my customers, I would want to know who the 20–25 per cent were, what made them so loyal and how I could find more customers just like them. This would influence where I invested my budget.

So, what has really changed with marketing communications strategy? After all, most of the basic principles stay true:

- You need to identify who the customer is. Of course, as discussed earlier, there are many different types of customers, not just one overarching customer segment or persona. The key is to identify a small number of segments or cohorts that you can focus on and where you can create a proposition that resonates for them.

- You need to work out how to get them into your store or onto your website.

- You need to understand the new channels that can help you to broaden your reach and drive more effective customer acquisition, including Google shopping and programmatic marketing.

- You need to know how to leverage 'growth hacking': working around the edges to get cheap viral marketing.

- You must understand that social media is too important only to be considered a part of marketing communications. While it is a marcoms channel or channels, it is far more strategic than that. See Chapter 14 for a full definition of the strategic role that social media should play in your business.

Growth hacking in more detail

Traditional marketing communications have a number of objectives, including increasing brand awareness. Growth hacking is focused on growth in the customer database, and subsequently growth of sales and profitability. By default, it is a 'test and learn'-led approach to lower-cost, high-growth marketing initiatives.

Growth hackers would argue that it is a mindset and not a tool set. It is a state of mind that has to permeate the organization in order to be effective.

To follow are a few examples of growth hacking.

Facebook's growth hack

Facebook is the largest social network in the world, with approximately 1.9 billion monthly active users. Facebook used growth hacking to drive engagement and new subscribers. They leveraged e-mail notification to drive significant levels of participation. Consumers were receiving e-mails stating that they had been tagged on Facebook. This drove an incredibly high level of activation and response with huge numbers signing up (Growth Hackers, nd).

Airbnb

When Airbnb launched, their objective was to scale quickly and grow their user base. To achieve this, they hatched an ingenious scheme whereby users who posted their property on Airbnb were given the option of adding the advert to Craigslist. Given that Craigslist had a huge database of millions of users, this gave Airbnb access to a large potential audience. When the user's post was uploaded to Craigslist there was a link that brought you back to Airbnb. This growth-hacking initiative enabled Airbnb to quickly scale its user base by tapping into someone else's customer base (Walsh, 2015).

Dropbox

Dropbox came up with a smart plan to leverage existing customers to drive customer acquisition through a referral scheme. Dropbox gave extra storage space to both the referrer and the new customer. This gains engagement and investment from the users in their core product (Veerasamy, 2014).

Hotmail

Hotmail developed a highly effective growth hack. They placed a message and hyperlink at the end of each Hotmail e-mail message distributed saying 'PS: I love you. Get your free e-mail at Hotmail.' Therefore, they were leveraging their customer base, who were unaware that they were inadvertently promoting Hotmail to the recipients of their e-mails to sign up for Hotmail accounts. It leveraged its own channel for free advertising and acquired a huge number of new users in the process (Card, 2017).

Ticketmaster

Ticketmaster has successfully used a timed countdown to create 'urgency' to encourage users to buy tickets more quickly. This hack has worked well to fuel growth (Kentico.com, nd).

Capabilities and skills required in modern-day marketing

Despite the ever-increasing marketing technology in play, including machine learning and programmatic, good digital marketers can help to ensure that you maximize the ROI from all of your activity. The challenge here is that digital marketers have not grown up in the traditional world. They have grown up on data, measurement and ROI.

Digital marketers have no idea about brand awareness as they are not measured on the top of funnel, only on conversion. Arguably, they are too focused on return on advertising spend (ROAS). Digital marketers know they need to do more up the funnel to build awareness but are not working with the right tools, eg paid search and display. The two functions can help each other, but most of the focus is on the one that can be directly measured, eg paid search.

Ultimately these sets of creative and analytical marketers need to join together, plan together and agree what the role of each marketing channel is in creating awareness, consideration and then purchase. Currently, marketing skills are too siloed. You work in social media or you are a paid search or search engine marketing (SEM) expert. Of course, this is not only about skill sets; the cause and effect is also due to businesses having too much focus on ROI and the business case. This leads to a decrease in investment in both test and learn as well as brand-building activities. The flipside of the challenge facing digital marketers is the challenge facing those from a traditional marketing background. TV has moved into programmatic. The focus is about reach and exposure rather than selling things. Traditional marketers understand econometrics but not so much data.

Marketing should be fun

An underutilized marketing channel is live video streaming. It doesn't only work for events. Consumers have high levels of engagement with live video streaming, primarily because it's real. It also makes your customers feel special and can be a very effective sales and conversion driver, particularly when it adds value to the customer by giving them a sneak peek at new products, or an inside view of your brand. We all crave authenticity, and live video streaming delivers this. Yes, it is risky, but it also enables a brand to show a 'human face' and, to some degree, vulnerability, which in this day and age of programmatic, machine learning and AI, can be no bad thing. It also plays to the big new trend of 'conversational commerce'.

You can leverage advocates of your brand to talk about why they love you and, in doing so, remind your customers of what makes you great and promote offers to them. Mark Zuckerberg, founder of Facebook, said at their earnings call in July 2016 that we are moving into a video-first world with video 'at the heart of all our apps and services' (Zuckerberg, 2016). Cisco said that by 2019 they expect 80 per cent of the world's internet traffic to be around video (Cisco, 2017).

Don't underestimate the value of viral marketing

Growth hacking is not the only driver of viral marketing. For the first 20 years of Ted Baker's life, the brand did not conduct any above-the-line advertising. Their shop windows were the core customer acquisition activity. What they lost out on in terms of reach through traditional media, they more than made up for by arguably pulling in more passing trade than other retailers, while also fuelling word of mouth driven by the often quirky and highly engaging retail theatre taking place both in the windows and instore. Craig Smith, now Digital Commerce Director, who was the Brand Communications Director previously, told me about how this played to the 'mystique' behind the brand. People often ask, who is Ted Baker? Ted Baker recognizes the role that digital marketing has to play and invests in different digital marketing activity to both drive sales online as well as footfall into its stores.

Proximity marketing: get closer to your customers at the 'moment of intent'

One of the relatively untapped marketing opportunities is in proximity marketing.

This is leveraged when a customer is either in – or in the vicinity of – a physical premises. I believe this will become far more pervasive than it is in 2018. After all, it has much to offer consumer-led businesses in terms of convincing someone while they are in the vicinity of a restaurant, a store or a car dealership. It can drive conversion both when a consumer has intent to make a purchase and also drive a spontaneous purchase decision. Web-push proximity marketing via smartphone devices is many times more effective than e-mail marketing. Yet, the vast majority of consumer-led businesses have yet to even trial web-push and proximity marketing. As we move towards the era of conversational commerce and voice-activated search, data and review structures will become hugely important as we will be even more influenced by what others like us felt about the restaurant or hotel we are looking to book. 'Find me the best restaurant nearby' or 'the best fashion shop for me' will require rethinking how we market ourselves.

Sumo group have found that the open rate of a web-push message is 46 per cent and click-through rate is 6.3 per cent compared to e-mail at a 17 per cent open rate and 2.3 per cent click-through rate – meaning 2.7x more people will open and click a web-push message (Sumo Group, 2017).

From 2005 to 2015, US department store sales declined by 31.2 per cent. Therefore, proximity marketing has a big role to play in both ensuring it helps to drive customer acquisition by targeting customers in the vicinity of their stores with relevant promotions and messaging, but also doing like-wise when customers are instore. Proximity marketing can help to drive conversion as well as increase average order values and the units per trans-action instore (Proximity Directory, 2017).

Ninety per cent of all consumers have a subscription through a proximity marketing business, where they can access coupons, promotions and special offers. So, clearly there is demand for proximity marketing solutions that add value to the customer. US retailers are earlier adopters of proximity marketing solutions than other countries. Walmart began implementing proximity marketing solutions in 2014 and Target a year later in 2015. Macy's has proximity solutions in all of its stores.

Proximity technologies also enable retailers and other consumer-facing businesses to do what they can already do online – and that is to more accurately track customer behaviour and adapt the footprint of the store to more effectively meet customer needs.

Here are some use cases, courtesy of Proximity Directory, of successful proximity marketing initiatives:

1 Mondelez International (Cadbury), teamed up with Mac's convenience stores in Canada (owned by Couche-Tard). They ran six types of offers over 30 days for customers who were logged into the Wi-Fi: 3,244 customers opted in; 14 per cent who received a coupon redeemed it. Customers who participated returned to their local Mac's 25 per cent more frequently than previously. Therefore, it drove an uplift in conversion, as well as retention.

2 Proximus, the electronics retailer in Belgium, leveraged 10 beacons around their store in Antwerp to message customers who had installed their 'MyProximus app' and grab their attention with a promotion offering different free gadgets, from selfie sticks to bracelets. This attracted 640,000 active users of the application.

3 Unilever and Magnum ran a proximity marketing campaign to promote the new Magnum pop-up stores. This saw over 85,000 push notifications being sent, of which 3,279 users opened the notifications and 1,785 users visited the store. This amounted to a conversion rate of 54 per cent of those who opened the push notifications.

(Proximity Directory, 2017)

'See now, buy now' fuels instant gratification

Although not the sole domain of proximity marketing, the rise of 'see now, buy now' has become a driver for instant gratification. This has been prevalent in fashion with a 'shop the runway' proposition. While previously fashion shows were the environment for designers to showcase their talent, often with products that would never see mass production, nowadays they can do both. They can showcase unique individualistic pieces but they can also show more wearable styles, both of which customers can 'buy now'.

I experienced this first hand when I was a guest of Alibaba's as a global retail and e-commerce influencer, at their Singles Day, 'global shopping festival'. During their gala, which is the lead-up on the evening before the event kicks off, they have many international and local pop stars, sports stars and other celebrities who appear and perform; they push the products worn by the celebrities or the products being highlighted to consumers on their Tmall mobile apps. This leads to a big spike in demand for these specific items.

Where do I invest my paid search budget?

Let's not forget that the majority of product searches start on Amazon now as opposed to Google. This is a game changer, both in terms of where you will maximize your reach through search but also where your brand and products need to appear in the first place.

Figure 12.1 The customer

Voice-activated search will also play a role here and has much potential. However, you are going to have to pay to be higher up the listings when someone asks their Amazon Echo (Alexa), Tmall's Genie or Google's Home, 'What wine should I buy for my meal tonight?' or 'Where can I find the best TV?'

Whatever activity you implement, make sure to send customers to landing pages with relevant content relating to the advert that took customers there in the first place.

Marketing is too often a silo

Many companies operate on a siloed channel basis. I believe everything is connected and, in order to drive growth, a holistic approach to planning cross-media and e-commerce is essential (see Figure 12.1). Acquisition and retention teams must work hand in hand with e-commerce traders to ensure every paid click is optimized to convert and return.

Attribution should lead to integration of teams and activity

PR departments, once used to just dealing with journalists and PR, are now having to work in the world of digital blogging. Yet the metrics have changed. This is not just about reach and awareness, but blogger outreach plays a key role in driving inbound links for SEO. Many consumer-facing businesses' marketing teams work completely separately from their digital SEO department, seeing SEO as dirty – using things such as 'keyword stuffing' – so they are reluctant to work together (and due to the differences in how they have both grown up and been trained are unaware of how to work together, nor what the benefits are of doing so).

Most director-level marketing leaders are traditional marketers. While many have valiantly attempted to embrace the new digital world, for most it has passed them by. They never implemented digital and therefore do not fully understand it. I think this is the biggest change to marketing – leaders who want to manage an effective organization need to recognize their own marketing skill gaps and ensure that teams are aligned and working together, thinking about the customer journey when planning their marketing spend, not the channel. This requires leaders to be brave – to get basic analytics training – to understand the KPIs that they are measuring their digital teams on and to understand how their creative and analytical marketers can work together better. With a minority of traditional marketers, some have gone too far into digital marketing and forgotten the importance of brand and above-the-line advertising. Of course, the customer doesn't care about any of this. All they care about is receiving joined-up marketing communications that add value to them!

You need to focus on all aspects of the customer funnel (Figure 12.2) to be successful online. With all the trading levers within your control, fast growth becomes more achievable. Marketing experience allows you to use the right channels for customer growth, not just the obvious ones, and your focus on retention ensures those customers return. Focus on data, analytics and user experience, to ensure you are experts at identifying and removing conversion blockers. Always look to maximize the customer experience to boost satisfaction and encourage repeat purchase.

As we discussed above and also in Chapter 7 when we talked about organizational design, one of the starting points to develop truly customer-centric marketing is to ensure that you have your digital, and more traditional, brand marketing functions working hand in glove. Otherwise the customer will not get the benefit of receiving consistent communications across all touchpoints with your business. To put this into context (see Figure 12.3), the path customers take is no longer linear.

Figure 12.2   The customer funnel

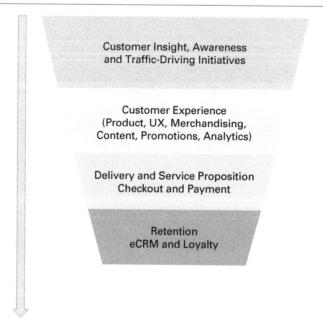

SOURCE Practicology

Figure 12.3 Consumer digital touchpoints

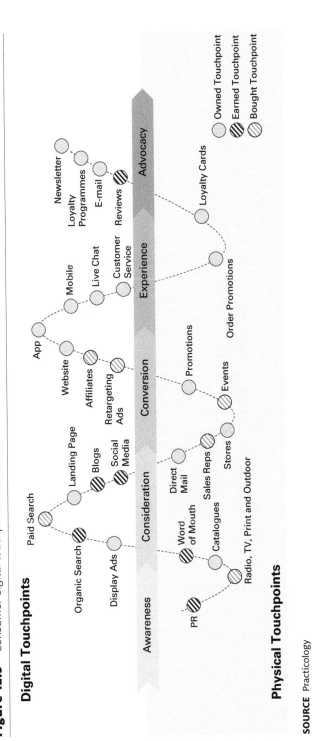

Digital Touchpoints

Organic Search

Paid Search

Display Ads

Landing Page

Blogs

Social Media

App

Website

Affiliates

Retargeting Ads

Mobile

Live Chat

Customer Service

Newsletter

Loyalty Programmes

E-mail

Reviews

Awareness

Consideration

Conversion

Experience

Advocacy

PR

Word of Mouth

Catalogues

Direct Mail

Sales Reps

Stores

Radio, TV, Print and Outdoor

Promotions

Events

Order Promotions

Loyalty Cards

Owned Touchpoint

Earned Touchpoint

Bought Touchpoint

Physical Touchpoints

SOURCE Practicology

The customer's path to purchase is no longer linear. Therefore, thinking of marketing communications in traditional terms such as 'above the line', 'below the line' or 'through the line' is not helpful in relation to thinking about the skills you need and the activity required to effectively acquire customers. Maybe a new way of thinking of it is 'inline'. The path to purchase might not be linear, but the line exists. It is just not straightforward any more! Thinking about being 'inline' with the customer's journey helps to ensure that you target them through the appropriate channel and methodology at the right point in their journey.

You will need to reach different customer segments through your own touchpoints, including your website, stores, contact centre; through touchpoints that you have bought such as advertising; and through earned touchpoints, including user reviews, PR and social media.

As a segway to social media, my local barber, Ego, in north London, who cut my hair every few weeks, have hundreds of thousands of followers on Instagram. They only have one salon but they have leveraged the fact they do some amazing haircuts as well as cut a fair number of soccer players' hair. They regularly post pictures and videos of their clients' haircuts. It is quite a phenomenal level of engagement for a business with only five staff! However, if you were thinking about going somewhere new to get your hair cut, they tick all the boxes in terms of making it obvious that they are really good at what they do and can cater for any potential style requirement you might have.

The moral of this story and of brands such as AO.com, who sell white goods and electricals, is that you don't have to invest $millions in marketing communications. Yossi Erdman, former Head of Brand and Social Media for AO.com, has told me they have 40 per cent monthly engagement on social media, which equates to hundreds of thousands of customers. Therefore, you can drive a lot of word of mouth/word of web by engaging customers with relevant content that inspires, educates and entertains them.

Don't shoot the messenger

Messenger apps are all the rage. Consumers are engaging with them in their billions. In July 2016, Facebook Messenger hit 1 billion messenger app users (Facebook, 2016). WeChat is the leading messaging app in Asia and is growing its user base globally. They have created a truly unique ecosystem, whereby WeChat is your Facebook, Messenger, Tinder, Twitter and numerous other apps wrapped up into one. It will be very interesting to see how the incumbent titans, including Facebook and Google, react to the threat and the opportunity this customer value proposition creates.

Beware of 'driverless marketing'

As we are increasingly served by AI chat bots, algorithms and machine learning, we expose ourselves to the risks of unethical advertising being served up – or, to put it another way, your brand being seen alongside content you would consider to be inappropriate. Take the challenge that YouTube faced whereby brands' adverts were appearing sometimes next to highly inappropriate content such as extremist videos (Grierson, 2017). Manual intervention would have helped to avoid this. If we leave everything to algorithms and machines, these sorts of issues will happen again.

It's not what you know, but who you know that counts

You need to decide upon which platform and which influencers will help you spread your message most effectively to the broadest but most relevant audience. Bloggers, vloggers and key opinion leaders (KOLs) carry huge influence. They have an army of followers who hang on to their every word and to all their recommendations. It is no surprise, therefore, that brands are tripping over themselves to have them promote their products or services.

Traditional marketing tools can play a big part

I have previously mentioned Metro Bank in the UK, of whom I'm a big fan. It is interesting how banks and many other organizations chain their pens to the counter so that customers don't take them. Metro Bank's pens are branded and they give away over 1 million a year! Not a bad piece of brand awareness don't you think?

Chat to my bot

I will discuss chat bots in more detail in Chapter 15 on AI. Suffice to say, automation is going to be used more and marketers should be thinking about how to target customers within these environments. More retailers are using automated chat bots to pre-empt customer questions. What can marketers do to leverage chat bots to learn more about customers and their behaviour and to ensure more effective messaging and conversion?

Top practical customer experience tips

1 Ensure you have the right mix of digital and brand-building and awareness activity.

2 Drive the attribution of all marketing activity: ensure you have the right mix of skills, and ideally in a more integrated and less siloed structure.

3 Make sure to focus on customer retention as well as acquisition.

4 Be clear about the customer's journey and where the owned, bought and earned touchpoints with the customer come into play and what your approach will be for each.

5 Think about growth hacking and how you can leverage viral marketing to more cost-effectively spread the word.

6 Look at leveraging proximity marketing to provide a better instore experience for customers.

7 Focus on experiential marketing as this will drive the engagement and involvement with your brand, products and services.

Expanded on below.

Ensure you have the right mix of digital and brand-building and awareness activity

The two go hand in hand. In most cases, I believe, businesses are still under-investing in digital marketing.

In a blog post, Forrester's VanBoskirk said investment in paid search, display advertising, social media advertising, online video advertising and e-mail marketing will pace to 46 per cent of all advertising in five years (VanBoskirk et al, 2017). Bearing in mind that the majority of store visits start on your company website, a digital environment, digital marketing can not only be used to drive traffic to your website but also footfall into your stores. That said, above-the-line advertising still has a part to play. It builds and maintains brand awareness and, with the opportunity to localize regionally and sometimes even targeted more locally than that, it can now be much more effective as a driver of sales and performance.

According to Forrester's latest US digital marketing forecast, over the next five years they see marketing budgets moving away from quantity to quality with a focus on brand, customer and instore experience (VanBoskirk et al, 2017).

Drive the attribution of all marketing activity: ensure that you have the right mix of skills, and ideally in a more integrated and less siloed structure

Most businesses have separate brand marketing and digital marketing teams. This cannot possibly help to ensure that the customer receives integrated and joined-up marketing communications, as both teams will invariably have different objectives and KPIs.

Make sure to focus on customer retention as well as acquisition

How many consumer-facing businesses do you know that have the job title Head of Customer Retention? In my experience, incredibly few do. Why would we focus all of our time, attention and most of our budget on acquiring customers and so little on retaining them? On building a relationship with them? Or at the very least, trying our best to stay a bit closer to them? It will always be more cost-effective to retain a customer than to acquire a new one, many of whom lapse fairly quickly. See Chapter 17 on key drivers for CRM.

Be clear about the customer's journey and where the owned, bought and earned touchpoints with the customer come into play and what your approach will be for each

Effective customer acquisition and retention requires the understanding that, as highlighted earlier in this chapter, the customer's path and journey is no longer linear. They will touch your business in different ways at different times.

Some of these touchpoints will be owned by you, such as your stores, your website, your contact centre; some will be bought, including TV or radio advertising; and others will be earned – these include user reviews, word of mouth etc.

Think about growth hacking and how you can leverage viral marketing to more cost-effectively spread the word

Who would not want to have lots of customers sharing their marketing communications and talking about their products or services? There are lots of opportunities to drive viral and word-of-mouth marketing; these include a fear of missing out, referral programmes and benefitting from a great deal.

Look at leveraging proximity marketing to provide a better instore experience for customers

We're all on the move these days and we're all using our mobile while we're doing so. Therefore, proximity marketing provides the best opportunity to drive both spontaneous purchase, or conversion, when customers are either in your store, showroom or office premises or when they are passing nearby.

Focus on experiential marketing as this will drive the engagement and involvement with your brand, products and services

Experiential marketing essentially boils down to getting customers to interact with your brand, product or marketing communications and to deliver an engaging experience in the process, one that they are unlikely to forget too quickly.

An extreme example of this is when skydiver Felix Baumgartner did the world's highest ever skydive. Sponsored by Red Bull, he dived from 24 miles above earth. The event was promoted for over a year beforehand and was arguably one of the most talked-about events during 2012. It also generated a huge amount of coverage on broadcast media.

Added-value experiences drive participation and participation drives engagement, and engagement delivers a return on involvement.

Over to Professor Malcolm McDonald

As pointed out in this chapter, we have fabulous new tools to help inform our commercial efforts, but, at the strategic level, the same age-old challenges remain – market understanding, segmentation, branding, insight, positioning, customer engagement, customer retention and, of course, understanding who are the 20 per cent of customers that account for 80 per cent of our business and how we can anticipate and satisfy their needs better than our competitors.

Having said this, however, these new tools, if understood and integrated, can take segmentation to different levels of sophistication to strengthen everything an organization does, from R&D right through to after-sales service. Incorporating product and brand-specific usage, attitudes and needs can make developing a far more nuanced segmentation possible, complemented by the new age of AI marketing and predictive analytics on consumer choice. Such a highly segmented approach will be needed to win and retain customer relationships.

To summarize, whatever the technological changes that are available now and the inevitable, continuous evolution of these over the next few years, it will always be about understanding your customers and their motivations. The customer of the future will expect you to interact with them more intelligently. It is certainly not about just remembering their birthday!

They will expect you to know about every single touchpoint they have had across sales, marketing and customer experience – and use that data to streamline brand messaging across multiple channels and to build up a picture of them as a prelude to offering them better service. They will disregard brands that do not do them this fundamental courtesy.

Martin provided one of the best figures I have seen for a long time in this chapter. To close this chapter, take a look back at Figure 12.3 on consumer digital touchpoints, an invaluable step to your customer-centric integration.

References

Card, J (2017) [accessed 15 December 2017] What is Growth Hacking and How Can It Help Your SME? [Online] http://www.telegraph.co.uk/connect/small-business/innovation/what-is-growth-hacking-and-how-can-it-help-your-sme/

Cisco (2017) [accessed 1 December 2017] Cisco Visual Networking Index: Forecast and Methodology, 2016–2021 [Online] https://www.cisco.com/c/en/us/solutions/collateral/service-provider/visual-networking-index-vni/complete-white-paper-c11-481360.pdf

Facebook (2016) [accessed 1 December 2017] Thank You! ♥ Messenger [Online] https://newsroom.fb.com/news/2016/07/thank-you-messenger/

Grierson, J (2017) [accessed 1 December 2017] Google Summoned By Ministers as Government Pulls Ads Over Extremist Content [Online] https://www.theguardian.com/technology/2017/mar/17/google-ministers-quiz-placement-ads-extremist-content-youtube

Growth Hackers (nd) [accessed 1 December 2017] 33 Growth Hacking Examples to Get Inspiration Grom [Online] https://www.growth-hackers.net/growth-hacking-examples-inspiration/

Kentico.com (nd) [accessed 15 December 2017] Growth Hacking: Not Just for Startups [Online] https://www.kentico.com/en/product/resources/whitepapers/growth-hacking/growthhacking.pdf

Proximity Directory (2017) [accessed 1 December 2017] Proximity Marketing in Retail [Online] https://unacast.s3.amazonaws.com/Proximity.Directory_Q117_Report.pdf

Sumo Group, I (2017) [accessed 13 December 2017] 2017 Email Signup Benchmarks: Here's How Many Visitors Should Be Subscribing, *Sumo* [Online] https://sumo.com/stories/email-signup-benchmarks

VanBoskirk, S et al (2017) [accessed 18 December 2017] US Digital Marketing Forecast: 2016 to 2021 [Online] https://www.forrester.com/report/US+Digital+Marketing+Forecast+2016+To+2021/-/E-RES137095?utm_source=blog&utm_campaign=US_Digital_Marketing_Forecast&utm_medium=social

Veerasamy, V (2014) [accessed 15 December 2017] Dropbox's Referral Program – How They Got 4 Million Users In 15 Months [Online] https://www.referralcandy.com/blog/dropbox-referral-program/

Walsh, P (2015) [accessed 15 December 2017] It's Time Your Business Hired a Growth Hacker – Here's Why [Online] https://www.theguardian.com/small-business-network/2015/may/29/hire-growth-hacker-silicon-valley

Zuckerberg, M (2016) [accessed 1 December 2017] Facebook Reports Second Quarter 2016 Results [Online] https://investor.fb.com/investor-news/press-release-details/2016/Facebook-Reports-Second-Quarter-2016-Results/default.aspx

A new framework for the marketing mix

13

The Customer Mix or 6Ws

WHAT YOU WILL LEARN IN THIS CHAPTER

- You will learn why the 4Ps, the traditional Marketing Mix framework, is no longer relevant for how to address the needs of the modern multichannel consumer.
- I will provide you with a new framework that will enable you to think even more effectively about what it takes to put the customer first.
- It will highlight the importance of doing so and what the key levers are to deliver a customer-first strategy.

The '6Ws' framework

- **Who** or whom are you targeting?
- **Why** do they want to buy from you?
- **What** do they want to buy?
- **When** do they want to buy?
- **Where** do they want their order fulfilled?
- **What's** next? (What's in it for them if they buy from you?)

Is the Marketing Mix still meaningful?

Developed in 1960, the original Marketing Mix framework for creating a marketing strategy – as conceived by American academic E Jerome McCarthy – included four aspects (the 4Ps):

- product;
- price;
- place;
- promotion.

The above four aspects were subsequently complemented by three more aspects to make the 7Ps (McCarthy, 1960):

- people;
- process;
- physical evidence.

This framework continues to be espoused and used to this day. But is it fit for purpose in the internet age, when the balance of power has fundamentally shifted from suppliers (retailers and product manufacturers) in favour of consumers? In particular, is it fit for purpose for a multichannel retailer or any other consumer-facing brand? I don't think so, the main reason being that it is not customer-focused. The 'people' aspect of the 7Ps refers to staff, not customers. While it may have been a useful framework in its day, the Marketing Mix has never spoken to the fact that the customer is king.

EXPERT VIEW

Nadine Neatrour, Ecommerce Director, Revolution Beauty, told me that she believes retailers need to move away from being product led to being customer led. A good example she cited was when she was head of e-commerce at Thomas Pink, the premium shirt retailer. They were still buying and ranging shirts with cufflinks when customer data and behaviour suggested that customers actually wanted button cuffs. As a result, the business was unable to meet demand for these as it was so focused on shirts with cufflinks. This was a by-product of range planning based on what the business thought were the right products rather than range planning based on customer data, customer needs and customer segmentation.

Be a victim or a victor – you decide

Winning and retaining customers should be like going to war. It is a battle-field out there, requiring careful strategy and deliverance, with a lot at stake. There are many other businesses who will gladly poach your customers. Customers should consume your every waking moment, at least when you are at work. If they don't, then you are simply not working hard enough for them.

Amazon has a role in their team known as 'the customer experience bar raiser'. There is a bar raiser in every project and their role is to push the team and the approach to consider whether or not the project they are working on will deliver all it can for customers or whether 'the bar could be raised' even further.

The Marketing Mix framework was originally created in a time long before everyone had access to the internet. Car dealers, travel companies, restaurants and retailers were not serving customers who have extreme choice, extreme price and product features transparency, and an almost limitless number of different customer journeys they can follow. Today all of these consumer sectors have a much harder time acquiring their customers, and an even harder time trying to retain them. As many businesses declare themselves to be customer focused, surely there should be a framework that really puts the customer at the heart of what is being delivered and gives them a chance of winning the battle for the customer?

Introducing the Customer Mix

How different would the framework be if we really put ourselves in custom-ers' shoes, rather than simply thinking about what we want to deliver to potential customers and how we deliver it? So, instead of the 7Ps, I have created a Customer Mix framework with 6Ws that aims to do just that. The following explains why it is the right framework for consumer brands today (see Figure 13.1).

The Marketing Mix framework does not properly consider customers' motivations, preferences and loyalties (or lack of). It does not consider that different groups and segments of customers might want very different things from the same business. The Customer Mix framework addresses this.

The Marketing Mix considers each purchase as a standalone transac-tion, rather than one of a potential group of transactions over time. For example, the 'process' element of the Marketing Mix refers to the customer

Figure 13.1 The customer mix

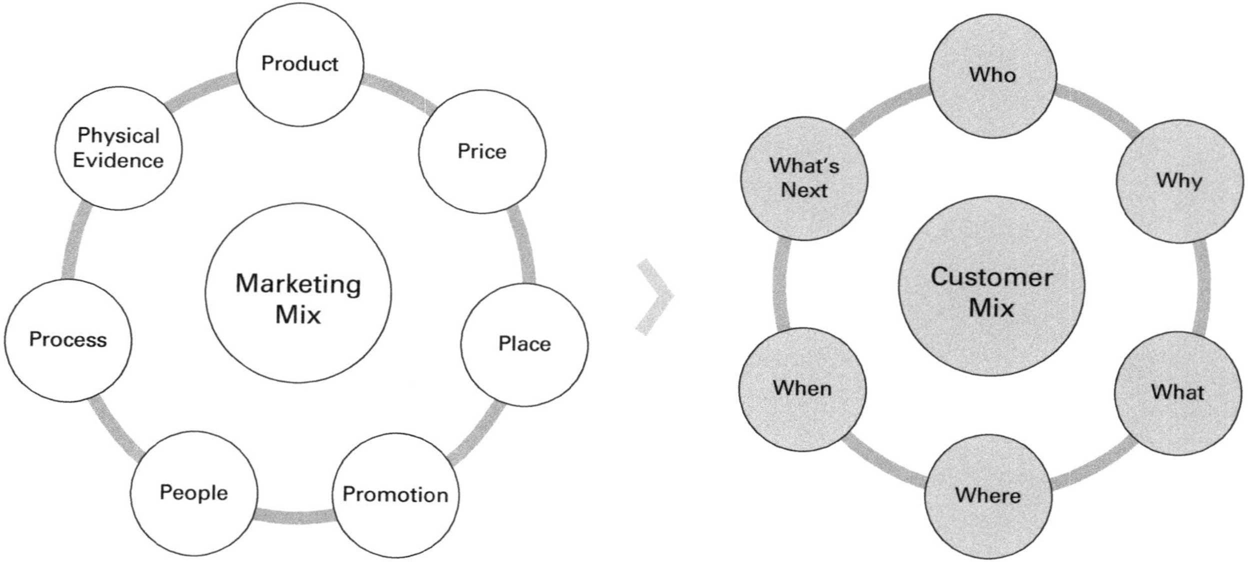

SOURCE Newman (2016)

experience delivered primarily before and during a single transaction. Due to the costs incurred in acquiring and serving customers, and the increasing levels of competition from the disruptors, modern multichannel businesses need customers who they can build relationships with, and so must focus on customer lifetime value.

If you don't focus on the customer's lifetime value, how can you possibly know how much you should invest in recruiting a customer in the first place if you don't have some idea of their potential worth to you? Again, customer segmentation will enable you to recruit more profitable customers with better lifetime value potential. I talk more about this in Chapter 17, CRM and customer insight. The Customer Mix looks past the next transaction, and thinks about what is required not just to sell an item, but to keep the customer's loyalty for future purchases.

So, what does each of the Ws within the Customer Mix really stand for and, more importantly what do they mean for a multichannel consumer-facing business?

Who

There is no P in the Marketing Mix framework that is focused on customers. In the Customer Mix we directly consider *Who* the different target customers are. Few retailers are niche enough to have a single customer type with one set of needs and desires. The majority of multichannel businesses have created a variety of ways to shop, primarily because they do not serve a homogenous customer base. You need to analyse your customer data to understand who your best customers are, and create key customer segments. In customer-centric organizations, these customer segments are developed into customer personas. Staff across the business can consider how their decisions on everything from products to prices to service will likely impact on these target groups. As Professor McDonald pointed out earlier, there is no such thing as 'the customer'. There are lots of customer segments. Without trying to be all things to all people, the key is to understand how best to serve your core customer segments.

Why

Combined with *Who*, *Why* informs us on our target customer segments and their motivations. It prompts retailers, banks, car dealers, restaurants and all consumer-facing businesses to consider not just why a customer wants a particular product or service, but why the channels used during the customer journey may be important to the purchase decision, as well as the fulfilment timeframe. An understanding of *Why* helps businesses to become more relevant to their customers. It can inform marketing, merchandising and product or service design decisions. For example, if a customer segment is time poor and cash rich, thinking about motivation might lead to the creation of premium services to engage them better, rather than a change to the product range being required.

I provided an example of this in Chapter 1 with 'You try, we wait'; Net-a-Porter's personal shopping assistants will deliver orders to their extremely important customers (EIP – extremely important people) at their home on the same day as they place their request. They will then wait until the customer has tried on the pieces they ordered, and take back anything that the customer does not want to keep.

What

This replaces 'product' in the Marketing Mix framework and focuses on what we believe our target customer segments will be most interested in purchasing. But it goes beyond product too, as *What* the customers want can include value, convenience or personalization of the offer. It can also include services, and in the Marketing Mix 'product' does not really lend itself to these additional requirements. Sometimes products and services cannot be separated. One example is the many online subscription-based e-commerce sites that have sprung up. The consumer is not just buying into the products provided, but the concept that they receive something in the post on a regular basis. As I mentioned previously, retailers and other consumer-facing verticals need to think like service providers and about what they can do to become more useful to their customers.

Where

Replacing 'place' in the Marketing Mix framework, *Where* considers locations for fulfilment, and also locations for every other aspect of the customer journey, including research and purchase. In a complex multichannel customer journey we can no longer assume that a product is purchased in a store or at a desktop computer, and fulfilled by either home delivery or being taken from the store at the point of purchase.

What is offered at a variety of locations may be important to a customer's overall decision to purchase, and decision to remain a customer too. A good example of this is in China. Unencumbered by legacy technology, processes and store footprints, Alibaba has opened grocery outlets under the 'Hema' brand. They have installed a 'ship from store' proposition with a fully automated system that takes the customer's order from the shop floor to the back of house where it will be packed and dispatched for delivery to the customer's home at a time of their choosing.

Another example is when an online grocery shopper can buy the same brands for a similar price from a number of supermarkets. In this case, having an app that allows the customer to add to their shopping list while they are commuting to work might be important, as might the grocer's ability to offer click and collect at their supermarket.

Considering *Where* leads consumer-facing businesses to question every aspect of their multichannel strategy. For instance, do their apps, mobile site and any other infrastructure support customers wanting to shop on the move, or complete transactions within the store/restaurant/bank on their own device? For online-only businesses without a bricks-and-mortar environment, do they need to consider physical collection points for customers who don't find delivery options convenient?

According to Salesforce, in 2017 stores remain the preferred channel globally. Even among technology-savvy generation Z shoppers, 58 per cent prefer the physical store shopping experience. But digital is where most end up starting their hunt, by nearly a 2:1 margin: 60 per cent of respondents are likely to start their hunt on digital, versus just 37 per cent in the physical store. Retailers are finding success when combining digital and instore to work together seamlessly. The research found that instore activity generates almost half of all online activity. They interviewed people to see how instore events and engagement matter and found that 26 per cent visited instore events and 58 per cent were more likely to purchase from that retailer in the future (Salesforce, 2017).

There are also an increasing number of good examples of brands that started as online pureplay e-commerce businesses who have opened up bricks-and-mortar stores. One such example is the fashion brand Missguided. A highly successful internet business, they opened stores in the two main Westfield malls in London. This enabled them to bring their brand to life in a physical environment, but also to provide the multichannel experience that many of their younger consumers demand. They have since gone into the wholesale channel and sell their brand through Nordstrom in the United States.

When

Combined with *Where, When* gives us a real sense of how important convenience is to the customer experience. But When is also important in its own right. Timeliness can be key to customer demand – particular products such as flowers, food or gifts may only be demanded if they can be fulfilled within a very specific timeframe. As consumers in developed economies become more time pressured, timeliness will only ever become a more important aspect of the Customer Mix. Again, questions about **When** can consider multiple points in the customer journey. Various clients of mine allow their loyalty cardholders early access to sales events, online and instore. Many retailers report differing success with their marketing e-mails, depending on the time of day they are sent out. Flash offers and price changes can be enabled in moments on the web, which makes time a much more powerful aspect of a consumer-facing business's tactics. Optimizing your marketing and trading calendars to maximize sales opportunities is crucial.

What's next

There is no 'P' for lifetime value or ongoing customer relationships in the Marketing Mix framework. In the Customer Mix this is crucial. As I mentioned in Chapter 7, very few businesses have a dedicated customer retention role. This correlates with the lack of any customer retention element in the Marketing Mix. Also, implicit in the **What's next** element of the Customer Mix is the idea that, in modern retailing, customer loyalty can rarely be earned with a single transaction. At the point they convert a customer for the first time, the best retailers already have a strategy in place for how they will continue to engage with them to keep them coming back. This requires proactive CRM, rather than the type of reactive and transaction-driven CRM programmes that are still widespread in the industry.

Customer lifetime value is a crucial measure of a retailer's success with its customers, and should be an indicator of both future sales and profitability. Improving the value and longevity of customer relationships involves considering some or all of the other five Ws to allow all consumer-facing businesses to meaningfully engage with their customers. The framework in Figure 13.2 is a good, practical example of how else you might think about adopting a customer-centric approach.

Insight not reporting

There is way too much data floating around most customer-facing organizations. Without insight, it is just numbers. Numbers on their own mean nothing. A KPI means nothing, unless you can explain why it is trending up or down. What were the factors that impacted it from one week to another?

Figure 13.2 The customer-centric approach

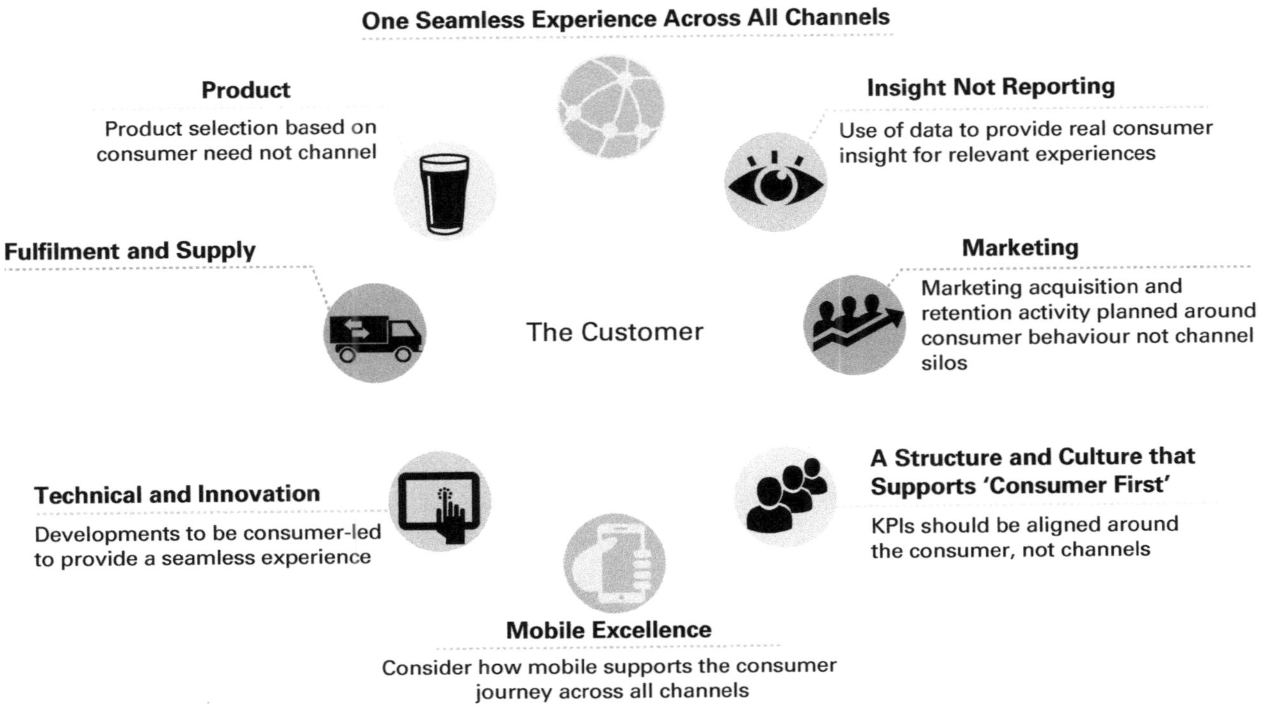

One Seamless Experience Across All Channels

Product

Product selection based on consumer need not channel

Insight Not Reporting

Use of data to provide real consumer insight for relevant experiences

Marketing

Marketing acquisition and retention activity planned around consumer behaviour not channel silos

A Structure and Culture that Supports 'Consumer First'

KPIs should be aligned around the consumer, not channels

The Customer

Fulfilment and Supply

Technical and Innovation

Developments to be consumer-led to provide a seamless experience

Mobile Excellence

Consider how mobile supports the consumer journey across all channels

To put the customer first, you must have insight about the customer. In Chapter 17, I discuss how to generate insight and how to build relationships with customers based on your knowledge of them.

Marketing

As I discussed in Chapter 7 on organizational design and in Chapter 12 on customer-centric marketing communications, too many businesses have siloed marketing teams. Brand marketing, which often looks after the 'traditional channels in the business', and digital marketing, which works across all the new channels, are more often than not working separately. The person who loses out is the customer. Marketing communications have to be integrated.

I have received communications in the past from retailers whereby I was sent an incentive to buy online 'for the first time', when I was already an online customer and had been for many years. I have had the same scenario occur when I have been encouraged to shop instore.

A culture that supports customers first

As I have discussed at various points throughout the book, if you want to change the culture of the business and its focus on customers, then you need to move towards KPIs and measures that give you a real sense of how customers feel about your business. When you buy a new car, do you, like me, have a great fear that the minute you drive away, if anything goes wrong, it is going to cost you? This is borne out of the focus on sales as opposed to service that you receive at most car dealerships. This can easily be remedied. But it is a cultural challenge and requires a root and branch re-set away from a sales culture to a customer service culture. If you serve customers well, they buy and buy again.

Mobile excellence

It should go without saying. However, we really do need to think mobile first. We need to think about the customer's cross-channel journey and all the touchpoints along the way, and how mobile can be leveraged to support and enhance their journey. Not only that, but we have to start planning for voice activation first with mobile. Within a very short time, we will no longer be pinching and scrolling on a mobile device. We will interact by voice alone. If you ever hope to do business in Asia, then you need to be aware that consumers do everything on their mobile. In China, particularly in large tier 1 and 2 cities, you rarely see people pay with cash. They use WeChat, Alipay and other mobile payment services, often activated through a QR code.

Technical and innovation

This is about planning for technology and innovation and not the development of technology for technology's sake. As I pointed out previously, you should not have to prove the business case for everything you do, otherwise you will never be agile enough to truly innovate. However, the reverse is that you develop technology where there is simply no use case for it. It must be about enhancing the customer's experience, with a potential commercial benefit to the business as a result of doing so.

Fulfilment and supply

Here we talk about having flexible delivery and returns processes. There are still some retailers today who charge customers for online delivery and for returns. All that does is create a barrier straight from the off.

Product and service

Product and service decisions should be made around the customer and not around the channel. Some very large retailers still struggle to surface all of their brands and products available instore on the website. So, guess what? Not only do they lose the potential additional demand they could generate, but they also suppress sales instore. Most customers use the web now as their first point of discovery before deciding whether or not to visit the store. If they cannot see the brands online on the retailer's website that they want to buy they may not visit the store in the first place. An exception to this is in China, where most customers start their journey on marketplaces such as Tmall or JD.com, as opposed to on the brand's own website.

Top practical customer experience tips

1 Adopt the Customer Mix – live it, breathe it, integrate its approach into all that you do.

2 Throw away the Marketing Mix, it is 20 years past its sell-by date.

3 Focus on 'what's next' for the customer.

4 Understand this: if you don't look after your customers, someone else will – it's a battlefield out there. Do you have a plan to win the war?

Expanded on below.

Adopt the Customer Mix – live it, breathe it, integrate its approach into all that you do

Irrespective of whatever consumer-facing sector you operate in – automotive, financial services, travel, CPG, retail, casual dining etc – it is a highly effective framework for thinking about how you can best meet the needs of different customer segments.

Throw away the Marketing Mix, it is 20 years past its sell-by date

The Marketing Mix is outdated and irrelevant in a customer-facing environment. Think about it. Even if you sell products ('product'), nowadays you also need to think of your business as a service provider. You cannot possibly think about price in the way you would have done 60 years ago when the Marketing Mix was created. Pricing has to be dynamic. It has to be flexible to cater for different customer segments. Place is also outdated. We have many different places, or channels, as we call them today, and channels tend to promote a siloed approach. Promotion 60 years ago was mainly about above-the-line advertising, on-pack promotions and some direct mail. Today, we need to engage with customers. This involves the creation of more experiential marketing.

Focus on 'what's next' for the customer

So few consumer-facing businesses pay any attention to what's next for a consumer. When was the last time an airline, travel agency, restaurant or car dealer communicated with you after you had engaged with them? If they did, did the communication have any correlation with what you had bought or your experience with them? I'm sure for 99 per cent of you the answer to that question will be a resounding 'no'.

I have bought new cars every three or four years for the past 25 years, always on a contract whereby, after three or four years, I hand the car back and start again. Only one car dealer or car brand (Lookers, Jaguar) has bothered communicating with me in the weeks and months after purchase to find out how I'm getting on with my new car and how the experience was when I purchased it. How many customers might have bought another new car from the same dealer if they had kept in touch with them throughout the life cycle of the car they acquired?

You must focus on lifetime value. You absolutely must do this. How can you possibly know how much you should invest in recruiting a customer in the first place if you don't have some idea of their potential worth to you? Again, customer segmentation will enable you to recruit more profitable customers with better lifetime value potential.

Understand this: if you don't look after your customers, someone else will – it's a battlefield out there. Do you have a plan to win the war?

You need to live and breathe customer-first. It should be the beating heart right in the middle of your business from which everything else, and I mean *everything* else, flows. Customers should be the first thing you think of every morning and the last thing you think of every night.

Over to Professor Malcolm McDonald

Models of marketing abound and, as times and practices change, each generation comes up with its own.

I was recently asked by a publisher to adjudicate on a manuscript entitled 'The 100 Ps of Marketing', although I did succeed in negotiating it down to 'The 20 Ps of Marketing'! Written by the Director of Procter & Gamble, the book sends out an interesting message and such models are useful vehicles to explain complicated concepts. Let us not forget that the world of finance after all these years still cannot agree on a definition of profit, with ROS, ROI, ROIC, EPS, EBIT, EBITDA, EVA, SVA and a host of others, each with its own advocate. So, marketing is not alone in this universe!

The '4Ps' model has served us well over the years and continues to do so to some degree. However, with the influx of technology and new platforms, perhaps now is the time to think about the Customer Mix as a more relevant, alternative model, not only to succeed in marketing, but also to place your company ahead of the curve.

For years, modern and astute marketers (of which I humbly include myself!) have used the 4Ps model intelligently, reacting to various changes and building in subtext where appropriate. For example, appreciating that 'product' encapsulates customer benefits, segmentation, branding, positioning and the like, while 'place' encapsulates customer service and channel management. 'Price' encapsulates value-in-use, and 'promotion', of course, although it has changed out of all recognition today, is still a useful way of understanding these changes. Over the years these submodels have advanced through different phases, including my own tried-and-tested '6Is' model, as shown in Figure 13.3.

Today, customer focus prevails and we as marketers have a duty to react accordingly to the increasing complexity of communications, embracing new ways to improve communication and productivity with our teams and clients.

Martin's fresh take on a 6Ws Customer Mix serves this purpose brilliantly, drawing our attention away from the supplier and back to the consumer. These are precisely the headings I have used for over 20 years in my books and papers on market segmentation – a quantitative process for

Figure 13.3   The 6Is of e-marketing

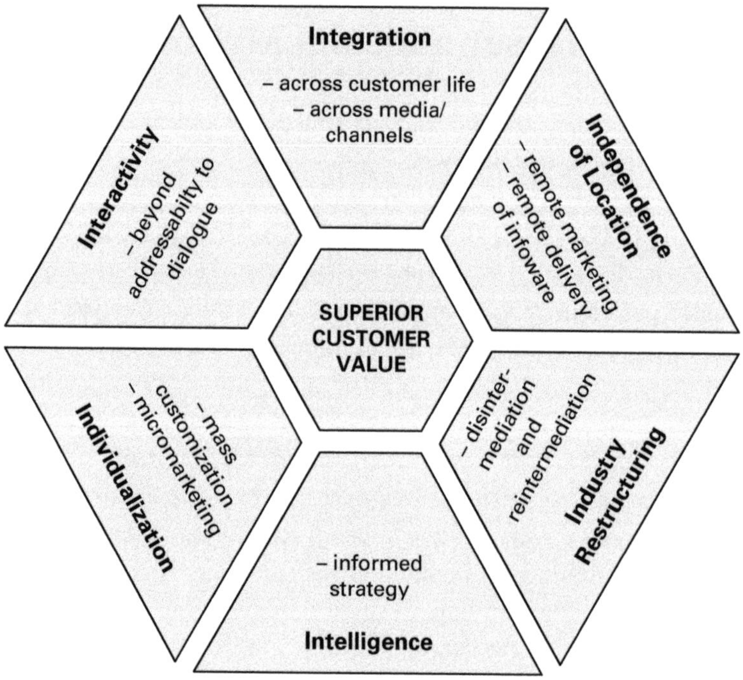

uncovering needs-based market segments. We as marketers should all be totally in agreement that, without these, most marketing will be misplaced.

The bottom line to this is that whatever model is used, or indeed in the inevitable frameworks that will emerge in the future, they should always be customer- rather than supplier-centric.

References

McCarthy, E J (1960), *Basic Marketing: A managerial approach*, Richard D Irwin, Homewood

Newman, M (2016) [accessed 1 December 2017] Introducing the Customer Mix [Online] https://www.practicology.com/files/4314/5043/1186/Practicology_Customer_Mix_White_Paper_2016.pdf

Salesforce (2017) [accessed 1 December 2017] Shopper-First Retailing: What Consumers are Telling Us About the Future of Shopping [Online] https://www.demandware.com/uploads/resources/REP_Sapient_Report_EN_27JUNE2017_FINAL_.pdf

Strategic social   14
media and its
importance to the
whole organization

WHAT YOU WILL LEARN IN THIS CHAPTER

- Social media should not be run by the youngest person in the business just because they are on Instagram and Pinterest every day!
- Understanding the strategic opportunities and imperatives of social media.
- The different parts of the business and areas that social media impacts, eg service, product development, customer sentiment etc.

All too often, social media responsibility is given to the 'youngsters' in the team, because they are on Instagram, Pinterest and Snapchat. This is indicative of the fact that social media is still treated as a tactical promotional channel as opposed to a strategic driver for multiple aspects of the business. As the social media model in Figure 14.1 suggests, there are a number of significant pillars to social media. Each of these pillars are discussed below.

Customer service

Increasingly customers expect instant feedback through social media channels. This increases if they have actually made their purchase online. But even if they purchased goods from you through your stores or ate in your restaurant, they expect to be able to message you on Facebook or Twitter and to get an immediate response.

Figure 14.1 The social media ecosystem

SOURCE Practicology (2017)

This is often not the case, with many brands still operating with 24-hour response service levels. This is simply not good enough. It leaves the brand owner exposed as customers grow angrier by the minute, when an issue could have been resolved in minutes. This in turn drives negative word of web, which is significantly worse than word of mouth – with the latter being a traditional form of telling friends and family of a bad customer experience, with the potential reach in the dozens. Compare this to a customer venting their anger online, which, depending upon the context, could at the very least gain exposure to a few thousand people on Facebook. In the worst-case scenario it could destroy your brand. Practicology undertook research of the top 30 non-food retailers in the UK and found that only 50 per cent responded to customers within 24 hours (Practicology, 2017).

I have mentioned AO.com previously, when discussing culture. Their founder and former CEO John Roberts used to spend 40 minutes per day responding to customers who had written in, e-mailed or posted on Facebook. He responded to both negative and positive customer sentiment. This closed feedback loop has helped to generate a lot of goodwill for the brand and a level of trust not afforded to too many organizations.

The Dutch airline KLM has extremely good service levels on social media. You can contact KLM 24/7 and you can expect a response within an hour on most social channels. You can ask questions on Facebook, Messenger, Twitter and LinkedIn or get specific support for these requirements:

- booking or changing a flight;
- check-in for a flight;
- choosing your favourite seat on board;
- ordering an à la carte meal;
- arranging extra baggage.

KLM have customer service available in nine different languages and now offer a 'Meet and Seat' service by which you can find out who will be on your flight via Facebook or LinkedIn profiles (Fritsch, 2017).

CRM

Social media is a great opportunity to build relationships with customers. AO.com has the level of engagement mentioned earlier because they have built relationships with their customers. Customers have a strong empathy for the brand. They trust AO.com. This is driven by a number of factors, including their service levels and the closed feedback loop on social media, both of which engender trust with customers, and not forgetting the fun element of the brand. Customers feel that AO is a friend, and a friend who understands them. This level of empathy is mutual and is at the heart of the brand's DNA.

Doubletree by Hilton is another brand with a strong customer focus. For those of you who have stayed there, you will know that the first thing you are greeted by when you reach the reception desk is a delicious, warm, chocolate cookie! Recognizing that you may well be tired and a little weary when you travel, Doubletree makes you feel at home straight away with this well-thought-through gesture. It also represents their dedication to their guests that ensures they feel special and cared for throughout their stay. I experienced this first-hand when staying in their hotel in Dublin. I woke up at 4 am (as I do too frequently) and I wanted to use the gym. I called reception expecting the usual feedback that 'the gym doesn't open until 6 am', which was the advertised time. To my delight, the receptionist said, 'Mr Newman, the gym doesn't normally open until 6 am, however, if you like, I'll come and open it now.' They have also taken the cookie proposition on to social media, running #sweetwelcome on various social media channels including Facebook, Instagram and Twitter. It is a good idea to remind customers how they felt when they checked in and how they go the extra mile to make you feel welcome. It keeps them top of mind for the next time you need to book a hotel. It demonstrates a strong focus on customer retention.

Multichannel

Social selling/social commerce: social media also drives sales. Those sales can either be true 'social commerce' driven online in the social media channel or generated through other channels. It is also an opportunity to generate leads and pent-up demand. Pinterest have also got in on the act when they launched 'Shop the Look'. Leveraging machine learning, this identifies pinned items that customers can buy. These include styles from large multichannel retailers. Data analytics from 'Shop the Look' can be leveraged to inform retailers when a sponsored post on Pinterest has resulted in a sale. This is a great example of true social commerce.

Advertising

There is cross-over between advertising and marketing, the former being more about specific campaigns and targeted activity with a clear intent to drive sales. Of course, social media channels present a great opportunity to influence customers. Let's not forget that social media is also the key tool that drives 'word of mouth'. As such, it can have a very strong viral impact with many customers increasing the reach of your message by sharing it with friends, family and colleagues they are connected with on social media channels. All customer segments are heavily influenced by their peers and therefore the response rates to products and services that are being promoted and have been shared with them will convert far higher than most other marketing communications.

Marketing

Marketing on social media presents the opportunity to talk to millennials and other customer segments about the causes your organization supports or your approach to corporate social responsibility.

Social media also provides the opportunity for sentiment analysis or opinion mining as it is also referred to in order to gain an understanding of what customers really think of your brand. This in turn can be leveraged to gain a good understanding of the health of your brand.

PR and influencer marketing

PR on social media is where you find and leverage influencers. In the west, we tend to refer to them as bloggers or vloggers. In China and Asia, they are referred as key opinion leaders (KOLs). These individuals have huge numbers of followers on social media. Some KOLs have 10–20 million followers! Their endorsement of your products or services can enable you to influence consumers in a way you could never possibly do directly yourselves.

Like the Kardashians, Chinese KOLs have as large a degree of influence as other western celebrities. A good example is Chinese superstar BingBing, who generated US $74 million in e-commerce revenue. Or Zoella, a vlogger in the UK who has well over 12 million subscribers to her blog. Bloggers, vloggers and KOLs carry a huge amount of influence.

There is also a plethora of category-specific bloggers such as Heather Armstrong in the United States who is a stay-at-home professional blogger. She launched Dooce.com as a place to write about pop culture, music and her life as a single woman – and she earns $40,000 a month for doing so (Smallstarter, 2017).

Some businesses have brand ambassador programmes. Ambassadors can be customers or celebrities. They are compensated with payments, products or other perks, and are asked to talk positively about the company's products or services. Just one example of this is Spotify's brand ambassador programme that leverages university and college students who host parties with curated Spotify playlists. It is a fun role and it helps to keep the company in touch with its core audience.

Hunkemöller, a leading European lingerie retailer, told me that they drive social engagement with younger consumers. They have 80 external ambassadors and 40 internal – all of whom wear products and communicate through social media and this is optimized through Olapic on the website. They have one of the biggest social media teams I've come across in a retail organization, with 12 full-time roles in social media driving engagement through all channels.

Social listening is the opportunity for a brand to identify sentiment and opinion, proactively address any concerns customers have and stave off the potential for a reputational issue before it becomes a crisis. There are many tools that you can use for social listening that will enable you to really understand what customers think of your business and your brand. Social media channels are also your first point of defence when it comes to reacting to any negativity you might be experiencing in the media. However, you need a crisis management plan for dealing with such events.

Think of United Airlines' scenario in 2017, when it was reported that a man who refused to leave his seat on an overbooked flight was 'yanked from his seat on to the floor and dragged off, blood visible on his face' (Gunter, 2017). This had a huge viral impact on social and mainstream media channels around the world, thus causing the brand serious damage to its reputation. A day later, United's CEO, Oscar Munoz, apologized on Twitter:

> This is an upsetting event to all of us here at United. I apologize for having to reaccommodate these customers. Our team is moving with a sense of urgency to work with the authorities and conduct our own detailed review of what happened. We are also reaching out to this passenger to talk directly to him and further address and resolve this situation (https://twitter.com/united/status/851471781827420160).

In contrast to the above, social media builds trust in a brand. For example, occasional diners surveyed in the United States are 1.79x more likely to be encouraged to eat at a restaurant if it is where other people their age go. It makes sense, therefore, to be talking about 'customers like them' on social media channels (Facebook Insights, 2017).

HR

On social media channels you can connect with candidates and employees, share company news and build your internal community. It is also the ideal opportunity to build the employer brand. Social media channels are a tremendous vehicle for spreading the word about your business, your culture and why yours is a such a great place to work.

Innovation and product development

Social media presents the opportunity to solicit open-source feedback from customers and their sentiments in relation to new developments to products and services that you are planning.

Know the channels that serve you best

Improve your credibility in an 'instant' – 46 per cent of beauty buyers in the UK agree they have greater trust in brands they see on Instagram (Spredfast, 2017). You need to understand what role the different social media channels play.

There's a lot of interest in Pinterest

One might argue that Pinterest has come of age. Pinterest drives significant engagement and is also paying its way as a driver of sales. For example, when KPCB asked people which social media service is a great place to browse things you might want to buy, in 2017 44 per cent said Pinterest, up from 33 per cent in 2015; and to buy things 24 per cent said Pinterest, up from 12 per cent in 2015 (Meeker, 2017). This was based on a survey of 12,000 global interest users.

Pinterest Lens

The ability to discover and potentially buy goods has been made far easier with the introduction of Pinterest Lens. Using the camera in the app enables users to discover ideas inspired by objects they see out in the real world. With fashion goods, related styles and ideas for what else to wear with the item can be found. With furniture, similar designs can be found as well as other items from the same era. Lens can also be used with food, whereby pointing the camera at an ingredient will result in a variety of recipes coming up. With 'Shop the Look' (currently available in the United States) the next step for Pinterest users will be to buy the goods they discover direct from retailers (Retail Insider, 2017).

Instore

Nordstrom leverages Pinterest to great effect. Their marketing team keep track of the most popular products by keeping an eye on Pinterest Pins and those that are trending. This data is leveraged to ensure the most appropriate products are being promoted within its bricks-and-mortar stores (Lutz, 2017).

A vacation on Pinterest

Pinterest is now one of the primary places people go to when researching and planning their next vacation; 62 per cent of customers use Pinterest to plan a future vacation. Travel is one of the top 10 reasons people come to Pinterest. In 2017, over 16 million people saved 780 million different travel ideas. Family travel was especially popular, with 2.7 million people saving over 36 million Pins (so was budget travel, with 1.2 million people saving over 12.7 million Pins) (Lux, 2017).

CASE STUDY Pets of (P)interest

Unlike many insurance companies, Petplan in the United States have developed a genuinely customer-centric value proposition borne out of their focus on pet health, delivered by high-quality and relevant content in addition to exceptional customer service. Their overarching objective is to enable communities who want to provide the very best health and protection for their four-legged family members!

Petplan wanted to showcase their expertise while also getting across their brand personality. They researched the pet-related topics that were trending on Pinterest and began creating Pinterest boards with relevant and engaging pet images from them with the pet health magazine *Fetch!* They subsequently developed and shared more educational content, including pet health tips and their 'Breed all about it' boards.

In only a few months Pinterest generated a large amount of referral traffic for Petplan, resulting in 69 per cent more page views and 97 per cent longer time on site, which rivalled Twitter and Facebook's performance. Petplan has clearly found a gap in the market and is doing a great job of leveraging social media to drive demand for its pet insurance products. Unlike the UK, which has close to 30 per cent of its pets insured, and Sweden up to 50 per cent, the United States had around 1 per cent of pets insured. Leveraging tactics such as adding the save button to their website, including Pinterest Follow buttons in their e-mail footers and social campaigns, and optimizing site content for Pinterest, Petplan was able to drive significant interest in both the importance of insurance as well as its specific insurance plans.

As a result of this focus, over the next quarter, Petplan enjoyed an 87 per cent increase in new visitors to its website, a 35 per cent increase in the number of page views, and a 12.5 per cent increase in requests for insurance quotes.

SOURCE Pinterest (nd)

Top practical customer experience tips

1 Treat social media as a strategic driver of opportunity for your business – it is not only a promotional vehicle.

2 Resource social media effectively – don't just give it to the youngest person in the room to look after!

3 Ensure that levels of service and response times are appropriate.

4 Don't be anti-social – social commerce is a tangible opportunity.

5 Think of the opportunities and the potential threats you are not currently addressing as a result of still treating social media as a tactical promotional tool.

Expanded on below.

Treat social media as a strategic driver of opportunity for your business – it is not only a promotional vehicle

As outlined above, social media can do everything from promoting your products and services to getting your customers involved in the product development process. It can enable you to pre-empt and handle a potential crisis; by using social listening tools it can also enable you to react well ahead of time to any potential threats or opportunities related to consumer sentiment towards your brand. You can leverage both engaged and existing customers as well as brand ambassadors and key influencers to spread the message about your business. You can promote the culture and values of your business and, in doing so, use social media for HR purposes. Use the framework above; it will enable you to leverage social media for the strategic business development driver that it is.

Resource social media effectively – don't just give it to the youngest person in the room to look after!

If you are really going to treat it seriously, and understand its strategic importance to the business, then you need the right people running social media. However, given that it feeds into so many different areas of your business, it is unlikely that you will have one person who oversees all of social media. Moreover, different departments will have teams responsible for their input into social media:

- customer service;
- marketing (brand, customer acquisition and retention);
- public relations;
- product development;
- HR;
- e-commerce.

Ensure that levels of service and response times are appropriate

You cannot leave customers waiting 24 hours for a response to a query on social media! Customers expect an instantaneous response, which is why messenger apps are becoming one of the key channels that customers use to communicate with a brand online. Poor customer service is one of the first triggers for negative sentiment and for consumers to use 'word of mouth/word of web' to tell others about their poor experience with you. See Figure 14.2.

Don't be anti-social – social commerce is a tangible opportunity

One of the best examples of social commerce that I have found is on GlassesUSA.com. They are an online e-tailer selling eyewear and lenses. They have a social shop where they showcase pictures of happy customers wearing their products. All images are tagged and users can click each image and buy the relevant frame or lenses there and then. It is a great example of the importance of user-generated content and the opportunity to leverage this by making it shoppable. It is a well-known fact that customers convert at far higher levels when they have read user reviews and comments or content from their peers. User-generated content also engenders trust and, according to Neilsen research, 92 per cent of consumers trust user-generated content more than they do traditional advertising.

Figure 14.2   Ovum get it right: deliver the omnichannel support customers
want (survey of consumers ages 18–80 in Australia, Europe,
New Zealand and USA, n = 400)

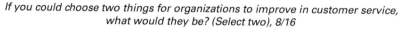

Social Media =
Can provide opportunity to improve customer service...

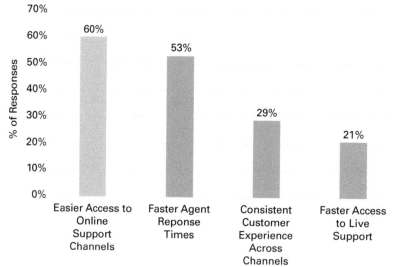

SOURCE Ovum (2016)

Think of the opportunities and the potential threats you are not currently addressing as a result of still treating social media as a tactical promotional tool

Believe me, at some point in time something about your business will kick off on social media. You must have a plan in place for how you will effectively deal with this.

Over to Professor Malcolm McDonald

The model at the beginning of this chapter is one of the clearest and best I have seen on the topic of social media, as it elevates to a strategic level what is mostly seen and treated as a tactical topic.

Although I have said earlier that it is impossible to have a social media strategy without a robust marketing strategy (remember, a strategy for what is sold, to whom and why customers should buy from us rather than a competitor), social media also requires its own strategy if it is to have a significant impact on the organization. In the same way that marketing needs a strategy, with its complex components – whether it is the 4Ps, the 7Ps, the 20Ps, the 6Ws – so does social media.

Also, as with marketing, Martin has pointed out in this chapter that there are several different teams that have an input into social media. It is my view, therefore, that a more formal document for social media is necessary if we are to avoid conflicting approaches and messages from customer service, PR, product development, HR and e-commerce.

To date, in spite of all the hype and skill sets surrounding social media, I have never seen a strategic plan for social media, so it would be extremely productive to devise a process for constructing one and agree what should go into it.

Let me remind us all that being efficient (tactics) is the worst thing we can do if we are doing the wrong things (strategy). Doing the wrong thing really well has to be the height of managerial stupidity!

So thank you for this model, Martin, which in my view sets out the potential components of a social media strategy.

References

Facebook Insights (2017) [accessed 1 December 2017] Cooking Up a Crave: The Role of Mobile in Fast Food Dining [Online] https://www.facebook.com/iq/articles/cooking-up-a-crave-the-role-of-mobile-in-fast-food-dining

Fritsch, E (2017) [accessed 19 December 2017] The Changing Retail Landscape [Online] https://www.sgia.org/journal/2017/sgia-journal-graphic-edition-septemberoctober-2017/changing-retail-landscape

Gunter, J (2017) [accessed 1 December 2017] United Airlines Incident: What Went Wrong? [Online] http://www.bbc.co.uk/news/world-us-canada-39556910

Lutz, A (2017) [accessed 14 December 2017] Nordstrom Will Use Pinterest To Decide What Merchandise To Display In Stores, *Business Insider* [Online] http://www.businessinsider.com/nordstroms-pinterest-in-stores-plan-2013-11?IR=T

Lux, C (2017) [accessed 1 December 2017] Using Pinterest and Promoted Pins for Travel Brands [Online] http://reprisemedia.com.au/blog/using-pinterest-and-promoted-pins-for-travel-brands/

Meeker, M (2017) [accessed 1 December 2017] Internet Trends 2017 – Code Conference [Online] http://www.kpcb.com/file/2017-internet-trends-report

Ovum (2016) [accessed 1 December 2017] Get It Right: Deliver the Omni-Channel Support Customers Want [Online] https://az766929.vo.msecnd.net/document-library/boldchat/pdf/en/boldchat-whitepaper-ovum-logmein.pdfPinterest (nd) [accessed 1 December 2017] Success Stories: Petplan Insurance [Online] https://business.pinterest.com/en-gb/success-stories/petplan-insurance

Practicology (2017) [accessed 1 December 2017] Omnichannel Customer Experience Report 2017 [Online] https://www.practicology.com/files/9414/8776/1948/Practicology_Omnichannel_CX_report_2017_DOWNLOAD.pdf

Retail Insider (2017) [accessed 29 November 2017] Digital Retail Innovations Report [Online] http://webloyalty.co.uk/Images/UK/Digital_Retail_Innovations_Report_2017.pdf

Smallstarter (2017) [accessed 14 December 2017] 7 Successful Bloggers Africans should learn from… and Become Like! [Online] http://www.smallstarter.com/get-inspired/7-successful-bloggers-to-learn-from/

Spredfast (2017) [accessed 14 December 2017] 8 Social Statistics on Beauty Buyers to Shape Your Strategy Now [Online] https://www.spredfast.com/social-marketing-blog/8-social-statistics-beauty-buyers-shape-your-strategy-now

The impact of AI, augmented virtual reality, machine learning and voice on customer experience

WHAT YOU WILL LEARN IN THIS CHAPTER

- Chat bots are all the rage. Who is using them and are they delivering better service?
- What other areas of customer engagement are likely to be impacted by machine learning and artificial intelligence (AI)?
- What parts of the value chain of your business can you improve by leveraging AI?

AI is the fourth industrial revolution

First, we had steam and machinery from 1760 to 1840. Then electricity and mass production from 1875 to 1925. In 1960 we saw the advent of the internet, albeit the world wide web was not invented until 1989. Now, the new millennium has AI and the fusion of digital and physical (see Table 15.1).

Table 15.1   The robots bring benefits: some key benefits of AI in a consumer-facing business

Aspect impacted by AI	Benefits to the business	Benefits for the customer
Customers are served more effectively by chat bots	• Deliver better service levels and sell more effectively • Increasing conversion and average order values	• They receive better service • They are happier with the products they buy
Distribution centres are automated	• Improved efficiency and productivity • Fewer miss-picks • Fewer breakages • Returns % reduced • Improved supply chain • Reduced shrinkage	• Correct items are sent • Customers receive orders quicker • Customers' goods are intact when they are delivered
Range architecture, product recommendation engines and on-site search	• An increase in conversion and sales • Ever-improving range architecture driven by data and machine learning	• Customers are presented with more relevant product choices • Better cross-sell options for customers
Payments and fraud prevention: applying machine learning to detecting user and payment fraud	• Reduce fraud • Reduce rejection of non-fraudulent transactions and customers	• More confidence in the security of the organization • Genuine, non-fraudulent customers are able to place orders
Marketing communications driven by machine learning	• Better return on investment	• More relevant incentives and communication

SOURCE Martin Newman

The robots are taking over – and we're not complaining

A Gartner report I read stated that more than 60 per cent of millennials in the UK express their appreciation of retailers who use AI to offer them products that are more interesting or more relevant. Subsequently, Gartner estimates that by 2020, over three-quarters of retail customer interactions will be handled by AI bots and agents (Gartner, 2017).

A voice-driven world

We have moved head-first into an era of conversational commerce. Before you know it, pinching and scrolling on your mobile or tablet will be a thing of the past. We are and will be using voice to search for products online, through our interactive devices in the home such as Amazon's Alexa, Google Home or Tmall's Genie. We will be getting into our cars and telling the car what music we want to play, what setting we want the air conditioning at and where we want to go. Conversational commerce is a great opportunity for brands in all consumer-facing sectors to promote to customers in their homes, cars and other more personal parts of their life that historically they have not been able to access.

However, for some brand owners, it comes with some challenges:

- Can AI-driven devices recognize the pronunciation of their brands?
- What if they search for the brand by the colour or labelling?
- What if consumers are uncomfortable asking for brands with difficult-to-pronounce names?
- Do brand owners need to trademark the likely mispronunciations of their brand and products?

AI drives multichannel engagement and supply chain efficiencies

Farfetch, the online marketplace, has created a unique model whereby they enable small premium and luxury brands to reach a broader base of consumers. AI enables Farfetch's partners to link their online inventory with the inventories of their bricks-and-mortar stores. This in turn enables them to deliver services and a customer value proposition that, due to the cost of implementation, would normally only be accessible to large multichannel retailers. These services include click and collect and instore returns. Farfetch also leverage AI to improve supply chain and product visibility.

Burberry launched a Facebook Messenger bot during London Fashion Week 2016. The bot enabled Burberry to offer customers a glimpse of their new collection before its debut on the runway. Customers could even buy the clothes immediately in one of the first 'see now, buy now' developments (Facebook, 2016).

AI may cause some short-term pain

One thing I believe we are yet to resolve is what happens when millions of unskilled workers lose their jobs as they are replaced by AI and robots. When they lose their jobs, many, many millions of US dollars of disposable income disappear at the same time. When unemployment levels are low, as they have been in the United States in recent years, bottoming out at 4.1 per cent in 2017, retailers who are looking to expand their stores could be faced with a shortage of manpower (US Department of Labour, 2017). This is where not only AI but other technology even more basic can play a part.

Uniqlo, despite having previously taken on the most expensive lease in US retail history for a property on 5th Avenue, New York, have opened vending machines of their clothing products in numerous locations in the United States, enabling them to increase sales and take the brand to new customers, without the cost of opening a raft of new stores. This is following the Best Buy model, as they have also opened vending machines at US airports. Best Buy now have more than 200 of these points of sale throughout the United States (Chapman, 2017). Vending machines can also provide the opportunity to sell 24/7. Tony Berthelot, an Oyster farmer in France, enables customers to purchase fresh oysters through a vending machine! Therefore, there is no need to pay for staff 24/7.

Site search (search traffic on the company's site) – which may be a preview to AI-based chat-bot adoption – is seeing significant usage. Shoppers using site search account for 9 per cent of all visits, and impressively that drives 23 per cent of all digital sales, with each figure up modestly over the past two years (Salesforce, 2017).

The following is from an interview I wrote in *Retail Week* in 2008 on the 'one click generation'. I've included it in the book as it is still relevant today and we are only just now moving into a world of integrated commerce, media and customer interaction. A world of 'see now, buy now'. Published with kind permission of *Retail Week*.

The experience of shopping in a store and shopping online will also be blurred. Ted Baker's Head of e-Commerce Martin Newman uses the term 'total commerce' or 't-commerce' to describe what retail will be like 20 years from now. He forecasts that consumers will move between the real world and virtual worlds seamlessly.

'Everything in e-commerce will be three-dimensional. I can't imagine how we wouldn't have advanced to that level by then', he says. 'Consumers will also be able to use any channel to buy and any channel they want to receive goods.'

Real-time product availability and product description information will be taken to new levels. Newman envisages a scenario where consumers can click on a character in a TV soap opera and immediately be taken to a page where they can buy the outfit that character is wearing.

AI delivers deeply personalized product recommendations

Thread is a styling service that provides personalized style suggestions. It combines the personal human touch with AI to gather insight on customers. Thread distributes questionnaires to customers with the objective of finding out more about each customer's preferences. They also ask customers to upload images of themselves as this will enable them to provide more accurate product matching. Their stylists review customer information to understand each client's needs. The AI algorithm then helps to sift through thousands of products to provide more relevant product recommendations. (See Figure 15.1.)

While visiting NRF, the National Retail Federation's annual 'big show' in New York in 2017, I met the delightful Pepper Robot.

Pepper Robot has been welcoming customers in Japan's SoftBank telecom branches for the past few years, conceived in 2010 in a collaboration between SoftBank and French robotic manufacturer Aldebaran. With the objective of creating a humanoid robot that could interact with SoftBank's customers, while also being able to read human emotions, Pepper has already developed a fan base in Japan, where it welcomes customers to SoftBank. It is definitely still early in the evolution of customer-facing robots in retail; nonetheless, even at this early stage it would appear that they have a positive impact upon word of mouth, traffic and customer engagement. Whether that only occurs in the interim or not remains to be seen (Softbank Robotics, nd).

Figure 15.1   Percentage of retailers planning to invest in AI by 2021

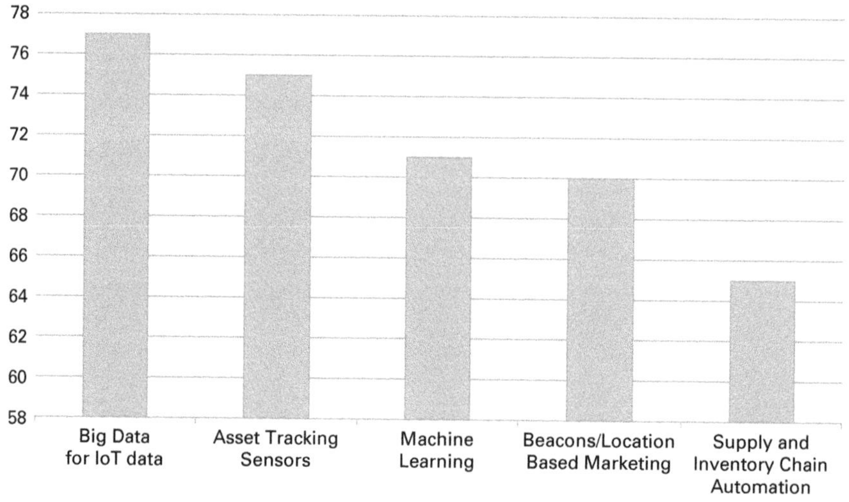

SOURCE Zebra Technologies (2017)

IBM Watson's cognitive computing is playing a big role in AI, particularly with product recommendations. In the United States, 1-800-Flowers.com launched a new proposition called Gifts When You Need, or GWYN – 1-800-Flowers.com has positioned this as an AI-driven gift concierge. Consumers are encouraged to provide information about a gift recipient, and IBM's Watson software determines personalized gift recommendations by comparing the information provided to those of similar gift recipients. Within two months, 70 per cent of online orders were completed through GWYN (Caffyn, 2016).

Logistics and delivery

Domino's robotic delivery

While most likely a long way off in terms of day-to-day use in the delivery of pizzas to its customer base, Domino's has been developing a delivery robot. Domino's claim is that the robot can keep its pizzas hot and drinks cold, while its sensors determine the best journey for delivery and help to keep the robot on the right route.

We have all been droning on about Amazon and their drones

We have all seen the videos. There has been a lot of noise about Amazon using drones for delivery some time soon. They are working with government and aviation agencies around the world to figure out how to implement the drones in a safe and manageable way. They are not alone. UPS and other logistics players are rapidly developing capabilities in this area. Drones are highly likely to become an established part of couriers' logistics and delivery capabilities, as they will improve the efficiency of the logistics companies by being able to deliver to customers more quickly and more cost-effectively – making more margin for the courier while delivering a better, more expedient service for the customer.

AI drives customer service and efficiencies

EXPERT VIEW

I spoke to Sean McKee, Director of e-Commerce and Customer Experience for Schuh, the leading footwear retailer. I asked him how Schuh are thinking about or actually leveraging AI within their business both from customer experience and efficiency perspectives. Sean told me that they started by considering what business problems AI might address if they had a self-learning system that could address business and customer issues, eg fraud checking – faster for the customer and less human resource required to deliver this service.

Other opportunities to leverage AI include more routine scenarios. For example, Schuh is a seasonal business. In September/October, students go back to college and university. Schuh has a significant student customer base who receive a student discount. Therefore, a large number of students need to demonstrate that they have student ID. Currently, this is a semi-manual process whereby their customer service team look at the cards through Facebook messenger in order to verify. In future, AI could play a part here to reduce the need for human intervention. It just needs to be efficient and secure.

Schuh's people are their unique selling point (USP) and they are a finite resource. Therefore, they need to ensure they use their people appropriately to deliver the best experience for customers where it also drives the most value for the business.

AI also drives price and margin optimization

Julian Burnett, Former CIO, Executive Director, Supply Chain, House of Fraser told me that price and markdown optimization is being driven by a machine-learning approach – taking the instinct out of decision making.

CASE STUDY   Payment services

Below are some examples of payment services using AI:

Amazon Go

In Seattle, Amazon have been testing an Amazon Go bricks-and-mortar proposition. They aim to create an environment where customers will be able to use the Amazon Go app to shop and go or pick up and go, creating a seamless automated shopping experience where the app tracks the objects that customers pick up and leave the store with, using AI systems. The customers' accounts are automatically charged when they leave the store (Fortune, 2017).

Net-a-Porter mash AI with human intervention

One of Net-a-Porter's USPs is that they have a huge number of personal shoppers. They cater for the needs of their not-insignificant number of high-value customers whom they refer to as extremely important people, or EIP for short. They are using AI to create a virtual personal stylist, which through machine learning is able to determine what products go together to create outfits that are best suited to certain customer types and needs. It also analyses external data such as weather and the customer's calendar. The focus for this AI-driven service would normally be to leverage the customer's purchase history to suggest what the customer might like to buy next. However, Net-a-Porter are able to deliver more relevant and granular degrees of personalization by also adding a layer of personal shopper recommendations on top of previous purchase data. For example, if a customer asks the virtual personal stylist (VPS) to search for an outfit for a party in Cannes on 4 April, the VPS will analyse local weather in order to recommend appropriate products (Arthur, 2017).

Otto/Blue Yonder

Forecasting sales has largely been an art but with AI and machine learning there is the ability to use science. Online retailer Otto is using technology from Blue Yonder (that builds on research undertaken at the CERN laboratory in Geneva) to crunch billions of transactions and 200 variables including past sales, web searches and things like weather information to predict what customers will buy in the near future. It has proved to be 90 per cent accurate in predicting what will be sold within 30 days, which has led to it now automatically purchasing 200,000 items a month. The surplus stock Otto holds has been reduced by 20 per cent.

(Retail Insider, 2017)

Driving around like a headless chicken... or human being

Never mind driverless cars, many organizations are developing driverless delivery vans. How long will it be before the motorways near you are full of robot-driven vans and trucks? Driverless cars are almost here. The impact of this will be beyond comprehension. What will happen to the huge number of lorry drivers? Will they lose their jobs? Will there be far fewer crashes and deaths on the road? Regarding the latter, I certainly hope so. What impact will that have on the insurance industry and on our insurance premiums? They should come down, shouldn't they? Or is that just wishful thinking?

EXPERT VIEW

AI will have a big impact upon payment solutions

I had the good fortune to interview Dr Leila Fourie who is a global thought leader in the area of payment solutions. I asked her how she thought AI would change the payment landscape. This was her response: 'AI will have a profound effect. However, as the great Roy Amara said, people overestimate technology in the short term and underestimate it in the long term.' I took from this that it may take a little time to achieve penetration, but it is coming.

Dr Fourie told me that the next 10 years will see profound changes to all aspects of the economy, as three interdependent trends mature – the extent to which everyone is connected, the opening up of networks, and the layering of rich services on these open and connected networks.

She told me that alongside this development, payments will become increasingly digital, integrated and seamless as a range of organizations, both globally and nationally, strive to deliver a secure and seamless payment experience.

Online and face to face will merge and payments will be invisible, for example China's Tenpay and Alipay apps that seamlessly pay for goods in the background and make purchasing the product more about selection than payment. Biometrics and non-traditional payment methods will quickly overtake traditional card POS payment channels.

One of the most interesting developments in AI is that technology will allow customers to initiate payments through natural language processing where a consumer can send a text message or use normal language, for example to say to Starbucks' app, 'Please give me my usual I'll be there in five.' Computers are now learning to adapt to less structured communications, which better reflects the informal way we speak. This means that computers are not limited to formal grammatically precise instructions but can better interpret our requests. As a Glaswegian, I cannot help thinking that this will be a good thing!

I asked her where else AI is being used. She told me that we are already seeing AI used in risk management and it is affecting the customer's experience, eg not everyone will be required to input a password due to tiny intelligence moments driving the interpretation of risk. Computers will have the ability to validate a user based on how they use their phone, eg if they are using a phone that does not belong to them, the computer will add additional layers of security for that customer.

I asked Dr Fourie about other changes to the payment landscape and what other innovative payment solutions are coming that will change the way we pay for goods or services. She highlighted Google's new product, TEZ. It involves audio QR codes where one phone talks to another without the requirement of any interaction on the part of the customer.

Top practical customer experience tips

1 Think about where AI can improve your value chain.

2 Leverage AI to improve customer service.

3 Use AI to deliver more personalized experiences.

4 Don't ever forget that you need a fall-back position when AI cannot answer the customer's question!

Expanded on below.

Think about where AI can improve your value chain

Do with AI what I suggested earlier in the book that you do with customer service, where you walk across all elements of your business and think about what you would do differently if you were a customer service business that just happened to sell the products or services that you do.

This time, walk across your value chain from product development to marketing, from merchandising to supply chain, from customer service to warehouse operations and determine where might you automate processes or leverage machine learning to improve the efficiency of what you do.

Leverage AI to improve customer service

Chat bots can definitely play a part in helping both to speed up the service levels for customers but also improve the quality and relevance of information they are provided with. For example, 90 per cent of Alibaba's customer service queries are handled by chat bots (Erikson and Wang, 2017).

Of Canadian auto shoppers, 63 per cent say they would prefer to check out cars on their own at the dealership. Maybe there is a good opportunity for car dealers to leverage bots at their physical branches to improve customer service and sales? This would remove the pressure and feeling from the customer that 'they are going to be sold to' (Facebook IQ, 2017a).

Also, 30 per cent of travellers said that they could make their travel decisions entirely with messaging apps. This is another area where chat bots can really drive value in terms of sales and conversion, by helping this customer segment to make a decision during their chat with you (Facebook IQ, 2017b).

Nonetheless, I would still suggest you have a good mix of human and AI customer interaction. But there is no question that AI in your customer service team will enable you to improve service levels, which in turn will drive a reduction in customer churn and an increase in word of mouth and advocacy. If your contact centre is also a sales channel, then it will also increase sales.

Use AI to deliver more personalized experiences

As mentioned above, AI can be leveraged to deliver ever more granular and relevant product and service recommendations for customers, whether that is a holiday or a car, a new house or a new dress. AI will ensure recommendations are tailored to the requirements of individual customers.

EXPERT VIEW

Robin Phillips, former Director of Omnichannel, Boots, once told me that they ran algorithms against the Boots range to determine relevant product recommendations based on the customer's skin type, which had already been identified. This is a great example of leveraging AI to drive tangible benefits for the customer.

Don't ever forget that you need a fall-back position when AI cannot answer the customer's question!

Hence my point above – don't get rid of all human interaction in your contact centre. That's a recipe for disaster!

Zalando, the leading fashion marketplace, has a personal stylist service called Zalon. They launched this in Germany in 2015 and have since rolled it out to other European markets. The unique service leverages existing customer data as well as information gleaned through telephone consultations conducted with shoppers by one of their 150 stylists. Following the call, customers are sent items that have been selected by the stylist. These product selections are made through a combination of the customer's profile, their existing data, an online questionnaire and a personal consultation. Outfits are delivered free and the customer can return any items they don't want to keep (Ecommerce News, 2017).

Over to Professor Malcolm McDonald

I guess most of us could write happily for hours about AI, but please don't worry, I won't do this! But I hope you do not mind my saying a few words, at least.

First, AI today is properly known as 'narrow AI, or weak AI' in the sense that it is designed to perform a narrow task, such as facial recognition, internet searches, chess (IBM's Watson), driving a car, etc. Many researchers have the long-term goal to create 'general AI, or strong AI'. Whilst narrow AI might outperform humans at whatever its specific task is, strong AI would outperform humans at almost every task except being able to exhibit human emotions such as love or hate, although they could be programmed to be intentionally benevolent or malevolent.

The truth, however, is that whilst some researchers at a 2015 Puerto Rico conference did not believe superintelligence will happen in our lifetime, many believed human-level AI would be with us before 2060. The point is that there is much safety research taking place in the scientific community to guard against the possible malevolent use of strong AI.

More to the point of this chapter, we know that narrow AI is already beginning to revolutionize hitherto professional domains such as law and accounting. For example, much of the basic work in law is predictable and repetitive, such as writing wills or conveyances, whilst accountancy firms such as Accenture and PwC are already using robots for many routine tasks because they can be done more cheaply and more quickly. In medicine, robots study X-rays, MRI scans, medical research papers and other data and pick up signs of disease that doctors sometimes miss. Lord Darzi, the surgeon who pioneered keyhole surgery, says 'Robots are more precise, have greater range of movement in keyhole surgery and no hand tremor, which makes delicate stitching easier ' (Pearson, 2017).

To pick up on Martin's earlier point, what of the impact of robots on our society? PwC's analysis suggests that up to 30 per cent of UK jobs could be at risk of automation by the early 2030s, particularly in transportation and storage (56 per cent), manufacturing (46 per cent) and wholesale and retail (44 per cent) (PwC Computational General Equilibrium Model for AI, 2017).

No one yet knows the answer to the question of what happens to our socio-economic structure when people have little or no value in the workplace, in an exponentially growing population with inversely proportional fewer jobs. What career advice would we give our children? I personally am one of that band of optimists who knows that society has always adapted to change, the way we did during the steel, oil and electricity and computer revolutions. We have indeed already entered the fourth industrial revolution and most predictions are that AI will boost profits in education, construction, accommodation and food services, wholesale and retail, etc.

There is one major proviso, however. During the first three industrial revolutions, businesses that did not adapt disappeared very quickly and the same will be true with this fourth industrial revolution. There will always be Luddites, of course, so avoid becoming one by paying careful attention to the important advice in this chapter.

References

Arthur, R (2017) [accessed 1 December 2017] Yoox Net-a-Porter Looks to the Future of AI and Mobile Commerce with New Tech Hub in London [Online] https://www.forbes.com/sites/rachelarthur/2017/06/27/yoox-net-a-porter-tech/#10f082e81564

Caffyn, J (2016) [accessed 1 December 2017] Two months In: How the 1-800 Flowers Facebook Bot is Working Out [Online] https://digiday.com/marketing/two-months-1-800-flowers-facebook-bot-working/

Chapman, M (2017) [accessed 1 December 2017] From Cars to Oysters: Could You Sell Your Products Through a Vending Machine? [Online] https://www.retail-week.com/topics/technology/could-you-sell-your-products-through-a-vending-machine/7025156.article

Ecommerce News (2017) [accessed 14 December 2017] Zalando Introduces Personal Shopping Service Zalon In Belgium [Online] https://ecommercenews.eu/zalando-introduces-personal-shopping-service-zalon-belgium/

Erikson, J and Wang, S (2017) [accessed 1 December 2017] At Alibaba, Artificial Intelligence Is Changing How People Shop Online [Online] http://www.alizila.com/at-alibaba-artificial-intelligence-is-changing-how-people-shop-online/

Facebook (2016) [accessed 1 December 2017] Burberry Facebook Post [Online] https://www.facebook.com/Burberry/photos/a.498187831424.298428.122792026424/10154547898026425/?type=3&theater

Facebook IQ (2017a) [accessed 1 December 2017] 63% of Canadian Auto Shoppers Say They'd Prefer to Check Out Cars On Their Own at the Dealership [Online] https://www.facebook.com/iq/insights-to-go/63-63-of-canadian-auto-shopperspeople-ages-1864-who-reported-that-they-planned-to-purchase-or-lease-a-vehicle-in-the-next-12-months-say-theyd-prefer-to-check-out-cars-on-their-own-at-the-dealership/

Facebook IQ (2017b) [accessed 1 December 2017] 30% of Travellers Said That They Could Make Their Travel Decisions Entirely With Messaging Apps [Online] https://www.facebook.com/iq/insights-to-go/30-30-of-travelers-said-that-they-could-make-their-travel-decisions-entirely-with-messaging-apps/

Fortune (2017) [accessed 14 December 2017] 5 Reasons Why Amazon Is Experimenting With Physical Stores [Online] http://fortune.com/2017/04/28/5-reasons-amazon-physical-stores/

Gartner (2017) [accessed 14 December 2017] Gartner Predicts [Online] https://www.gartner.com/binaries/content/assets/events/keywords/digital-marketing/ml3/gartner-2017-marketing-predicts.pdf

Pearson, D (2017) [accessed 2 May 2018] Artificial Intelligence [Online] http://www.davidcpearson.co.uk/blog.cfm?blogID=543

PwC Computational General Equilibrium Model for AI (2017) [accessed 2 May 2018] The Macroeconomic Impact of Artificial Intelligence [Online] https://www.pwc.co.uk/economic-services/assets/macroeconomic-impact-of-ai-technical-report-feb-18.pdf

Retail Insider (2017) [accessed 29 November 2017] Digital Retail Innovations Report http://webloyalty.co.uk/Images/UK/Digital_Retail_Innovations_Report_2017.pdf

Salesforce (2017) [accessed 1 December 2017] Shopper-First Retailing: What Consumers are Telling Us About the Future of Shopping [Online] https://www.demandware.com/uploads/resources/REP_Sapient_Report_EN_27JUNE2017_FINAL_.pdf

Softbank Robotics (nd) [accessed 1 December 2017] Pepper, the Humanoid Robot [Online] https://www.ald.softbankrobotics.com/en/robots/pepper

US Department of Labour (2017) [accessed 1 December 2017] The Employment Situation [Online] https://www.bls.gov/news.release/pdf/empsit.pdf

Zebra Technologies (2017) [accessed 1 December 2017] Reinventing Retail: 2017 Retail Vision Study [Online] https://www.zebra.com/content/dam/zebra_new_ia/en-us/solutions-verticals/vertical-solutions/retail/white-paper/2017retailvisionstudy-whitepaper-en-global.pdf

The rise of the 'ations' in driving differentiation   16

WHAT YOU WILL LEARN IN THIS CHAPTER

The rise of what I call the 'ations':

- Premiumization.
- Customization.
- Personalization/me-ization.

Aside from the fact that all three end in 'ation', I feel that there is a direct correlation between premiumization, customization and personalization and their importance in delivering the right proposition for customers, but also enabling you to differentiate what you offer.

Premiumization

Premiumization has seen the ever-increasing move towards the creation of products or services that have a perceived higher value through their branding, packaging and product or service value proposition. If we buy them, consuming or experiencing them is more rewarding than doing the same with less premium brands.

According to the Oxford Dictionary, premiumization is the action or process of attempting to make a brand or product appeal to consumers by emphasizing its superior quality and exclusivity (Oxford Dictionaries, 2017), one example of this being the 'premiumization' of bottled water.

There have been many new bottled waters launched in recent years. Some of those include:

- Voss Artesian Water;
- Hildon Natural Mineral Water;
- Evian Natural Spring Water;
- Fiji Natural Artesian Water.

The launch of Fever Tree as a premium mixer has shaken up (excuse the pun) that particular product category. We have also seen this in the alcoholic beverages sector. A few examples of premium brands launched in existing core categories include:

- Whisky:
  - Haig Club;
  - Barrelhound;
  - Prometheus.
- Gin:
  - Hendricks;
  - Monkey 47;
  - Martin Miller's;
  - Tanqueray No Ten.
- Vodka:
  - Grey Goose;
  - Absolut;
  - Belvedere;
  - Stolichnaya.

Premiumization has provided the opportunity for any new entrants to come into established product categories with new, innovatively packaged and branded products, charge a premium and, in some cases, displace well-established market leaders. However, as more and more new brands enter different categories, it will over time become harder for consumers to differentiate in their own minds between the plethora of options available. It is almost like the creation of the long tail of premium brands.

If a company has a high perceived price and low perceived benefits it will sit to the left-hand side of the value equivalence line (VEL) (Figure 16.1) and will be at a competitive disadvantage and lose market share. Companies on

Figure 16.1   The value equivalence line

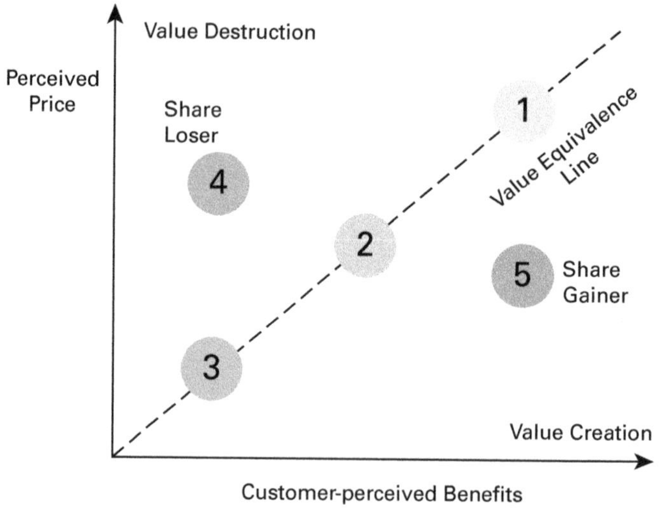

SOURCE McKinsey (1997)

the right-hand side of the VEL will have larger market share and could be in a position where they can raise prices and capture more value (netvaluescore. com, 2015).

A customer move to trade up rather than down

While I believe there will always be a segment of customers who look for the best-value product or service, which to their mind will most likely be the cheapest, increasing numbers of customers will look to trade up, with their concept of value not derived from a cheaper price. To the contrary, they will perceive that they will enjoy more value by paying for a product or service that delivers more longer-lasting benefits. This in turn lends itself to premiumization.

Customization

With so much homogeneity around, I believe consumers will increasingly look for products or services that can be customized for their own specific requirements, or simply to give their product a point of difference. We can order specific models of cars, but as we move towards an era of driverless vehicles, I cannot help thinking that consumers who still want to drive themselves – which I'm sure will be the majority over the next decade – will seek to differentiate our cars more: by 'wrapping them', ordering them in unique colours, changing the wheels. Pimp my ride if you like!

Sports equipment: I'm sure we will be able to customize our sports equipment far more than we do at present. Whether that is changing the colour of your golf driver, adding your own branding to your golf bag, tennis racket or skis, I cannot help thinking that we will strive to customize our products and services more and more in order to maintain a degree of our personal requirements, as things around us become increasingly homogenous.

Sports brands Nike and adidas have for a number of years been offering customers the ability to customize their sneakers. This can be done both online and instore, enabling the customer to fully customize and personalize their new footwear. Many other brands offer this facility, including Levi's and Converse. This does not just apply to products. We increasingly look for vacations and short breaks that we can create ourselves. Even when we stay somewhere in the same place for two weeks, more often than not we have booked the flights and hotels separately ourselves. Package holidays work when you are at a certain life stage or demographic.

How about going into a restaurant and asking them to make you something you want to eat that isn't on their menu? Obviously, they would need the ingredients and the recipe! But the latter would not be too hard to find online. What if you were able to go into your bank or speak to your insurance company and ask them to create a package of insurance cover for your family covering household insurance, car insurance, pet insurance and so on? Why can't you do this?

Customization is also having a very positive impact upon the lives of disabled people. Remap is an organization that customizes equipment for disabled customers, enabling them to lead more independent lives. This can be anything from showers to golf clubs, from head-operated computers and feeding devices to bespoke fireguards (Remap.com, nd).

Me-ization/personalization

According to Salesforce (2017) 58 per cent of shoppers who attend instore events are likely to make purchases and 70 per cent of customers receiving personalized promotions or offers are more likely to visit a store again. Consumers have so much choice both in relation to the channel and the brand to buy from. Whatever you sell – cars, holidays, dining out, dining in, fashion, electricals, homewares, insurance – you must at the very least offer customers the option of a more personalized and customized proposition.

The marriage of localization and personalization

Amazon have launched a personalized shopping service that offers products based on the shopper's local weather conditions. This makes personalization far more relevant as the product offers are contextualized and current. For example, on a sunny summer's day, you will find sun cream, sunglasses and bathing suits being promoted, while on a wet, rainy day, umbrellas, anoraks and rain boots. Amazon has developed an algorithm that studies weather data in order to recommend weather-relevant items, which are also based on the consumer's location. So, it is a very localized weather-driven proposition (Jahshan, 2017).

Retailers are slowly starting to get personal

Some fashion retailers are beginning their journey towards delivering personalized experiences for customers. Shop Direct Group's flagship brand Very.co.uk delivers personalized homepages to customers. This is a highly effective way to segment your customer base and deliver more relevant and engaging content based on the individual customer's preferences. For example, younger consumers who shop for fashion will immediately be served up with styles that Very know they will be interested in; those looking for homewares on a budget will see discounted products or those that fit with their budget. Shop Direct Group have been one of the early innovators within e-commerce. Over a number of years they have built up their data science capabilities and created their own in-house algorithms that they leverage to predict customer behaviour. They have a huge amount of customer data, which when fed through their algorithm can rank the relevance of offers to individual customers.

This is not where it ends. According to *Retail Week*, Very.co.uk can create 1.2 million versions of its homepage, with flexible elements including the type of promotional messages and their position on the page. They also leverage AI to deliver personalized product recommendations for customers (Retail Week, 2016). The challenge when it comes to fashion is how you balance highly personalized recommendations with the 'surprise element' that particularly younger consumers like to experience when it comes to fashion.

Grocery multiples such as Coles in Australia and the online grocer Ocado in the UK leverage personalization to deliver convenience to customers through pre-populated shopping bags and lists based on previous purchases.

Personalization doesn't begin and end online.

As outlined in Chapter 15 with the example of Zalando's 'Zalon' personal stylist service, and with Net-a-Porter's 'you try, we wait' service, e-tailers are trying to bring the personal touch to their proposition. Multichannel retailers are also looking to leverage the abundance of customer data they hold from online transactions in order to deliver more relevant and more effective offline experiences and deliver personalization through all channels and touchpoints.

According to *Retail Week*, Monsoon Accessorize has achieved this by arming store staff with iPads to transform them into personal assistants. The iPads give staff access to live stock information and product pages, featuring recommendations so that they can promote alternative or complementary items (Retail Week, 2016).

As described earlier, US retailers are under huge pressure, partly due to Amazon taking market share but also due to the increasing customer migration to online. This means that retailers have too many stores. Some have been looking to repurpose these with smaller, more experiential store formats. One such brand is Kohl's, a US department store who also have a firm focus on personalizing the experience for customers. They have created a personalized experience across all touchpoints, both physical and virtual – from the deals and products that the customer sees when they hit a landing page on the website to personalized offers aimed at stopping the customer from abandoning their shopping cart. Kohl's also delivers customers with tailored marketing campaigns and now leverages data science to assist merchandising allocation.

In Australia, David Jones, one of the leading department-store chains, will have a Johnny Walker bar. Taste it, buy the bottle, have it engraved and personalized.

This personalized product experience will definitely increase as retailers look to differentiate and provide more engaging experiences.

Top practical customer experience tips

1 Deliver personalized experiences for core customer segments.

2 Provide the ability for customers to customize their products.

3 Consider the opportunity to create more premiumized products or services.

Expanded on below.

Deliver personalized experiences for core customer segments

The more you personalize the customer's experience, the more you will sell. Yes, it is as simple as that. A personalized experience means more relevant product, services, content and overall experience. As a result, more customers will convert, they will spend more, they will come back more often and they will tell others about you.

A big contributor to Alibaba's 61 per cent year-on-year growth in sales in Q3 2017 was their ability to deliver deeply personalized content and product offers for customers (Michael Evans, President).

Provide the ability for customers to customize their products

While not widely available currently, I believe this will become a given and any consumer-facing business that does not enable customers to customize their insurance policy, car, suit, dining table and so on, will simply lose out.

Consider the opportunity to create more premiumized products or services

Most of us are happy to pay more for more quality. That's why premium and luxury brands exist. So, think about whether there is an opportunity for you to premiumize some of your products or services

Over to Professor Malcolm McDonald

This chapter identifies a commercial phenomenon that many business people don't either appreciate or understand, particularly economists. That is, 20th-century economists popularized the nonsensical notion that consumers are rational. In other words, they maximize utility at the margin using perfect information. To give just one illustration, consider the scientific jargon that many are drawn into on adverts, from yoghurt to hair loss

treatment and skincare! It is designed to sound overintelligent and encourage consumers to make a seemingly rational decision, regardless of whether
the yoghurt is bog-standard or premium quality.

The only problem with the economist view is that it just isn't true, otherwise we would not have brands, for example.

In this context, let's discuss premiumization and Martin's point in using
pricing strategy as the differentiator for customer choice. Premium brands
in particular defy the logic of economists. In most markets, such as education, price is seen as an indicator of value. Despite economist predictions,
nearly every time price goes up for luxury goods, sales also go up.

It is also interesting to note that during every recession most sectors
suffer, but hardly ever do premium brands suffer. Most of them just keep
thriving and prospering. Figure 16.2 illustrates this phenomenon.

From Figure 16.2 it can be observed that during a recession most of
the companies in the mass middle market are forced to reduce their prices
(mostly because they do not understand the crucial importance of market
segmentation), whereas the premium brands just keep growing, with a few
rare exceptions. So premiumization is certainly worth considering, providing the consumer perceives real value in a brand.

Customization and personalization are also growing trends, as spelt
out by Martin in this chapter. Fortunately, we now have the technology to
enable brands to interact with consumers more intelligently and certainly
way beyond just knowing their name and birthday. We can expect brands
to have a record of every single touchpoint and every single experience and
to use that data to achieve, where appropriate, customization and personalization, as long as it doesn't err on the side of intrusion into our privacy.
The new General Data Protection Regulation (GDPR) of May 2018 is

Figure 16.2   What happens in a recession

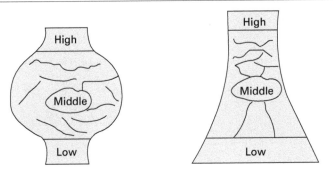

testament both to the ethics of this increased data use and the awareness of the consumer of how their identity is being used and circulated beyond their control. Ensuring the customer feels safe and trusting of where you are using their data will build a unique and authentic differentiator to your organization.

References

Jahshan, E (2017) [accessed 1 December 2017] Amazon Launches Weather-Based Shopping Service [Online] https://www.retailgazette.co.uk/blog/2017/04/amazon-launches-weather-based-shopping-service/

McDonald, M (1996) *Strategic Marketing Planning*, Kogan Page, London

McKinsey (1997) [accessed 29 December 2017] Setting Value, Not Price, *McKinsey Quarterly* [Online] https://www.mckinsey.com/business-functions/marketing-and-sales/our-insights/setting-value-not-price

Netvaluescore.com (2015) [accessed 14 December 2017] Price Against Benefits – Value Equivalence Line [Online] http://netvaluescore.com/price-benefits/

Oxford Dictionaries | English (2017) [accessed 14 December 2017] Premiumization | Definition of Premiumization in English by Oxford Dictionaries [Online] https://en.oxforddictionaries.com/definition/premiumization

Remap.com (nd) [accessed 19 December 2017] [Online] http://www.remap.org.uk

Retail Week (2016) [accessed 1 December 2017] Personalisation: Retail Technology That Enhances the Customising Shopper Experience [Online] https://www.retail-week.com/topics/technology/innovation/personalisation-retailers-blazing-a-trail-on-the-customer-journey/5079455.article

Salesforce (2017) [accessed 1 December 2017] Shopper-First Retailing: What Consumers are Telling Us About the Future of Shopping [Online] https://www.demandware.com/uploads/resources/REP_Sapient_Report_EN_27JUNE2017_FINAL_.pdf

Understanding customer behaviour 17

Turning data into actionable insight and the key drivers for customer relationship management

WHAT YOU WILL LEARN IN THIS CHAPTER

- What are the current barriers to achieving a single customer view?
- What can be achieved with a single view of the customer?
- The importance of personalized communications.
- I demonstrate that there is a hierarchy of customer relationship management (CRM), from sending gender-relevant e-mails to full personalization.
- I provide case studies of brands that communicate highly effectively with customers.
- How do you surface a deeper understanding of customer behaviour?
- What should you be looking for in the first place?
- How can this insight help you to deliver an even better customer experience?

I want the penultimate chapter of the book to cover what I feel is the most underserved and potentially undervalued opportunity for consumer-facing organizations: customer *relationship* management (CRM).

If you don't have a single view of the customer, then you cannot truly know who your customers are, what they like, what they don't like, which channels they like to buy from and when, which marketing activity they respond best to, and whether or not they ever engage with your contact centre.

We live in a multichannel world. To this end, I would hope that most businesses know that the value of a customer who engages through more than one channel is exponentially higher than that of a single-channel customer. Not only is their value higher, but they are also more loyal. Hence the imperative to have a single view of the customer. I know that legacy systems and technology are often to blame for the inability to deliver this, but I also know that very few businesses are prioritizing it.

Clean up your act, or at least your data

When shopping in numerous retailers, more often than not, when I am asked for my details the staff cannot find me in the system. This suggests various potential issues. Some relate to the requirement for data cleansing, some could be system related. Either way, brands need to ensure that if they are going to offer and promote any form of loyalty programme they can ensure that all of the customer's transactions are recognized and that they are rewarded appropriately for their level of spend, irrespective of the channel in which the order was placed.

GDPR: General Data Protection Regulation

Implemented on 25 May 2018, the General Data Protection Regulation is the biggest shake-up of data protection rules since the introduction of the Data Protection Act in 1998. Introduced by the European Union (EU), it is directly applicable in all member states without the need for implementing national legislation.

The GDPR applies to any organization that offers goods or services to individuals in the EU no matter where they are in the world. So, it is not just about retail, it covers all consumer-facing verticals and more. The GDPR also applies to both data controllers and data processors. This is particularly important for companies that use external data agencies, and as a controller you must ensure your contracts are up to date and your agencies are meeting the correct standards. The GDPR is very similar to the Data Protection Act 1998, which it is replacing, and all the legal obligations covered by the Data Protection Act still apply. There are some additional obligations and safeguards. For example, the Data Protection Act applies to all personal data but personal data just got bigger. The GDPR's definition of personal data is more detailed and is clear that it includes online identifiers such as MAC and IP addresses. The definition is broad to account for changes in technology. If you can identify an individual from it, it is included.

Unlike the Data Protection Act, GDPR also applies to individuals in a business. Previously you could send unsolicited e-mail to people at a business e-mail address but this no longer applies. You must ensure your opt-in status on your marketing lists is perfect. The best bet is to get advice to ensure you are compliant.

ROI = return on involvement

Are there any brands really building 'relationships' with customers? I would say no, and if there are you can count them on one hand. Later in this chapter, I demonstrate that there is a hierarchy of CRM, from sending gender-relevant e-mails to full personalization. If you can get customers 'involved' in your brand, then there is a far higher likelihood of them buying more of whatever you have to sell.

If you were a fashion retailer, you might want to invite your top customers to the launch of your new range in your flagship store or in another salubrious environment. You would also want to ensure that top customers had the first option to buy from you when you have an incentive running. If you were a tour operator, running vacations, you might want to proactively ask your customers to tell others about their experience. If you were a vacation and tour operator, wouldn't you want to invite customers who have travelled with you before to come to an evening when launching a new destination you've added to your proposition?

If you were a car dealer, instead of thrusting salespeople upon new customers, you might give existing customers the opportunity to tell them why they love their new car so much. I'm sure you could find a way of rewarding them for this.

Engaged customers talk about you. They are advocates. They attract other customers, and they buy more frequently. As Figure 17.1 highlights, their lifetime value is significantly greater.

I mentioned earlier in the book that AO.com has 40 per cent monthly customer engagement on social media channels. That is approximately 720,000 of their followers on Facebook! Let me remind you. They sell fridge freezers, washing machines, tumble dryers. Yes, they also sell TVs now, but

Figure 17.1   Customer lifetime value

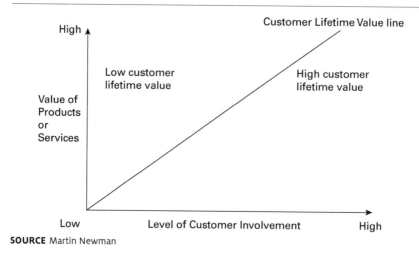

SOURCE Martin Newman

whatever way you look at it, it is a phenomenal level of customer engagement. Even more so given what they sell. I can think of dozens of brands who are better known, in what you would think would be product categories that lend themselves to greater customer engagement, but they have far lower overall numbers associating with them on social media and way lower when it comes to regular engagement. These customers have also become a huge army of advocates for the brand.

Wiggle and Rapha, both key players in the cycling sector, understand what it means to engage and involve customers in their brand. While it is primarily an online business, the former does so by running a lot of offline events. Sportives and involvement with other cycling events have enabled Wiggle to reinforce its credibility with its core, loyal, customer base, while also broadening the reach of the brand. Rapha has created community hubs in its store, turning a retail environment into a place where cyclists want to spend time, meet their friends and engage in all things cycling. Both of these brands generate a lot of word of mouth through brand advocates, and that goodwill is at least in part driven by how they involve customers in their brand.

Price x involvement drives lifetime value + advocacy = value-added sales

Alibaba have coined the term 'retail-ment' to describe how they believe that retail environments need to become more entertaining and to bring the customer experience to life. I could not agree more. However, the term I would prefer to use is 'retainment'. Sorry, but I think it neatly describes the same thing: the mash-up of being able to buy things in an environment that entertains us, that is the 'tainment part, but also from a brand that wants to 'retain' us. It describes a business that is focused on ensuring we come back. Entertainment on its own will not always ensure that is the case. But it will certainly help. We need to extend the relationship with the customer beyond the store and beyond our websites. We need to find other ways of keeping them 'involved' with our brand. Then, along with an engaging and entertaining experience, we have a real chance of winning the war for the customer.

CRM drives involvement and engagement and it absolutely drives sales

I asked Philip Mountford, CEO of Hunkemöller, a leading European lingerie brand, how he had leveraged CRM to drive sales and engagement. This was his response: 'It has helped to be able to move the average customer age down by 11 years, making the brand more accessible to a broader and also a younger audience.'

The brand conducts data mining, segmentation and personalization to drive customer engagement and sales. The KPIs certainly support their success to date: 1) they have 10 million customers who are members of their CRM programme; 2) 5 million of whom are active in a year.

They created a programme called 'sexy comes in all shapes', which in turn has provided a level of detail and understanding about their customers that has enabled them to radically reduce returns rates and drive a deep understanding of the customer's shape.

This in turn led to the creation of the following customer shape-driven segments:

- Perfect plunge.
- Delicious demi.
- Fabulous full cup.
- Beautiful balcony.

This enables Hunkemöller to only send customers bras that fit their size and shape. They are only sent personalized communications and relevant promotions that fit their profiling.

The business also has a very innovative loyalty programme whereby customers are not only rewarded for the purchases they make (they get

£5 after a £50 spend). Customers get points for tweeting, product recommendations and are rewarded for other social interactions; 5 per cent to 7 per cent of CRM-related customer rewards are given for non-transactional touchpoints. Crucially, they have a single view of the customer and are therefore able to provide more effective service and incentives for customers as a result of understanding their behaviour. They are also using geo-fencing and iBeacons to push relevant promotions to customers when they are instore.

Move from customer transactional management (CTM) to CRM

Unfortunately the best practice demonstrated by Hunkemöller above is the exception rather than the norm.

CRM is another of those terms that has been bandied around since 2002. It implies that we are going to build a relationship with customers when, in reality, CRM is normally no more than a crude loyalty-based points programme or an incentive to spend more and save. In the retailer's case, I would argue that too often they give away margin without really knowing what the impact is on customer lifetime value and behaviour.

Tesco Clubcard, Boots Advantage and similar programmes such as CVS Pharmacy's ExtraCare have their strengths in driving propensity to buy, but at their core they are spend-and-save schemes. They are not building a lasting, long-term relationship that correlates with the life stage of the customer. I believe the acronym that best describes what this currently represents is customer transaction management (CTM). As consumer-facing businesses, we manage customers' orders, we don't build relationships.

Of all the retailers I buy from, I cannot think of one that sends me truly segmented, trigger-driven, behavioural e-mails based on who I am and what I buy, and therefore what else I might like.

So how can retailers deliver true CRM?

Join up your customer data across all channels, including the call centre, so that they have a single view of customers and their behaviour through all touchpoints. Their marketing communications should also be joined up so that they send relevant communications via e-mail and other channels, which are aimed at adding value to me based on my behaviour. A single customer view (SCV) is not only for the benefit of the customer in the context that you can send them consistent and relevant communications. It can also be used to inform your business decisions. For example, Nadine Neatrour, Ecommerce Director, Revolution Beauty, told me that when she was head of e-commerce at Thomas Pink they were one of the first retailers to have an SCV. One of the main benefits was that she was able to prove through empirical data that e-mail marketing was driving 30 per cent of sales across all channels, and not just online. This understanding of attribution is hugely important.

Clientelling solutions instore and the use of iBeacons to bring a more personalized instore experience will be hugely important. Whatever the correct term is, I don't believe that CRM on its own is enough, even when the true definition moves towards relationship management. Maybe it should be customer life cycle management (CLM), as only once a consumer-facing business builds relationships that deliver relevant products, promotions, content, service and added value – that recognizes where the customer is in their life cycle – can they truly hope to build a meaningful long-term relationship with their customers.

Automotive brands and dealers have a great opportunity to drive an increase in customer lifetime value by communicating with customers more regularly at different stages throughout the lifetime of their car ownership.

I have a number of friends who only ever buy the same brand: Porsche, Audi, BMW, Mercedes, Ford et al. Yet, the communication they receive, both from the car brands directly or the car dealers, is sporadic. Car buying has a life cycle, often dictated these days by various contracts, be that contract hired for business or personal contract purchase (PCP) for personal usage. There are clear windows of opportunity to engage with a new car buyer: within a few weeks, just to ensure all is well; within a few weeks of their first service being due to remind them to book in their car; at various other times when the car requires a service. A car dealer has the opportunity to e-mail you about the fact you may require new tyres, or to offer you the option of having your alloy wheels resurfaced. Also, of course, when you are within six months of the end of your contract they should be targeting you with the latest offer or option to trade in for a new model. If you are as loyal to one of these brands as some of my friends are, then you could easily be on some form of loyalty programme:

- get a new model quicker – no need to join the end of the waiting list;

- a free upgrade to the model above;

- free servicing;

- free insurance;
- a discounted second car for your partner etc.

With a number of the car manufacturers now creating a direct-to-consumer model, disintermediating the car sector by bypassing the car dealerships, this may well change.

The hierarchy of CRM

1   Do nothing, eg customers even receive non-gender-relevant e-mails.

2   Spray and pray: everyone gets the same message.

3   Minimal personalization: I'm recognized by name albeit nothing else is personalized in the e-mail.

4   A welcome programme: I'm sent some fairly generic incentives or communication based on having made my first purchase.

5   Surprise and delight: I receive the same general communication as everyone else, but the brand gives me a surprise gift on my first purchase, or potentially at another point in my life cycle. For example, when I first bought Lab Series skin crème directly from the brand, they sent me a very luxurious dressing gown. It made me feel special and wanted as a customer.

6   Basic points-driven loyalty programmes and communications.

7   Recency, frequency and value: this is where a brand targets you based on how recently you bought, how often you buy and how much you spend. It is a good, quick way to target your best customers. However, make sure to reward this customer segment as well and don't simply try to sell them more stuff.

8   Behaviour driven: the communications I receive relate in some way to what I purchased previously and the loyalty programme gives me the flexibility to choose what I get discounts on. Both Waitrose and Boots offer this for loyalty card holders.

9   Full personalization: all of the communications I receive are relevant, they use my name, my purchase history and frequency, they recognize my multichannel behaviour etc. All of the incentives, loyalty and promotions are tailored towards me.

EXPERT VIEW

Robin Phillips, former Director of Omnichannel at Boots, told me that he looks to create an actionable view of the customer's most recent behaviour so that they can layer over relevant offers and content for different customer segments.

There can be no doubt that many customers want a brand to know who they are, and to recognize all of their behaviour. That way they will receive more relevant communications and content from the brand.

EXPERT VIEW

I asked Morgan Tan, President of Shiseido in Hong Kong, from her own experience as a consumer what she believes makes for a great experience (either online or offline). She told me that when they know it is YOU online, when companies are able to connect all of your interactions together and know that it is YOU, that is when you get the best experience.

I want my data back, and I want it now

One other key thing to keep in mind is that in the future it is highly likely that consumers will be able to demand their data back from a brand that they no longer choose to engage with. I don't just mean that you will not be able to communicate with them, as that exists today, I mean that you will have to give them all the data and insight you have built about them. This risk means that being customer-centric has never been more important, as failure to do so means customers will walk with their data.

I've got data coming out of my ears... what about insight?

Brands often complain about not having enough data, when in fact they have plenty of data but what they lack is actionable insight. I have the personal experience of sitting in literally hundreds of trading meetings on a Monday. I had more KPIs than I could shake a stick at:

- sales;
- margin;
- average order values;
- conversion rates (for web and stores);
- traffic for the web (unique and repeat);
- abandonment rates;
- bounce rates;
- footfall for stores;
- returns rates;
- dwell time;
- best sellers;
- worst sellers.

The list goes on and on. But when asked by my boss at the time why the KPIs were behaving the way they were, why they were up or down, I had no tangible answers.

Data, and more importantly insight, is hugely important. They enable you to make fact-based, objective decisions and remove excuses for poor performance from the conversation. They also remove 'the hippo effect', the 'highest-paid person's opinion', just as they provide insight into what is working well and therefore why you should invest more in activity that is delivering good results for you.

If you were a restaurant, wouldn't you want to know if there were options on the menu that customers simply didn't want to eat? Or if the mix of desserts was not appropriate for the starters and main courses that preceded them? You would be able to see this through the data.

You might follow the example of FMCG brands who regularly run taste panels with their suppliers. Get your real-life customers to taste new dishes or even provide you with ideas on how to improve the menu. Now I fully appreciate there are head chefs recoiling in horror at this suggestion! But this is simply about putting the customer first. Letting them make a contribution to helping you shape your menu.

One of the largest accessories and fashion brands in the world, Xiaomi, who have 50 million fans, leverage customers in the product development process. Customers are able to vote for the styles the brand is thinking of producing, also giving them the opportunity to recommend amendments to products that would make them more desirable.

Volvo's strapline and key campaign message for the past couple of years has been 'first we listen, then we make', in their inimitable Swedish 'matter of fact' approach. Essentially it says, 'we listen to our customers' then we decide what to develop.

How often does a financial services company speak to its customers to get their feedback on the products and services that would make a difference to them? I mentioned in an earlier chapter that if financial services providers did involve their customer base in determining the relevance of their products, they would most likely offer a very different proposition, such as a package of different products and services for the whole family. They would find ways of creating a value-added ecosystem. Yes, price architecture is an important factor; however, customers are often prepared to pay for something with the appropriate level of perceived value.

All consumer sectors should leverage customer sentiment

Customers return products to retailers every day. Whether they were purchased instore or online, customers take things back. This is often because they don't fit, or they have simply changed their mind when their goods have been delivered. There can be many other reasons for returning products. This insight is invaluable and can be leveraged in various ways. At a generic level, you can discover patterns. These can highlight issues with certain categories of products. This data enables retailers to develop more effective ranges of products. At a personalized level, you get to know what customers don't like. That should help to inform what you try to sell them, the content you produce, marketing activity and other ways you serve individual customers.

How many holiday companies have a really granular view of which elements of the customers vacation they did or didn't like? How many US travel operators know that, according to Facebook stats, US Hispanics are 1.34x more likely than non-Hispanics to have booked their most recent trip as a package vacation? (Facebook IQ, 2016). You may well review your offer and how you market to each of these segments.

If you were an insurance company selling car insurance, what could you learn from customers who did not renew their policy with you? I don't ever remember being asked by an insurer why I didn't renew with them. I think they too often make the assumption it is purely about price. That may be one of the main criteria for purchasing insurance; however, customers also care about what happens if they have an accident. If I have to call you, what is the experience like? An insurer who can focus on how they go the extra mile to help you out with a courtesy car, getting you a taxi home and so on, has a good chance of reducing customer churn and possibly even being able to charge more as a result of having better levels of service.

Propensity modelling

This is one level up from the most basic form of targeting customers. That is, sending them communication, content and offers that bear some relevance to what the customer has purchased before or to their purchase behaviour around how recently and how often they buy, and how much they spend. Despite this, the vast majority of consumer-facing businesses have not even got out of the starting blocks with this.

The beauty of the digital world is that you can test and learn. You can fail fast. You must never assume that because one business achieved a certain result from their e-mail marketing you should expect the same result. Everything has to be contextualized for your customers, your products, your business. Test and learn, test and learn, test and learn. Do it quickly. Learn and move on – and never stop learning.

Top practical customer experience tips

1 Build a relationship with customers, don't pay lip service.

2 Understand the hierarchy of CRM and how it helps customers.

3 Segment your customer base – there is no such thing as 'the customer'.

4 Measure and work towards the lifetime value of your customers.

5 Build a list of what is important to your business as actionable insight in order to improve performance.

6 Test and learn: fail fast, learn what works best and continue to improve it, learn what doesn't work, and don't do it again!

7 Loyalty is not a given. It has to be earned.

Expanded on below.

Build a relationship with customers, don't pay lip service

CRM is one of the great misnomers of business rhetoric. It suggests that we build relationships with our customers. But that is seldom the case.

Once you buy a new car, the only time you hear from the dealer you bought your car from is when they want to make more money from you, isn't it? It is time for your car to be serviced, Mr Newman. It may well be. Of course, it is vital that you can demonstrate that your car has a full-service history. But this is still very short term and sales focused, as opposed to relationship building with a focus on my lifetime value to the dealer or brand. One brand that has addressed this is Hyundai. They offer a five-year warranty.

My recent purchase of a car saw multiple e-mails and survey requests asking me to rate their service and how I was getting on with my new car. Traditional direct-marketing models would tell you that it is not profitable to continue to communicate with me until it is time for me to trade in my car for another new car. However, I believe that in this day and age that is a flawed model. After all, if you knew I would buy another new car, wouldn't you consider it a worthwhile investment to keep in touch with me – if nothing else, to ensure you were my first port of call when I did want to trade my car in, as opposed to leaving me to choose a different car dealer to engage with?

How about if you were able to get to know more about me, for example, who else is in my life? After all, referrals should be a focus for every business.

One automotive brand that sees the longer term, customer lifetime value opportunity, is Nissan. When you buy one of their electric cars, they lend you a petrol car for driving holidays where electric cars are not practical.

It pays to be sociable. Waitrose offer a free tea or coffee for anyone on their loyalty programme. This is a customer retention driver.

Understand the hierarchy of CRM and how it helps customers

You have to question whether or not you are simply wasting hours and budget by sending the same generic e-mail to all of your customers. This will limit the level of response and in some cases simply turn customers off your brand for good as you haven't made the effort to communicate with them personally, to send something that relates to who they are, what they like and what they have previously purchased from you.

Your technology may not enable you to go straight to fully personalized communication, but at the very least you need to have a road map that clearly lays out the steps and timelines required to get there.

This might take the approach of the following model:

- review quality of existing customer data;
- define customer segmentation;
- define engagement and CRM plan for each;
- review systems and internal capabilities to acquire and manage data and derive insight from all customer touchpoints;
- join data and create a single customer view;
- define contact and communication strategy and plan for all core customer segments;
- measure, refine and communicate.

Segment your customer base – there is no such thing as 'the customer'

As Malcolm mentioned in the early chapters, there is no such thing as 'the customer'. There are multiple types of customer segment. If you don't know whom your core customer segments are, how can you develop your holidays, cars, houses, homewares, financial services, apparel, accessories and so on? How can you know how much to invest in targeting and acquiring these different customer types?

Measure and work towards the lifetime value of your customers

Nadine Neatrour, Ecommerce Director, Revolution Beauty, is very clear that customer lifetime value should be determined at margin/profitability level not at gross sales level, ie once the cost of goods and delivery has been removed. I would agree. Otherwise, how can you know how much to invest in recruiting and retaining customers?

Build a list of what is important to your business as actionable insight in order to improve performance

What are the things you really need to understand in order to know what to do to continually improve performance? As highlighted earlier in this chapter, as opposed to the typical KPIs we all measure, this would include things such as:

- Customer satisfaction levels for different elements of their experience with your brand. How many customers received their order first time?
- How many customers only rated your holiday with three stars out of five?
- Why was that? What didn't they like?
- Why are customers returning their products purchased online?
- Why are customers contacting your contact centre?
- What questions are customers asking through live chat?
- Why did customers not buy on your website? What was it about the products or experience they didn't like?

Test and learn: fail fast, learn what works best and continue to improve it. Learn what doesn't work and don't do it again!

I mentioned that you cannot always prove the business case for everything you want to do. Therefore, you must test and learn. In any case, testing and learning should become a core part of your business culture. Good is never good enough. You can always improve what you do and deliver a better experience for customers as well as deliver a better commercial performance for your business.

You should continually test products, services, the customer journey, promotions and service levels. Customers will always tell you what you do well and what you need to improve.

Loyalty is not a given, it has to be earned

The way to earn it is not only by giving points or discounts. It is by adding value and by delivering great service. Yes, customers often like to complain, some more than others. But there are many customers who will also happily promote your business to their friends or colleagues if you have been able to serve them well.

According to Nielsen, 67 per cent of consumers agree that they shop more frequently and spend more with retailers who have loyalty programmes (Nielsen, 2016).

Over to Professor Malcolm McDonald

As this is the last chapter I shall comment on, I want to finish on a positive and optimistic note, having first, however, put this whole product and branding issue into context.

We are all time poor today, yet we are bombarded by communications from a thousand different directions, most of which are irrelevant to us. The fact is that people have less time and attention available. The result is that consumers are doing everything within their power to spend less time on the communications being pushed at them. The response from marketers has been to push even harder, especially with digital technologies that use algorithms to process real-time data streams (programmatic). As a result, many consumers are blocking, skipping, avoiding, ignoring and clicking away, so it is vital to differentiate your efforts.

We simply don't care about product categories that are irrelevant to us. Brand choice is often no more than a mild feeling of preference, the brand name simply a way of cutting out on a lot of purchasing decision-making hassle. Having bought it, we simply don't want (nor do we have the time) to have an abstract relationship with it, thank you very much! What Martin says in this chapter is so right, in that many companies have confused customer habit with customer loyalty. For those categories in which we are really interested, if one supplier can demonstrate an understanding of us and show they care about us, we will be more willing to switch and stay with them.

As Mark Ritson said (*Marketing Magazine*, 3 December 2008, p 20) 'Great brands shine brightest when the sky is darkest. In austere times great brands bestow pleasure, maintain their premium and take a long view.' To conclude on this issue of brands, a great brand is not just a logo, it is a way of life, a way of doing business.

On the issue of CRM, I could not agree more with what Martin has said. Billions of dollars are wasted every year on so-called CRM systems. One of the main reasons they don't work is of course the failure of companies to segment their market into segments of customers who share the same or similar needs. Purchasers then expect this CRM system to give them a single view of the customer and so obviate the need for thinking!

Recent research reports in the industry are increasingly coming around to this idea, supporting our view very strongly. For example:

> Most marketers broadcast identical messages across all channels.
>
> (Salesforce, 2017)

> Consumers believe B2C marketers fail to align their communications with how they prefer to engage. Irrelevant content is the number one reason they don't engage more often.
>
> (Marketo, nd)

Finally, I share full support of Martin with regard to overcomplex food menus – using 100 words for a simple concept can, with such overcomplex phrasing, often sound more pretentious than inviting! Think of a simple steak and chips in a fresh roadside café, or the food generally in Italy. The high quality and authenticity speak volumes, offer a substantial portion and often taste a million times better!

I have thoroughly enjoyed working on this excellent book with Martin. I have 48 business books behind me, but it is safe to say that this one is different. It is current, desperately needed and based on Martin's long and deep experience of working with world-class companies.

To close my contribution to this wonderful book, I have just one last request to the customer-experience community.

In the spirit of losing my way so many times through a wilderness of call-centre buttons and recorded messages, please can we instate an option for 'if you have by now lost the will to live, please press 7!'

References

Facebook IQ (2016) [accessed 1 December 2017]A Field Guide to the US Digital Travel Booking Journey [Online] https://fbinsights.files.wordpress.com/2016/09/facebookiq_mobilecompassfieldguide.pdf

Marketo (nd) [accessed 14 December 2017] The State of Engagement [Online] https://uk.marketo.com/analyst-and-other-reports/the-state-of-engagement/

Nielsen (2016) [accessed 22 December 2017] Get With the Programme [Online] http://www.nielsen.com/content/dam/nielsenglobal/de/docs/Nielsen%20 Global%20Retail%20Loyalty-Sentiment%20Report%20FINAL.pdf

Salesforce (2017) [accessed 14 December 2017] Salesforce Research Fourth Annual State of Marketing [Online] http://www.salesforce.com/assets/pdf/datasheets/ salesforce-research-fourth-annual-state-of-marketing.pdf

So where do you 18 start to transform your business?

Customer-centric transformation journey framework

If you have got this far, then you must know **why** you need to put the customer first.

I sincerely hope I've done my job well enough and that you have now also got a fairly good idea of **what** you need to do, and **how** to do it. But I appreciate it is a lot to take in. As a Practicologist, I would hate for you to read this book and not know the practical steps for how and where to start your transformational journey. Therefore, I thought it might be helpful to end with a short chapter providing the key recommended steps on how to transform your business to deliver a customer-first approach:

1 **Appoint someone to the role of chief customer officer.** Or customer director. Someone who has a mandate from the board to define and deliver the new customer-facing business you want to become. They will help to answer '**what you need to do**' and also ensure that you are delivering your promises consistently.

2 **Appoint a change agent:** someone who can make it happen. The change and transformation lead will answer the '**how we need to do it**' question.

3 **Create a cross-functional 'customer enablement team'.** This does not necessarily need to be exclusively made up of directors and functional heads. It will help to 'keep it real' if you include some of your colleagues at different levels of your business. It is a steering group empowered to ensure that the new customer-first approach is being delivered across the business and within each of the core operational areas.

4 **Talk to your customers:** you can never do this enough. This is where your best insight will come from – not from algorithms, machine learning or AI.

A good place to start is in your physical environment if you have one. Just start having conversations with customers in your store, car showroom, restaurant, bank etc. Also, run a short, sharp survey on your website. Ask customers what they liked, what they didn't like, whether they made a purchase or not or responded to any calls to action, and if not why not. These are really easy and cost-effective to pull together through Survey Monkey or another similar site survey tool. The most effective leaders I have ever worked with are those who 'walk the floor'. They talk to customers, and they do it frequently. Customers will tell you all you need to know about what's good and what's less good about your business.

5   **Define customer experience for core customer segments:** only once you have determined what you need to do to deliver the right experience and to build up a rapport with your core customer segments can you possibly move on. This will help to answer **'what you need to do'**. You will be considering the experience of core customer segments across all channels and touchpoints of your business and what this needs to be moving forward.

6   **Lead from the front:** you don't have to be a digital native or customer-driven marketer to have the right skills to deliver the change your business requires. You just need to have the foresight of a Greg Wasson, former CEO of Walgreens who recognized he did not necessarily know exactly what the new customer journey needed to be nor how best to leverage technology to deliver it. However, he knew how to 'clear the path' for the people in his business who did have these answers. That was the best role he could play to ensure the successful delivery of the new customer-centric strategy.

EXPERT VIEW

Morgan Tan is the President in Hong Kong of one of the world's leading beauty brands, Shiseido, and recently listed in Hong Kong's top 50 retail leaders. I asked her what are the qualities she believes are required to be a successful CEO in this day and age? The following is her response:

> The greatest value a leader brings to organizations is recognizing that they are there to be in service to others. Helping others succeed in achieving their own goals is a leader's main purpose. Getting results becomes a means to an end, as the focus is on people building and rewarding efforts to

innovate. What makes it challenging is having to do so amidst uncertainties and changes in today's landscape. This is because consumers are changing how they engage and connect with brands. The difference between great and good leaders is having the courage and capacity to do things that others cannot.

I really like this, and just as the example before with Greg Wasson, Morgan recognizes that empowering her people and giving them the tools to be successful is key and that her job is one of enablement.

7 **Begin cultural change:** then you need to do some serious navel-gazing. Do you really have a customer-first culture? Your values, what you stand for, how you treat you internal customers, your colleagues, are all hugely important factors, as is your attitude towards investment. You cannot successfully complete this journey unless you move away from only having a short-term return to shareholder focus. I fully appreciate this flies in the face of what you have always had to do. But surely if your investors can see a difficult landscape ahead and the challenges you face versus the medium-term opportunity to become a customer-centric business, and the commercial benefits of doing so, they will have a different mindset? If not, you may need to look for different investors.

8 **Look at people, structure, capabilities and technology at the same time:** technology may help to plug some gaps in capability and in fact may even be a better option. Moreover, you need to determine what technology is required to deliver the level of customer-centricity you are aiming to deliver.

People, capabilities and structure. It is highly likely that you will have some obvious capability gaps. These are likely to be in the areas of data science, technology development, customer service and marketing. However, as outlined in Chapter 7, you may also need to become more integrated and move away from the channel siloes you currently have.

9 **Go after quick wins:** you don't need to answer the whole transformation piece before you can do this. You can drive an immediate commercial upside.

Think about how you can make things better for customers straight away and therefore drive a better commercial outcome. I would suggest you focus on the following in the short term:

Checklist

☐ How to improve the website experience and usability and remove barriers on the customer's path to purchase – make it easier to buy.

☐ Optimize marketing with more experiential marketing and ensure digital and brand marketing are working hand in hand – make it easier to find you.

☐ Ensure content synergy across channels and touchpoints.

☐ Treat social media more strategically.

☐ Are all your processes and service levels as customer facing as they could be? For example, order fulfilment, returns, customer service etc. Probably not. Now is the time to put that right.

☐ What KPIs can you implement in the short term that will give you a better sense-check of how you are performing in the eyes of your customers? Some examples are:

 – Net Promoter Score (NPS);

 – customer satisfaction levels;

 – rating and reviews of your products and services.

10 **Be socially responsible:** less of the corporate, more of the social and responsible. You need to live and breathe this. Start by implementing a code of conduct for suppliers and partners.

11 **Improve processes:** you will have to change the way you work. If you do what you have always done, then you will get what you have always got. Start by walking through your business, end to end, to determine how each part of your value chain can become more customer-centric. Everything you do, and I mean everything, will impact customers in some shape or form.

12 **Set up your technology team into two parallel streams of activity:**

 – The first is there to keep the lights on and the business running as usual. This team looks after your core systems: point of sale (POS), enterprise resource planning (ERP), order management system (OMS), warehouse management systems (WMS), customer relationship management (CMS), web platform (if in-house) and your legacy technology. The second is there to implement all the new developments required to put the customer first: this might include some of the above technology as well as others listed below.

When you are ready to, you swap out the old for the new.

Create a technology-development road map that enables you to begin to implement incremental improvements to the journey and experience for different segments of customers.

The big changes are likely to include the following:

- Enable you to have a single view of stock and inventory to ensure that stock is allocated to where the demand is (ERP).

- A single view of the customer and their behaviour (SCV) through all channels and touchpoints (data warehouse ingesting and housing all customer data).

- The ability to manage customer returns/reverse logistics through all channels and touchpoints, most likely through an OMS.

- Business intelligence (BI) tools that enable you to understand customer behaviour more accurately and therefore to serve different customer segments more effectively (Google 360, fast no-SQL databases, advanced analytics tools, interactive data visualization, single customer view – SCV).

- The ability to deliver more efficient customer service (chat bots and contact centre systems that are integrated with all channels and core systems).

- The removal of friction instore, including mobile POS, digital mirrors and the endless aisle.

- The removal of friction online (user testing, Google 360, split and multivariate testing tools – MVT).

- The ability to reward customer loyalty through all channels and also to enable customers to redeem loyalty rewards through all channels. Leverage the SCV in real time across the organization/channels.

- The ability to more effectively communicate with customers and build relationships with core segments (CRM, omnichannel campaign management).

- Personalization solutions that deliver personalized content and product or service offers. Tools will be a combination of SCV, clientelling, campaign management, CMS, and third-party plug-in tools.

- The ability for customers to customize products and services (extensible eCom platform, flexible CMS).

- The ability to have more agility and control around the creation and management of content (product information management – PIM, content management system – CMS).

13 **Marketing plan**: your messaging will change, it will be more customer facing. You will want to let customers know about your new, more customer-centric culture and focus. Remember the example I gave earlier about Avis? When they wanted to gain market share against the market leader Hertz they created the tagline 'we're second, but we try harder'. In other words, we're not the biggest, but we go the extra mile for you. Whatever line and overarching positioning you determine is appropriate, it is crucial that you are able to demonstrate the delivery of this across your business.

14 **Training**: to the point above, you may well need to train your colleagues in order to get them to a place where they can help ensure you deliver on your promises to customers. At the very least, you will need to think about the internal marketing plan. After all, I'm not talking about a gimmick, I'm suggesting root-and-branch change and transformation of your business. A new way of thinking. A new focus. A clarity of purpose. A new way of working. A new way of measuring the performance of your colleagues. New processes. All of which will require a programme of change and transformation and, at the outset, needs to be very clearly communicated to all.

15 **Competitor analysis**: keep your friends close and your enemies closer – this also means understanding who your enemies are. As I stated at the outset of the book, your competitors will now include the disruptors such as Amazon, Alibaba, Uber, Airbnb, Deliveroo, Instacart and so on. You need to ensure you have a strong focus on them. Is there anyone in your business whose job it is to keep an eye on competitors? If not, then give that task to someone or recruit someone in to do it. Things are moving so quickly that if you don't have a day-to-day view of what these competitors are up to and how the landscape is changing, you could find yourself in serious trouble one day.

What are you waiting for? Good luck on your journey

I really am hugely excited about the opportunities that exist for many businesses as they become more customer focused.

Thank you so much for reading my book. I'm truly humbled that you have taken the time to do so and I sincerely hope that it makes a big difference to your business.

100 practical ways to improve customer experience

1 Always start with the customer. Otherwise, how can you possibly know what you need to do to be successful?

2 If you can't beat them, join them: it's okay to mimic successful businesses.

3 Think of yourself as a customer service business that just happens to sell stuff.

4 Think customer empowerment: what can you do at every step of the way to truly empower your customers?

5 Always empower your staff to deliver the right experience for customers.

6 Exclusive products can help you to defend your position.

7 Listen to the voice of the customer.

8 Don't cut off your nose to spite your face... marketplaces are an effective route to market.

9 Deliver a seamless multichannel experience.

10 Consider offering an Amazon Prime-type delivery proposition.

11 Keep your friends close and your enemies closer.

12 Walk through the customer's journey – regularly.

13 Rethink your customer value proposition.

14 Adopt customer-facing KPIs.

15 Learn from other verticals.

16 Train your colleagues to remove friction from the customer's path to purchase.

17   Always start with ensuring you get the basics right.

18   Let customers help define how you might improve things for them.

19   Leverage disruptive thinking to drive innovation.

20   Become an agile business.

21   Create a culture of innovation.

22   Continually review how you might remove friction for the customer through all channels and touchpoints.

23   Think about how you merchandise and provide discovery and access to products.

24   Leverage digital technology in the changing room to drive sales.

25   Use mobile tills to remove friction and drive engagement at the point of sale.

26   Capture Net Promoter Scores instore (and through all channels).

27   Drive product and brand immersion.

28   Extend your range and offer through the endless aisle.

29   Add more benefits to customers above simple points-based loyalty cards.

30   Always think mobile first.

31   Balance the approach to apps versus mobile web.

32   Leverage iBeacons and free Wi-Fi to drive engagement instore.

33   Review our best-practice checklist for apps.

34   Plan for conversational commerce.

35   Develop new roles that can help drive customer-centricity.

36   Give someone ownership of the customer and their experience, and crucially the mandate to deliver the change required to become a customer-first business.

37   Create a customer-first culture throughout the entire business.

38   Create a cross-functional team with accountability for delivering customer first.

39   Adopt a two-tier organizational structure in areas such as IT, one focused on business as usual (BAU), one on the road map for new developments.

40   Ensure you have a leader who understands what putting the customer first really means.

41 Use the 6Vs framework to develop your customer-first business culture.

42 Surprise and delight customers.

43 Lead by example: culture comes from the top.

44 Create a cross-functional team to ensure your culture is maintained.

45 Always be fully transparent with customers.

46 Develop a marketing plan to communicate your culture to both external and internal customers.

47 Culture eats strategy for breakfast. Never forget that.

48 Drop the word corporate and focus on social responsibility.

49 Implement a code of conduct for colleagues, suppliers and partners.

50 Make purchasing decisions that put sustainable products first.

51 Support your local community.

52 Encourage your customers to take part in your CSR initiatives.

53 Implement an EP&L. Be clear about the value of being socially responsible.

54 Can you make customers' lives easier by enabling them to pay a subscription or for auto replenishment of big, bulky or frequently used products?

55 Enable customers to interact with a live chat service online.

56 What services can you offer that enhance the experience of the customer buying from you? Can you help them build, install and maintain what they have purchased?

57 Ensure that there is clear 'shop my way' messaging in all channels and touchpoints.

58 Use the service framework created.

59 Choose the right country to expand into.

60 Understand local-market consumer behaviour.

61 Localize customer communication.

62 Localize for culture and climate.

63 Offer localized customer service.

64 Understand the value chain and proposition of your competitors.

65 Offer the appropriate currency and payment types.

66 Know what good conversion looks like and how to deliver it.

67 Consider the most appropriate channels to market.

68 Think localized content.

69 Crew: consider staff resourcing and structure for internationalization.

70 Determine how you will gain trust in new markets.

71 Ensure you have the right mix of digital and brand-building and awareness activity.

72 Drive the attribution of all marketing activity: ensure you have the right mix of skills, and ideally in a more integrated and less siloed structure.

73 Make sure to focus on customer retention as well as acquisition.

74 Be clear about the customer's journey and where the owned, bought and earned touchpoints with the customer come into play and what your approach will be for each.

75 Think about growth hacking and how you can leverage viral marketing to more cost-effectively spread the word.

76 Look at leveraging proximity marketing to provide a better instore experience for customers.

77 Focus on experiential marketing as this will drive the engagement and involvement with your brand, products and services.

78 Adopt the customer mix. Live it, breathe it, integrate its approach into all that you do.

79 Throw away the Marketing Mix. It's 20 years past its sell-by date.

80 Focus on 'what's next' for the customer.

81 Understand this: if you don't look after your customers, someone else will. It's a battlefield out there. Do you have a plan to win the war?

82 Treat social media as a strategic driver of opportunity for your business. It is not only a promotional vehicle.

83 Resource social media effectively. Don't just give it to the youngest person in the room to look after!

84 Ensure that levels of service and response times are appropriate.

85 Don't be anti-social: social commerce is a tangible opportunity.

86 Think of the opportunities and the potential threats you are not currently addressing as a result of still treating social media as a tactical promotional tool.

87 Think about where artificial intelligence (AI) can improve your value chain.

88 Leverage AI to improve customer service.

89 Use AI to deliver more personalized experiences.

90 Don't ever forget that you need a fall-back position when AI cannot answer the customer's question!

91 Deliver personalized experiences for core customer segments.

92 Provide the ability for customers to customize their products.

93 Consider the opportunity to create more premiumized products or services.

94 Build a relationship with customers, don't pay lip service.

95 Understand the hierarchy of CRM and how it helps customers.

96 Segment your customer base – there is no such thing as 'the customer'.

97 Measure and work towards the lifetime value of your customers.

98 Build a list of what is important to your business as actionable insight in order to improve performance.

99 Test and learn: fail fast, learn what works best and continue to improve it. Learn what doesn't work, and don't do it again!

100 Loyalty is not a given. It has to be earned.

INDEX

Note: Chapter references, expert views, key performance indicators and top practical customer experience tips are indexed as such. Page numbers in *italics* indicate Figures or Tables.